To: Kathryn

Hope you enjoy

Donna Lee

Comer

By: Donna Lee Comer

"A CHILD A MOTHER SHOULD LOVE"

VOLUME ONE

COVER DESIGNED BY SAMUEL COMER
@ COMER COMPUTER SERVICES

PRINTED AND BOUND IN THE UNITED STATES OF AMERICA
By CREATESPACE
CHARLESTON, SC
JULY 2011

ACKNOWLEDGMENTS

A Book is a Good Place to go and Dream

SPECIAL THANKS TO MARY TAYLOR
FOR HER CONTRIBUTIONS

AND TO MY FAMILY FOR THEIR CONSTANT
SUPPORT

AND A GRATEFUL
THANK YOU TO MY SON
SAM FOR THE BOOK COVER

CHAPTER ONE

Annie sat on the porch swing clutching Betsy, her doll, as she rocked back and forth. She rubbed the silky ribbon on the doll's dress between her fingers, a habit she had developed in the past few months. The feel of the fabric gave her comfort in her troubled times.

The bright sun shining through the trees hurt her eyes when she looked up at a bird she heard singing in top of the old oak tree that dominated the front yard. Annie wanted to fly away with the birds. She wanted to go to a place where nobody screamed or called you names and hurt you. She wished she could fly to the top of the tree and live there forever.

Annie hummed a simple melody as she rocked. She didn't remember the words, only the tune. She loved to watch Big Bird and Elmo on Sesame Street whenever her mother thought she deserved a few minutes of the show. Once she asked her mother to wait until the show was over before she turned the TV off, but a sharp slap across her cheek was her answer, so Annie never asked again. She tried to memorize the songs and sing them to herself when her mother locked her in her room. She would hum the melody and softly sing the words that she could remember as she disappeared into herself.

Annie heard her mother calling her from inside the house and trembled. She knew she should run as fast as she could to find out what her mother needed, but today her legs hurt so badly that she sat still. Annie wanted to pretend that this was a good day in the few seconds she shared with Betsy.

Jill, her mother, was getting agitated. She needed Annie to move a heavy trunk to the other side of the room. Why was that girl so hard to find all the time? It never failed, when she needed her, she was never around. Jill's agitation grew each time she yelled Annie's name. Finally, she went to the door and saw Annie on the swing.

"Annie, didn't you hear me? I was calling for you. I want you to come here this instant. Don't bring that stupid doll; you know I hate the filthy thing. I threw it away last week. How did you find it? Never mind, just get in here. I need you to move something, now!"

Annie sat the doll in the corner of the swing, slowly followed her mother inside, and waited until her mother grabbed her hand and drug her to the living room. "I want you to move this trunk under the window. I bought this quilt to drape over it. Hurry up, I don't have all day."

Annie got down on her knees to push the heavy trunk. It took all her strength to budge it. The carpet rubbing against her blistered knees hurt but she knew she had to ignore the pain and do what her mother told her to do. Jill stood over her but didn't offer to help. Slowly the trunk started to move, and Annie kept pushing until it was under the window. After she straightened the trunk, she turned to her mother and asked, "Is this all right?"

Her mother got her yardstick and got down to measure each side. The trunk wasn't centered and she reached out and slapped Annie's face. The action surprised Annie, but she didn't shed one tear.

"You stupid girl, can't you see it's not straight. Here I'll hold the stick while you move it. I'll let you know when to stop."

Annie got down and scooted the trunk back. After a few pushes her mother was satisfied and smiled widely and said, "Yes, that's perfect. I'm so glad I thought of putting it here. Now, go away while I fix the quilt."

Annie slowly walked back out to the porch and picked up Betsy. She crawled back on the swing and rubbed the ribbon while she hummed. The bird sang again, but Annie didn't hear. She rocked back and forth closing her mind to everything but the song.

Jill had found the quilt at a flea market the week before and just knew that the stars would match the blue in the living room sofa. She painstakingly spent the next half an hour making sure that the pattern was perfectly straight and the quilt was hanging the same distance from the floor on each side. It drove her crazy to see anything crooked. When she had it just right, she stood back to admire it. She saw something on the floor in front of the sofa, and picked it up to examine it. It took a few seconds until she realized that it was a cookie crumb. Jill stormed to the porch and grabbed Annie by the arm pulling her along behind her to the living room.

"Do you see what I see? What's that doing on the floor? Get down and lick it up. You told me you were careful. I declare you are the world's stupidest child. I'll never trust you to eat in here again."

Annie got down to the floor to lick up the crumb. She thought she was going to escape punishment, but a hard kick to her back caused her to cry out. Her mother waited a few seconds after kicking her, turned, and marched out of the room.

Annie tried to stand but the pain was excruciating. She tried not to cry but the tears started flowing anyway. Her chest felt as though it was on fire and she labored for each breath. The poor child lay on the floor in anguish.

Jill went to the kitchen to prepare dinner, and never once thought of Annie as she scrubbed the potatoes and sprinkled the spices on them. She looked out the kitchen window at the new patio set on the back deck. The striped color of the cushions had worried her at first. At the department store, she wasn't sure about the green and cream stripes, but now as she looked out, they did blend beautifully with the white mums she'd planted so carefully in each pot.

"Yes, I picked the right color. Why do I always doubt myself?" she asked.

Jill heard her husband's car pull in the driveway and park in the garage. She quickly set the timer for the chicken and potatoes and went to meet him. She glanced at her hair as she passed the hall mirror and hurried to the door. John, her husband, was getting out of the car when he spotted his wife.

"Honey, I'm so glad you're home. That daughter of mine has been impossible all day. I don't know why she never learns. Anyway, I'm making your favorite supper. I can't wait until you taste the chicken and the potatoes with parsley and butter. I have an apple pie with a crumb top for dessert. Are you hungry?"

John braced himself for the evening; it wasn't starting out too good. If Jill met him at the door with complaints about Annie, it usually got worse. He never knew what to expect and hoped Jill hadn't hurt Annie again.

Jill chattered away as she reached for John's hand to walk with him into the kitchen. She took his briefcase and laid it on the desk along with his suit coat and tie. John had a habit of removing his coat and tie on his way home trying to relax as much as possible before he faced his wife each evening.

John walked to the kitchen and opened the oven door a crack to peek at the food he smelled. Jill would ruin dinner if he didn't rave about her cooking. He asked about Annie and heard Jill's statement about leaving her in the living room. The dread of what he would see grew stronger as he headed to the fancy living room that Jill guarded like a soldier.

He spied Annie's feet in front of the sofa and he hurried to her side. He carefully picked up the young girl and cradled her in his lap. He saw the tear stained cheeks and instantly knew that she was hurting bad. Annie learned not to cry unless the pain was over bearing.

"Annie sweetheart, are you okay?" he asked her. "Where does it hurt? Did your mother do this?"

Annie whispered softly, "I'll be okay. It doesn't hurt too bad. Can I lay down a while, please?"

John gingerly picked her up and headed for her bedroom. He laid her on the bed as easy as he could and got a cover from the bench.

"Do you think you should go to the hospital? I'll take you this time. I promise I'll stay with you. I hate your mother for doing this to you. Soon we'll leave and she'll never hurt you again. I'm sorry, Annie."

Annie took a small breath and shook her head. "Don't worry daddy, I'm okay. Can I lay here and rest. Please tell mommy I'm not hungry."

John touched Annie's forehead and thought it felt hot. He was worried about Annie this time. He hadn't seen her cry for quite a while. He didn't want to upset Jill so he told Annie to rest and he would be back to check on her soon. Annie tried to smile as John left the room and closed the door.

John headed back to the kitchen and saw that Jill was taking the food out of the oven and the table was set with her special dinnerware. He wondered what she wanted this time. A request always followed the special dishes. Every time she used her good china, it cost him lots of money.

Jill smiled at him while she finished setting the table. She pulled his chair out from the table and told him to sit down. The wine glasses were gleaming in the sunlight that streamed through the window. The white wine cooled in the bucket in the middle of the table.

He asked, "Jill, what did you do to Annie? She looks bad this time. If she's hurt, I'll take her to the hospital this time, and I won't care what I tell them. What did she do to you? Nothing can be bad enough for you to hurt her this way. Jill, did you hear me?"

Jill looked up from the candle she was lighting. "What do you mean, did I hurt her? She dropped a crumb on the living room floor and I made her lick it up. I can't help it if she is so messy. I warned her the last time, and she promised me she would never eat in the living room again. I didn't hurt her. Enough about Annie, sit down and eat."

"No, you have to stop hurting her. I swear I'm going to take Annie and leave one of these days. Why did I get mixed up with such a crazy woman?" John knew he made a mistake when he saw the redness crawl up her neck.

"How dare you call me crazy? You know what kind of a girl Annie is. She never listens to a thing. She lives in her own world and I only discipline her. I'd never harm my own child. Don't threaten to leave me John. You can never leave me. What would happen to your precious Annie then? Think about her John, and make sure you don't use idle threats against me. I know what I'm doing. She's not your child, and you have no idea how hard it is to be here every day with her."

John sighed and kept quiet. He knew he could never leave Annie here alone with Jill. He resigned himself a while back to sacrifice his own happiness for hers. Jill would probably kill Annie eventually if he left, and no court in the world would award him full custody of a child that wasn't his. So he shut his mouth and started eating from the plate Jill sat in front of him. His appetite was spoiled but he made an effort to eat to avoid another screaming fit.

He complimented Jill on the chicken and listened as she talked about her latest project. She wanted to redo the kitchen and install stainless steel appliances that matched the new dishwasher she just had to have. He didn't care about the money since he had plenty.

11

He wished he could join her enthusiasm but he had grown to hate the woman he married. If only he could take Annie and hide. She didn't deserve to grow up with a hateful mother. Annie was a sweet innocent child with a gentle heart. She didn't hate the mother that had kicked her an hour ago.

After he finished eating, John went upstairs to Annie's room. He sat down on the bed and was shocked at the sight of the little girl's face.

Her breathing was shallow and she was as white as a sheet. John bent to listen to her chest and felt for her pulse. He could hardly feel her heart beat and he was afraid that she might die.

John ran downstairs and screamed, "Jill bring the car around front so I can take Annie to the hospital. Your child is barely breathing and I don't have time to argue. Just go get the car."

He ran back upstairs and wrapped Annie in a blanket. He scooped her into his arms trying to be gentle with her. When he got to the bottom of the stairs, he saw Jill sitting at the table calmly eating her chicken.

"What are you doing? Did you not hear me tell you to go get the car? What's wrong with you? Do you want Annie to die?"

Jill continued eating and ignored what he was saying to her. She honestly didn't need to be bothered with a spoiled child. When she didn't make a move to get up, John carried Annie to the nearest sofa and said, "Annie I'll be right back. I'm going to back the car out."

Annie didn't respond and John was afraid of losing her. "Dear God, help this poor child. She doesn't deserve this. Please don't let her die," he prayed as he got in the car and backed it out. He ran to the passenger door and opened it. He ran inside, carried Annie out, and put her in the backseat. He hoped she held on until they reached the hospital. The thoughts of guilt and shame of not stopping Jill before this happened tore away at his heart as he drove.

It took twenty minutes to drive to the hospital. John parked in the emergency parking and jumped out of his car. He picked Annie up and rushed in and almost ran over a team of nurses. He handed Annie to them and they hurried down the hall with her. Someone directed him to the desk to fill out the forms.

One of the nurses returned a few minutes later and asked him what happened to his daughter.

"She is my step-daughter, Annie Lawson. My wife punished her. I don't really know what happened. Is she going to be alright?"

The nurse asked a few more questions and told him someone would be out in a few minutes to talk to him. She handed him a clipboard with some forms. John tried his best to concentrate but his eyes were drawn to the door waiting to hear about Annie. He was scribbling down the insurance information when he heard someone come up beside him. He looked up and saw it was a police officer. The officer introduced himself as Officer Thompson and asked, "Are you John Hawkins?"

"Yes, I'm John Hawkins Officer Thompson. Is there a problem? Is Annie okay?"

"Mr. Hawkins, I have to ask you to come with me. I need you to answer some questions, if you don't mind. There's a room over there we can use."

John stood and followed Officer Thompson to the empty room and sat down.

"Please tell me if Annie's going to be okay. I need to get these papers finished so I can go see her. I promised her I wouldn't leave her alone."

Officer Thompson said, "Mr. Hawkins, I understand you are worried about your daughter. First I need to know what happened to her. Her injuries may involve internal bleeding and the hospital informed us that this isn't the first time that your daughter has been admitted with suspicious injuries."

"Annie is my step-daughter. My wife Jill tends to get a little carried away with her discipline. Is Annie going to live? Please let me go to her. Annie will be scared and she needs me."

"Mr. Hawkins, I have to tell you that the paper work states that you abused your step-daughter in the past and your wife didn't want to press charges and the other incidents were dismissed. Now, we have a huge problem. Your stepdaughter's ribs are broken, which caused a collapsed lung. I'm not sure what other injuries she has at this time. I can't let you near her until we determine if you're a threat to her. Where is your wife, sir? Did she come with you?"

"No, I promised Annie I would bring her this time. My wife wouldn't allow me to come along the other times. She said she was the mother and she would handle it. Are you telling me that she told the hospital I hurt Annie? That's not true. I love Annie as though she were my own child, and I'd never hurt her. I want to press charges against my wife. She can't be alone with Annie and I'm afraid for her safety. I was too scared to say anything before because she said I would lose Annie if I told. She knows I could never get custody because I'm only the step-father."

Officer Thompson asked John to excuse him and wait while he checked on something. John couldn't believe that Jill would be cruel enough to tell a lie and say that he hurt Annie. He mumbled to himself in disbelief, "Why would they believe her over me? Don't they see that she's crazy?"

The officer returned with several files in his hands. "Mr. Hawkins, these are the reports from Annie's previous visits. I see here that the first time your wife brought in Annie. she had a fractured collarbone. Do you recall this incident?"

"Yes, I came home and Annie was crying and said she fell off the swing I built for her in the back yard. I convinced my wife to bring her here when Annie continued to cry in pain. I believed what she told me. I had no reason at that time to doubt my wife."

"Mr. Hawkins, are you saying that Annie didn't fall off the swing? Did you hurt her then?"

"No, I wasn't home at the time and I didn't see what happened and when I questioned Annie about it she said she had fallen off the swing. I didn't question the fall until I saw a pattern, and now I know that my wife hurts Annie. I'm so ashamed to say that all this time I was gullible and believed everything my wife told me. Several months ago, I saw Jill hurt Annie and I started to piece things together and now I'm certain that all of these previous injuries were at the hand of my wife."

"Mr. Hawkins, please don't say anymore until you have an attorney present. I'm certain that charges will be filed after this incident for the sake of your stepdaughter's safety. Can you call your wife and have her come here? I need to get her side of this."

"No, I don't want Annie upset. If her mother comes here, it will be worse on her. She's too scared to talk when Jill's in the room," John told him. "She needs me to be with her. My wife doesn't care about her. She abuses Annie on a daily basis and I have been too cowardly to stop it. Now, can I please see my daughter?"

"Are you saying that you don't want your wife here? Are you afraid of what she'll say about you? We can call her, and we will. I don't care what you say, and I will ask your daughter who has hurt her as soon as I can. Let me ask you about the other injuries. Your wife brought your daughter in six months later with her lips split and teeth missing. Do you know how that happened then?"

"Again, my wife said Annie fell off her bike. I didn't doubt that either."

Officer Thompson said, "And the third time, a broken ankle. Later she was treated for burns to her arms and her hands. And then again there was an incident that your wife brought her in and she had a bald spot on her head where her hair had been pulled out by the roots. The doctor noted that it looked as though someone may have pulled the hair out. The list is ridiculous and an investigation is necessary. If you have abused your daughter, you will go to prison. A parent that hurts a child is the worst criminal I can think of. A child loves until someone turns that love to hate."

"I'm telling you the truth. I didn't hurt Annie. I promised her I would stay with her. I just want to make this right. I didn't hurt her." John leaned over and as his head rested in his hands, he cried for Annie. He silently prayed for her to be okay and that someday she would forgive him for not protecting her.

CHAPTER TWO

In the emergency room Dr. Howard was on call. He heard the buzz about the little girl that had been brought into the ER, and understood the reason for it when he entered Annie's room. Dr. Howard had a daughter the same age and had an excellent reputation with children. He tried to make Annie feel at ease and joked with her as he checked her injuries.

He sensed the fear from Annie and sent one of the nurses to find the puppet he kept in his desk drawer. The other staff members watched in awe as Dr. Howard changed from serious doctor to Turbo the Turtle. He used the turtle often with children to ease the fear of the hospital. He crept up the side of the bed with the puppet and was glad when he saw a smile on Annie's face.

"Hi, I'm Turbo the Turtle. What's your name little girl? I love your brown eyes. I wish my eyes were brown. They're just turtle green. YUCK!" Turbo said.

Annie said, "Oh, your eyes aren't ugly. I never talked to a turtle before."

Turbo replied, "Oh, I talk to girls all the time, but none of them are as pretty as you are. Will you be my friend?"

Annie shyly nodded her head. "Why am I here? And where is my Daddy? He said he would stay with me."

Turbo said, "I'm sure he had papers to fill out. He should be able to come to be with you soon. Do you mind if I ask you what happened to you?"

Annie turned away and said nothing.

Turbo crawled up on her stomach and said, "Don't be afraid of me, I want to make you feel better. We need to know what happened so we can fix it. Will you tell me?"

Annie shook her head no. She knew if she told, her mother would hurt her more than she ever had before, so Annie didn't say a word. Her chest hurt and she was so tired. "Mommy hurts me because I am bad. I wish I could just be good," she thought.

Dr. Howard used Turbo's hand to grab onto Annie's hand. He hoped to settle the child down so he could finish his exam. His gut told him that this little girl had already suffered so much and he needed to reach an understanding with her in hopes that she could trust him. He signaled the nurse to increase her medication running through her IV. The sedative was weak but he wanted to take the edge off the pain he knew she was feeling.

"Annie, would you like me to tell you a story? I promise I will make you better. If you want to, you can tell me a story too," Turbo said.

"I love stories. Mommy lets me watch Sesame Street sometimes and I try to learn each song that Big Bird sings. Sometimes I forget the words, but I remember all the stories."

16

"Well, my story goes like this. Once there was a little girl named Susie. She loved playing with her dolls. She liked the one with red hair the best. It was her favorite of all. But, Daddy didn't like the red haired doll so he took it and broke it in many pieces. Susie was so sad because she loved her doll. When she cried, her daddy got mad and hurt her. She was hurt so bad, that Daddy had to take her to the hospital. A nice doctor was going to make her better but he needed to know who hurt her. Susie told what happened and the doctor made sure that she was never hurt again."

Annie's pulse speeded up when she heard the story. Do other mommy's and daddy's hurt their kids too? Maybe I should tell what mommy did. "I just want her to love me", she thought.

"Will you tell me a story about your daddy? Did he break your doll too? Is that why you are afraid," Turbo asked.

"No, my daddy loves me and he would never hurt me. I fell down and hurt myself. Mommy tells me to be more careful, but sometimes I don't listen. I don't want to get in trouble and I try to do what she says, but I don't pay attention," she said.

Dr. Howard didn't want to upset her so he told her that she needed to go to sleep for a while and when she woke up, they would tell more stories. "Don't worry Annie; I'll take care of you now. You just relax and try to sleep, okay?"

He walked over to the IV and increased the sedative to help calm her down. As the drug took effect, he watched Annie drift to sleep. He waited a few more minutes and started to examine her.

Doctor Howard started with her arms and upper body. What he saw made him wonder what this poor little girl had suffered. He saw many scars on her arms that looked as though someone had cut her. From the initial exam, it looked like her right wrist had been broken and never set properly.

When he pulled the covers the rest of the way down to expose her legs, his heart broke. Annie's legs were red and swollen. After examining her, the only explanation that made any sense was someone had put her into scalding hot water and burned her legs. Who would do this to a child?

Dr. Howard asked the nurses to prepare her for the O.R. He had to inflate her lung so she could breathe. He wanted to put her under anesthesia so she wouldn't feel the pain. While she was under, he would confer with Dr. Willows. She was the best doctor on the staff to handle child abuse and this case certainly fit the description.

While the nurses transported Annie to the operating room, Dr. Howard put in a call to Dr. Willows to meet him in Operating Room 3. He went to scrub and wait for her.

The nurses had orders to do a complete body x-ray. A technician set up the machine and it took only a few minutes. He told them he would bring the results back in fifteen minutes.

Dr. Willows arrived at the O.R. and immediately examined Annie. When Dr. Howard came in, she agreed that in light of the evidence, someone had definitely hurt this child. They both needed to document every fracture and injury in hopes of making sure that whoever it was would never harm her again.

The technician brought the x-rays while Dr. Howard started the procedure to inflate Annie's lung. Dr. Willows gasped when she looked at them. Annie's body was riddled with old scarring left from quite a few hairline fractures in her arms and legs. She agreed with Dr. Howard's diagnosis that the wrist had been broken and the bone had not healed properly. They agreed that Annie wouldn't have complete and full use of her right hand from the neglect.

When Dr. Howard was finished inflating the lung, he told the nurses to take Annie to the recovery room and he would check on her in a little while. He asked Dr. Willows to come to his office after she finished changing. She arrived shortly after he did and they discussed Annie's injuries while they enjoyed a much-needed cup of coffee.

Dr. Willows said, "I hate this. It's so unfair when a parent hurts their children. I heard from the nurses that the authorities suspect that the stepfather is to blame. Have you met him?"

Dr. Howard answered, "No, I haven't met him yet. I might go down to the emergency department and talk to the officer that's on duty. Maybe he can fill in the details."

"I have my rounds to do, and I'll contact you to continue my report as soon as I'm done. We have to make sure that this beautiful little girl doesn't go back into the hands of whoever has hurt her. When I'm done, I'll call you," Dr. Willows said.

"Okay, I'll let you know what I find out," Dr. Howard said. He picked up the phone after she left and gave instructions to the staff that Annie's legs should be coated with a burn medication. He didn't think that the burns would leave any scars and for that, he was grateful.

The emergency room at the Holy Spirit Hospital was packed. The nurses did their best to keep the cases moving. In between patients, the talk centered on the little girl named Annie. All the nurses agreed that her eyes held a sadness that was heartbreaking.

The officer on duty called in Social Services and was waiting on Nancy Branson, one of the agents covering that day. When she arrived, the officer filled her in on the events of the evening.

Nancy asked to meet with the stepfather and when she opened the door, she saw John Hawkins pacing around the table.

She introduced herself and asked him to have a seat.

"Mr. Hawkins, I'm Nancy Branson from Children Services. The officer at the hospital called me to review your stepdaughter's case. I'm waiting on the file from the doctor in charge and as soon as I can, I'll take your statement. I understand that this isn't the first time that your stepdaughter Annie has been admitted here."

"Yes, my wife brought Annie in several times before. I didn't realize until a few months ago that the situation at our home was this severe. My wife kept telling me that Annie was accident-prone and all her injuries were just that, accidents. She told me that Annie fell off her bike, or tripped on the stairs, or fell off the swing. A few months ago, I saw my wife, Jill, deliberately hurt Annie when she didn't hear something she told her to do. I was under the impression that Annie was a difficult child. Now, I believe that my wife has abused Annie all her life."

"So, it is your story that your wife, and not you, hurt your stepdaughter? I'll have to talk to your wife before I allow you to see Annie. I'm in charge of the case now. I'll have guardianship of Annie until we get to the bottom of this. Are you aware that Annie had fractured ribs and a collapsed lung when you brought her in this evening?"

John said, "No, I haven't talked to the doctor yet. I didn't know what was wrong with Annie, but I knew when I brought her in that she was barely breathing. I promised Annie that I would stay with

19

her. She isn't used to strangers and I'm sure that she's scared to death. I need to see her; please, she has been through so much. I would never harm her. I love her as though she were my own child."

"Mr. Hawkins, what happened today that caused Annie's injuries? Do you have any idea how she got three fractured ribs and a collapsed lung? Remember before you answer, what you say may be used against you later. Please, do yourself a favor and tell the truth now."

"All I know is that when I arrived home Annie was lying in the living room floor and she asked me to carry her upstairs to her bed. When I went to check on her, she looked terrible and she was crying in pain. Annie only cries when the pain is unbearable. She knows better than to cry when my wife punishes her, it only angers my wife, and Annie suffers more."

"Are you aware that there is evidence of past abuse and your wife made a statement to the hospital authorities that it was indeed you that hurt Annie? I'll know more when I see the other files on her previous visits, but even if this was the first time, I'm so glad that the hospital reported this. No child deserves to be beaten as Annie has been."

"I can't imagine why my wife blamed me. I regret not taking Annie and leaving her long ago. I stayed for Annie. My wife used her as bait for me to stay with her and told me that she would hurt Annie more if I left. How can I prove to you that it was my wife and not me?"

"Mr. Hawkins, I'm trained to protect the child. Whether it was you or your wife, we will remove Annie from your home until we are satisfied she is safe. Do you have a lawyer you can call? Do you want to call your wife and ask her to come here, or should I do it?

"No, I'll call her. I'll be glad to have her confronted for what she's done. I have no love left for her and if you allow me to keep Annie, we'll leave her. She is an evil and vindictive person, and I will testify to anything if it helps Annie."

Mrs. Branson noticed the tears in his eyes and wondered if he was acting. In her experience, mothers normally do not harm their own children. Since he was a stepfather, it was more likely he was the guilty one. She hoped for the child's sake that this would be the last time Annie ever felt fear or pain from either parent.

CHAPTER THREE

Mandy, the nurse in the recovery room checked Annie's blood pressure. The sweet little girl seemed to be doing fine. As she studied her, she thought to herself that when she had her own daughter, she would want her to look just like Annie. Her light brown hair was shiny and naturally curly and her eyelashes were so full most grown women would pay to have them. She was small for five and a half, and thought her mother was probably a petite woman. Mandy brushed the hair from Annie's eyes and leaned down to brush her cheeks with a kiss. She said, "Now, what did I do that for? Maybe you just needed a little tender loving care."

Dr. Howard went to the nurse's station to find Annie's charts. He read the information from her previous visits. He was shocked to see the diagnosis and number of times Annie had been hospitalized. The broken bones and extent of her injuries made him think that someone was to blame for not catching this pattern quicker. He wanted to consult with Dr. Willows and hoped that between the two of them they could convince the hospital to protect this young girl from being sent back to the same environment.

As he was reading the last page, he heard someone asking for Annie's files at the desk. He approached the woman and asked why she wanted to read them.

"And you are who?" she asked.

"I'm Dr. Howard, and I treated Annie for a collapsed lung. I'm going to be taking care of her while she is here."

"Dr. Howard, I'm Nancy Branson from Children's Services."

"So, the hospital called in Children Services? Do you think this is a case of child abuse? I'm not used to treating patients with a history like Annie Lawson. What do you need from me to help protect her?" he asked.

"First, I need to ask you from a medical standpoint if these injuries could be abuse. Have you treated Annie before?"

"No, I haven't seen her before today. I was just looking through her file, and I'm very concerned. I'm not sure what the guidelines are for abuse. I can verify her injuries that I'm treating her for now. She has three broken ribs, one of them punctured her lung, and I took her to the O.R. for treatment. It could have been from a strong blow to her body. Also, both of her legs have 2nd degree burns."

"The burns are on both legs?" she asked.

"Yes, her bottom torso is red with some small blisters. The burns probably came from placing her in the tub while the water was too hot. Hopefully, there will be no scars."

"How could a parent intentionally put their child in scalding hot water? Could it have been an accident if they weren't aware the water was that hot?"

Dr. Howard thought a moment before he answered. "I don't want to accuse anyone of neglect if it isn't warranted. I would say in my professional opinion most parents check the water before placing a child in the bathtub. Annie was kept in the water long enough to cause 2nd degree burns. The burns to her lower torso are extensive. She had to be in the water for more than a second. Any child placed in hot water would scream immediately and the parent would take them out of the water."

"So, you're saying that Annie was forced to stay in the tub for some time and that's what caused the burns to her legs?"

"Yes, that is my first impression. According to her chart, some of her other injuries probably were at the hand of someone else. Either one of the parents, a daycare, or someone that spends a lot of time with her is to blame. Have you met the father?"

"Yes, actually he's waiting for me to return. He says that his wife, Jill Hawkins, Annie's natural mother, is to blame. I have a report that states Mrs. Hawkins put the blame on her husband John for the previous incidents. We must do whatever it takes to protect Annie and that probably means I'll petition the court to be her guardian and neither parent can be with her. In your opinion, would it be possible for her mother to cause the injuries, or would she be too weak? What I mean, would a stronger person have to be to blame?"

"No, a woman is certainly able to harm a small girl in this way. I see no reason to think that a man has to take the blame. But can't you ask Annie who hurt her?"

"Yes, we can. In most cases, the parent warns the child not to tell or the next time will be worse. I'm not sure Annie will tell us."

"I can't believe that any woman, or man for that matter, would do harm to such a precious child. I have my own and my first instinct is to keep them from harm. Will you keep me informed? Annie is asking for her father, and I'm not sure she'll stay quiet if she doesn't see him. Is it possible for her sake to have someone stay in the room while the father reassures her?"

"I'll see what I can do. If you find it will enable her to stay calm, let me know. I can't imagine if he were that kind of father, she would want him in the room. Right now, we must put Annie's well being ahead of anything else. I don't want the father to be with her right now until I'm sure who the criminal is. Thank you for your help, Dr. Howard. I'll keep in touch with you."

"Here's my card with my numbers, and my pager number. Call me for any reason if I can help."

Nancy headed back to the room where she left John Hawkins waiting. When she entered, she saw he'd been crying and it did touch her heart. "This is going to be a difficult case to decide unless Annie is willing to point the finger to the guilty one," she thought to herself.

"Mr. Hawkins, I'm sorry to keep you waiting. I'm going to have the officer bring you a phone so you can call your wife. As soon as she arrives we'll try to sort this out."

"Please, can you tell me if Annie is alright? I'm so sorry for what she has endured. I'll stay away if it'll do more harm to her. Right now, she's the most important one in this mess."

"I spoke to her doctor and he says that the puncture to her lung was corrected and her burns on her legs are being treated."

"Burns, what burns? I remember Jill giving her a bath last night and I heard Annie scream, is that when she was burned? Jill said she got soap in her eyes and she was being a baby and screamed as if someone was trying to kill her."

Again, she wondered if Mr. Hawkins was acting innocent. She would wait until she met the mother to decide whom she believed.

The officer brought in a phone and she handed it to him. John dialed the number and as she listened to his side of the conversation, her confusion grew.

"Jill, this is John. The hospital has admitted Annie and they need you to come down to fill out papers. What? Yes, it really is necessary for you to come here. No, I didn't tell them what you did. I care about Annie don't you? How can you say that? She's not a baby. Her lung collapsed from you breaking her ribs. Yes, I know you just kicked her. I want you to come down as soon as you can. No, it can't wait until tomorrow. Jill, an officer will come and get you if you don't come right away. Okay. If that's how you want to play this, I'll tell them you aren't coming and they'll have to come and get you. Are you sure? Yes, I'll tell them. Good bye."

John turned to Mrs. Branson and asked, "Did you hear enough? Someone will have to get my wife. She says she doesn't have the time to come here for something so minute. So, you will have to send someone to the house."

"Did your wife admit to kicking Annie just now? Did I hear right?" she asked.

"Yes, she told me she kicked Annie for dropping one cookie crumb on the floor. She told Annie to lick it up, and she must have kicked her while she was down on the floor, and that's where I found her."

"I'll contact the police and have an officer dispatched to pick her up. I hate to handle it this way, but Annie's safety is the utmost priority. I'll make the call now."

John asked, "Can I see Annie now? I promise I won't upset her. I just want her to know I'm still here."

"She's in recovery, and I'll ask the doctor when she wakes up if you can see her for a few minutes. You understand that if I change my mind, you will accept that decision," she said sternly.

"Yes, I understand. I just don't want Annie to think I don't love her."

Mrs. Branson went to the desk to use the phone. She called dispatch and asked for a patrol car to pick up Mrs. Hawkins and bring her to the hospital.

CHAPTER FOUR

The officers knocked on the door to the Hawkins home. Jill came to the door and stared in disbelief when she saw them. She didn't think that John would have the nerve to call the police.

"Can I help you officers?" she asked.

"Mrs. Hawkins, we have orders to transport you to the Holy Spirit Hospital."

"Why, is someone hurt? Is it my daughter or husband? Was there an accident?" she cried as she held her hand over her heart. She acted as if she was going to faint.

"Mrs. Hawkins, are you alright? No, there was no accident. Your daughter and your husband are at the hospital, but I'm not sure of the details. I think they need you for paperwork."

Jill quickly sat down in the closest chair. She didn't want to be bothered going to the stupid hospital and she hoped that she could play up to the police officers and maybe they would feel sorry for her and she could go back to making plans for her new kitchen.

"Mrs. Hawkins, do you need to take anything with you, a purse, or a jacket? We'll give you a few seconds."

"Oh, I feel faint, and I don't think I can make it. Do I really have to go? Can I lie down for a minute?" she swooned.

"No, ma'am we need to leave now. If you need your purse I'll wait for you, but please go get it now."

Jill really didn't need this crap. She saw the officers meant business and were serious, so she went to get her purse. She changed her attitude with them and they knew she was agitated.

They put her in the back seat of the patrol car and headed for the hospital. One of the officers called dispatch and told them they were on their way and asked where Mrs. Hawkins was to go when they arrived. Dispatch told them to take her to the emergency department and ask for Mrs. Branson.

The officers escorted Jill to the desk and asked to talk to Mrs. Branson. When Mrs. Branson saw Jill, she was surprised to see how beautiful and well-dressed she was. She didn't show her surprise and walked over to introduce herself.

"Mrs. Hawkins, my name is Nancy Branson from Children

Services. I need to ask you some questions concerning your daughter Annie. I have spoken to your husband John, now I need to speak with you. If you will follow me please, we'll find a room so we can talk."

Jill followed Mrs. Branson to an empty room and sat at the table. She told herself to be careful and be ready to turn on the tears when she talked about Annie.

"Now, Mrs. Hawkins, are you aware that we admitted your daughter Annie tonight? I know your husband did call you."

"Yes, he told me Annie was staying tonight but I really don't understand what happened. Were they in an auto accident? I was so scared when the officers arrived at my door, but they wouldn't tell me what happened." She started the tears and reached in her purse for a tissue.

"No, your husband and daughter weren't in an accident. Your daughter Annie came to the ER. with a collapsed lung. Do you know how that happened?"

"No, I don't know anything. I need to speak with my husband. Where is he? Can I talk to him now?" Jill asked.

"Right now I need your co-operation and then you can see your husband. Do you need something to drink before we get started?" Mrs. Branson asked. She took note that she didn't ask to see Annie.

"Yes, could I have some coffee? All this stress gives me a headache. And could I have two creams please."

"Sure, give me one second," Mrs. Branson said as she went to find the coffee.

Jill told herself to keep it under control. "You can't let them see that that child gets on your nerves. I have to convince them that John hurt Annie, I just have to," she thought.

When Mrs. Branson returned, she made sure the coffee was the way Jill wanted it and she pulled the file out of her briefcase.

"Mrs. Hawkins, your husband told me that you kicked Annie tonight and he was the one that decided to bring her to the hospital, and you didn't want him to. Is that true?"

"Oh no, John is lying again. I told the hospital the last time I was here it was John that hurt Annie. They wanted me to press charges but I was afraid for my own safety so I didn't do it."

Jill took time to blow her nose and continued, "I thought he would get better. He promised that he'd stop. I hate to see Annie hurt. I tried to stop him but he got angry when he found out she ate the cookie in the living room and knocked her to the floor and kicked her in the back."

"Mrs. Hawkins, are you sure you're telling the truth? Your husband said you hurt Annie. He told me he stays to protect her. I must tell you that Annie probably won't go home with the two of you until the court is satisfied she'll be safe. There will be a hearing to decide if charges are brought against either you or your husband, whichever one is the threat."

"Please believe me when I tell you that I love Annie. I didn't know John was like this when I married him. I thought we were so happy. Then I saw him hit Annie one day and I have feared him since then."

"Has Mr. Hawkins ever hit you? Do you try to keep him from hurting your daughter?"

"Yes, I tried several times to get in front of Annie but he just knocks me out of the way. He dares me to interfere, and I know he would kill me and then he would kill my daughter. I wanted to tell someone for a long time, but I'm afraid of losing Annie. I couldn't stand it if I lost her."

Mrs. Branson hesitated and wondered how she could catch Mrs. Hawkins in a lie. She was leaning to the assumption that it was Mrs. Hawkins, not Mr. Hawkins, which was guilty.

"Can you tell me about your daughter's previous injuries? A few months ago, your daughter was here with teeth missing and her lips split open. Do you know what happened that time?" Mrs. Branson asked.

"Yes, Annie didn't want to eat her green beans and John became so angry he hit her right across the mouth so hard the chair fell backwards and she ended up in the floor. It took almost an hour for me to convince him she needed medical attention. He finally agreed when I told him that if someone else saw her that way, that they might ask questions. I told him that I put in the report that she fell down the stairs. She doesn't see very well close up and I told him that I told the doctors that's why she fell. He seemed satisfied so I dropped it and hoped he wouldn't hurt her ever again."

Mrs. Branson decided to take a break and asked Mrs. Hawkins to excuse her for a few minutes.

As soon as the door shut, Jill allowed the smug look to take over her face. "I should get an A+ for this performance," she thought.

Nancy Branson went back to the room where John waited. She told him what his wife had told her. John hung his head and looked completely defeated.

"I wanted to tell you that for tonight Annie is safe here in the hospital. I'm going to wait to talk to her tomorrow. You and your wife are free to leave but this isn't over. An investigation will continue through Child Services and I'll file a petition tomorrow for guardianship until we decide which one of you is telling the truth. Would you like to see your wife now?" she asked him.

John stood and said, "Yes I may as well get it over with. Will you do me a favor and check on Annie. Would it be possible for me to go and tell her good night? I'd like for her to know I'm still here for her."

"Yes, I'll go to the desk and ask for permission for her to see you just for a minute. I'll find out what room she is in and make sure she's up to seeing you and your wife. Understand though, I will be in the room with you at all times."

"I appreciate it, and thank you for caring," John said.

Mrs. Branson went to the nurse's station and asked for the room number. They told her Annie was in 3211. Mrs. Branson motioned for John to follow her and she led him to the room where his wife waited. When she opened the door and Jill spotted John she could see the look of apprehension on Mrs. Hawkins's face. John didn't say a word to her.

Mrs. Branson led them to the elevator, went to the nurse's station, and asked if Annie was able to have a few minutes with her parents. The nurse told her that Annie was awake and doing well but they could only stay for a little while.

Mrs. Branson told the two of them to wait until she went in and talked with Annie. When she approached Annie's bed, her heart went out to the small girl with so many problems. She went to the side of the bed and said, "Annie honey, my name is Mrs. Branson, and I wanted to check and see how you were doing. Would you like to see your parents for a few minutes before they leave?"

She watched Annie's face and saw the fear and hesitation. "Is my mommy here too? My Daddy said he would stay with me. Can I see him please?"

Mrs. Branson was surprised when she asked for just her Daddy.

"Yes, your mommy and daddy are here. Do you want to see them now?" she asked her.

"I want to see my daddy first. Can I please have some water too?"

"Yes, honey I'll get your water. I'll bring your daddy back with me but he can stay only a minute, okay?"

"Okay and thank you."

She went out in the hall, asked the nurse for water, and told the parents that Annie wanted to see her daddy first. John looked over at Jill with a look of pure hate and followed Mrs. Branson into the room.

Annie smiled when she saw her father and reached up her arms to hug him. He asked her, "Pumpkin, how are you doing sweetheart?"

"I'm fine daddy. Is mommy mad at me? I don't want her to be mad. I should have stayed at home. Now, she knows I'm in here and she'll be mad at me."

"Annie sweetheart, don't you worry about Mommy. I'll take care of her. I promised you I would be right here when you woke up. I just wanted to say good night and tell you that I love you. I don't want you to worry about a thing. You just get better so I can take you to the zoo like I promised. Would you like to go when you get better?"

"Yes, daddy I'd love to go to the zoo. But, will mommy let me go? She never let me go before. I want to see the monkeys. Wouldn't it be fun daddy? I love you daddy."

Mrs. Branson was beginning to have little doubt as to which was the evil one in this family. She didn't see how a child could hide genuine love for her father.

"Annie honey, would you like to say good night to your mommy. She's right outside," Mrs. Branson said.

"I guess I can say good night to her. Will you stay with me daddy? I don't want her to be mad."

"Yes, pumpkin, I'll stay right here. Just say good night to

mommy. I'll be back tomorrow to see you. Okay?"

Mrs. Branson went to the door and asked Mrs. Hawkins if she would like to see her daughter.

"Yes, I suppose I should see her," Jill said. She entered the room and walked towards the bed.

Mrs. Branson was standing on the other side and she saw Annie's little body shake, as her mother got close.

"Annie, are you alright," Jill asked. "I was so worried about you. I was so scared when they told me you had to stay here. I love you Annie."

Annie tried to control her fear. She was glad that her daddy was here with her. She looked at her mother and said, "I love you too mommy. You are the best mommy in the whole world. Daddy said we could go to the zoo when I get better. Is that alright?"

"Sure honey, that's fine. We just want you to get better, okay. Mommy and Daddy have to go now so you get some rest and we'll see you tomorrow."

Mrs. Branson waited for them to hug Annie and the three of them walked out of the room. She asked them to wait for her down the hall. She wrote an order on the chart that no visitors were to be in the room unless she gave her permission.

She joined the parents, looked at Mrs. Hawkins, and said, "I will find out who hurt that child. If you ever want to see your daughter again, I suggest that the two of you get your stories straight and admit what happened. Remember no one is to be in the room with her unless I'm there. We'll continue this later." With that said, she walked to the elevator and pushed the button.

Jill glared at her husband. "Now, look what you've done. She thinks I'm a bad mother."

John ignored the comment and walked to the elevator. He didn't say a word while they walked to the car and headed home. When they arrived, he unlocked the door, went straight to the bar, and poured himself a drink.

"Now what John? How are you going to get us out of this one? Do you think for one moment that I will settle for the reputation as a child abuser? Why did you have to take her? She would have gotten over it just like all the other times. I have to think about this and decide what to do now. This child is going to ruin me yet, I just knew it."

"Jill, let me say one thing to you. I don't want to stay with you anymore and I want to take Annie and move. I'll make sure you have plenty of money. You can buy all the clothes and furniture you want. I'll trade you money for your daughter. You think about that and let me know." John walked to the study and closed the door.

CHAPTER FIVE

The nursing staff on the third floor all agreed that Annie was one of the sweetest little girls they had ever seen. Each one of them made several stops in her room by lunchtime. Missy, the nursing assistant assigned to the west wing of the third floor, found a few coloring books in the storeroom and a big box of crayons. She took them to Annie's room and was thrilled when she saw the excitement on her face.

"Can I color any picture I want?" Annie asked.

"Yes, sweetheart, you can color all the pictures if you want. I'll bring some more books tomorrow. Do you like to color?"

"I don't get to use crayons at my house. Mommy says I might ruin the furniture. I spilled a box of pencils once and she told me I could never use any of my crayons or books again. She threw them in the trash."

What Annie said surprised Missy. She thought to herself, "What kind of mother would throw away her child's crayons?"

Annie seemed afraid to open the pages in the coloring book, so Missy sat beside her on the bed and helped her find a picture to color. They chose a picture of a small kitten in a yard filled with flowers.

Missy's pager went off, she told Annie to have fun, and she'd be back in a few minutes. The patient in the next room was on crutches and needed to go to the bathroom. It took ten minutes until she could get back, and she peeked in the room and watched the concentration of Annie's face as she worked on the picture.

31

Annie glanced up and saw her standing in the doorway and instantly shut the book.

"Are you finished with your picture? Would you like some soda or ice cream? I'll bring you some if you want."

"But I'm not supposed to have desserts except on Wednesday. Is today Wednesday? Mommy says that bad girls can't have dessert whenever they want, so I'm afraid I can't have any until Wednesday."

"Annie, if you want ice cream you can have it. I don't think you are bad. I think you are one of the cutest little girls I've ever seen. Are you afraid of me? You don't have to be. I'd never hurt you. No one in the hospital is going to hurt you. We want to make you better."

Missy recalled that the talk at the nurses' station that morning was that Annie's stepfather probably hurt her and that was why she was here. She moved to the side of the bed and touched Annie's hair. "Would you like for me to brush your hair?"

"No, mommy says I shouldn't worry much about the way I look. She told me I was an ugly duckling and nothing would make me pretty so I'm not allowed to have a brush in my room. I have to go to the bathroom if it's not too much trouble. My legs feel funny. The nurse rubbed some stuff on them and I can't feel them like I usually can. I don't know if I can stand on them by myself."

"Oh, honey, the medicine is so you can't feel the pain. Your legs have blisters, and the doctor told us to put medicine on them. Sure, I'll help you."

Missy walked to the head of the bed and unplugged the IV cart. "Which side of the bed is easier for you to get out of?"

"This arm doesn't work right; I'll get out on that side."

Missy had noticed the disfigurement of Annie's right wrist. She helped Annie out of bed and walked slowly to the restroom. She helped Annie on the toilet and told her to yell for her when she was finished.

Missy used the few minutes to straighten the bed. When she heard Annie say she was finished, she went and helped her back to the side of the bed. "Would you like to take a walk down the hall?"

"Yes, I guess I could walk for a little while, if you'll go with me."

"Sure, Annie. I'll stay right with you, I promise."

Missy tied the strings tighter in the back of the gown and they walked out into the hall. She watched Annie's face as she glanced into each room where the other children were. At one room, Annie stopped and stared at the girl in the bed.

"Her name is Lucy. She has a brain tumor but she's doing better. Would you like to go in and say Hi? I'm sure she wouldn't mind. She could use a friend."

"Okay, if you're sure she won't mind. Is she going to die?"

"I'm not sure. She's been a very sick little girl."

"Why doesn't she have any hair? Did her mommy cut it off?"

"No, honey. She lost her hair because she had chemo. Do you know what that is?"

"No."

"Children that have cancer have to have chemotherapy and it makes their hair fall out. It kills the cancer, so we have to give it to them. Let's go in and say hello, alright?"

Annie nodded her head yes. They approached the bed and Lucy looked up and smiled when she saw Missy.

"Hi, Missy. Who's this?" Lucy asked.

"Lucy, this is Annie. We were going for a walk and we wanted to say Hello. How are you doing today? I was going to come and see you as soon as I took Annie back to her room, but this is better. I can make your bed while you two get acquainted."

"Hi Annie, my name is Lucy. How old are you?"

"I'm five and a half. Does your cancer hurt?"

"No, I'm a whole lot better. What is wrong with you?"

"The doctor had to fix it so I could breathe better. I fell and hurt myself. What is that thing?"

"Oh, that's my picture of my cancer. Every day we cut out some more of it and soon it will be all gone. The nurses made me this picture. I will be going home tomorrow. Do you come to the hospital a lot?"

"No, my mommy doesn't want me to come here. I fall all the time and she tells me to not be bad, but sometimes I don't listen. I like your necklace."

"My daddy gave me this. I try not to cry when I get the needles, and he got me this cause I'm a big girl."

"My daddy gets me stuff too. Is your mommy nice too?"

Missy was a little concerned with the tone of the conversation, so she changed the subject by saying, "Girls, it's almost time for lunch. Would you two like to eat together?"

"Yeah, I want Annie to eat here with me. Can she stay please?" Lucy asked.

"Yes, I think I can arrange that. Would you two like to read a book together while I check on your lunch trays? Which book would you like Lucy?"

"I want to read The Little Red Caboose. Have you read that one, Annie? I love when the red caboose reaches the top of the hill. Daddy says I can be strong like the red caboose."

"No, I don't have any books to read. My mommy says I don't deserve any."

"Here Lucy, read this one to her. I'll be back in a second." Missy handed the book to Lucy and hoped that she didn't realize what Annie was saying. She didn't want Lucy to get depressed about what Annie was telling her. She would make herself a note to talk to the nurses about what Annie said about her mother and the situation at home.

Lucy opened the book and Annie climbed up beside her on the bed. The girls were laughing with each other when she came back with their trays. The girls both had hot dogs and macaroni for lunch. She brought another table for Annie and made sure they had what they needed. Her pager beeped and she went out to the desk to check another chart. She passed the head nurse on the way back and asked her if she could meet with her a few minutes.

"Sure, what did you need?" Mrs. Anderson asked.

"I took Annie to Lucy's room and they are eating lunch together."

"Oh, that's nice. I'm sure that Lucy enjoys the company. She is due for her treatment this afternoon and she wasn't in a good mood this morning."

"Yeah, I thought Annie would cheer her up, but I'm worried about a few things that Annie said to her. She told Lucy that her mother wouldn't allow her to read books and she keeps saying how bad she is. Do you think that it's bad for Lucy to talk with her?"

"Oh, you mean because of the abuse in Annie's home? I don't think that Lucy is old enough to understand what abuse means. I wouldn't worry about it unless she does get real upset. It's good for Lucy to have company. I feel sorry for Annie, how awful it must be for your parents to hurt you. I know the hospital has put restrictions on visitors for her, so be careful if anyone wants to visit her, okay?"

"Yes, I read that on her chart. So far, no one has visited her."

"Okay, Missy, was that all you needed?"

"Yes, that's it Mrs. Anderson. Thank you."

Missy headed back to the room. Both girls were almost done with lunch, and Missy asked if they wanted to watch the movie that Lucy's dad brought her.

"Annie, have you seen Snow White before? My dad brought it yesterday, and I can't wait to watch it."

"No, I don't know what Snow White is."

"You never heard of Snow White?"

"No, I never did," Annie said.

"Hold on girls. I'll set the movie up, and Lucy you can tell Annie all about it, okay?"

"Hurry up Missy."

Missy set up the VCR and started the movie. She stood back and watched as Annie saw the images on the screen. She wondered what Annie had missed and had suffered. The world we live in could be so cruel, especially to innocent children.

CHAPTER SIX

Jill woke up and turned to look at the clock. She couldn't believe it was 7:00 a.m. already and she had so much to do. She glanced at the other side of the bed and remembered John slamming the door in her face and telling her that he hated her.

She grabbed her robe and cursed under her breath. She knew it wasn't going to be easy to get him to forgive her this time. Oh well, she would have to work extra hard at being the beautiful se-ductress, it had worked up until now. If only she would have given that child of hers up for adoption when she had the chance, her life would be perfect.

As she hurried to the bathroom, she caught a glimpse of herself in the hall mirror. She'd have to call her beautician today and schedule an appointment to touch up her hair; after all it took hard work to look as good as she did. Even though she couldn't spare the time, her mind drifted back to when she was in grade school.

Jill remembered the first day of school, and how she held on tight to her mother's hand that day. Her mother, Betty Buckner, scolded her for dragging her feet.

"You must hurry Jill, we'll be late, and the teacher won't be happy with you. Now straighten your dress and remember to say yes ma'am and no sir, like I told you. Come on now, it'll be fine." They headed for the principal's office.

Jill didn't want any part of this dumb school. Why did kids have to go to school anyway? I could just stay home and learn from the TV.

The principal stood as they entered the room and asked Mrs. Buckner and Jill to have a seat. "How are you today? Ah, this must be our new pupil, Jill."

"Thank you Mr. Sims. We're just fine, aren't we Jill. We're looking forward to school. Jill is shy but I hope that she makes new friends quickly. Even though she is getting a late start, Jill will work hard and I'm sure she will do fine. Right, Jill?"

Jill looked up at her mother and made a stupid face. She wanted to say she wanted to go back home, but she knew it would get her nowhere.

"Okay, let's get her registered and we'll let Mrs. Grove know that Jill is here. What is your correct address Mrs. Buckner?"

"We live on Stamper Road, actually 4492 West Stamper Road."

"And that is in Centerville, and the zip code is 22546?"

"Yes, that's correct."

"And Jill, may I ask what your birthday is?"

Jill didn't answer and her mother nudged her arm.

"My birthday is June 16. I'm six years old," she timidly answered.

"Thank you. Now, are you ready to meet your teacher and some of your classmates? I just know you'll like it here at Clearview Elementary. Mrs. Buckner, are you going to walk with us to the room? I'd like for Mrs. Grove to meet you too."

"Yes, I'd love to meet her."

Mr. Sims led the way down the hall and as Jill looked around, she was scared to death. The hallways were huge and the rooms seemed to stretch on forever. She hated school already and it was only the first day.

Mr. Sims opened the door to the room and Jill peeked around her mother's legs to stare at the other kids. She didn't recognize any of the kids, and she knew she wouldn't like any of them.

"Mrs. Grove, I'd like you to meet your new pupil, Jill Buckner. And, this is her mother, Betty. Class, this is Jill. She is new to this school and I know you all will make her feel welcome."

The other kids stared at the new girl. Two of the boys in the back leaned toward each other and after whispering to one another snickered. Mr. Sims threw a look their way and waved his finger at them. All was quiet.

"Mrs. Buckner, I'm Mrs. Grove and I'll be Jill's first grade teacher. I'm glad to meet you. And Jill, I have a desk here in the front for you. Now class, take out your workbooks and start on page 6 while I do Jill's paperwork." As the children found their books, the sound of pages turning filled the room.

"Mrs. Buckner, I'm sure Jill will be fine and I'm glad I had the chance to meet you. Jill, if you would please take your seat, I'll collect your books from the back shelf."

Mr. Sims opened the door and gave a second look at the boys who did the snickering and motioned for Mrs. Buckner to follow. As the door closed, Jill could feel the other children staring at her back, and tried to calm down and not show her fear. She knew the boys would laugh if they saw her knees shaking.

"Jill, this is the book we are working on now. You've not been here for the first two weeks, but I'm sure with a little help, you'll soon catch up with the rest of the class."

Mrs. Grove opened her book to page 6, returned to the front of the class, and went to the blackboard. Jill looked at the book, but had no idea what the lines meant. She heard the teacher talking about the letter A. She had a tablet on her desk and watched the girl beside her making a straight line on her paper, so she picked up her pencil and copied the action. They worked on a few more letters, and she tried hard to concentrate. Her head started to hurt, and she was glad when she heard a bell ring and the teacher said it was time for recess.

Out on the playground, one of the girls came over to her and said, "Hi, my name is Mary Ann. I like your dress. Do you like to swing?"

"Yes, I like to swing."

Jill followed Mary Ann to the swing, and the girls were soon flying high in the air. The rest of the day wasn't so bad. Jill was glad she had a least one friend.

Mrs. Grove went to the office after the kids boarded the buses. She asked to see Mr. Sims, and waited for a few minutes until he opened the door and asked her to come into his office.

"What can I do for you, Mrs. Grove?"

"I wanted to ask you a few questions about Jill Buckner. I was wondering why she wasn't here for the first two weeks of school. Her mother seemed very nice, and I thought they might have moved into our neighborhood. Do they have any other children?"

"No, I think Jill is the only child. I don't want to say too much until I understand the problem."

"That's fine; I didn't mean to pry."

"Actually, Jill was sick and in the hospital for two weeks. According to the report I received, Jill's doctors were concerned with her heart rate. I don't think it is an immediate problem, and according to the therapist, stress tends to make her heart speed up. I hope to get a full report from the school nurse and would like to set up a meeting between the three of us later in the week."

"That would be fine, just let me know when."

Mrs. Grove thought about Jill on her way home. She thought she was such a pretty girl and hoped she could help her settle into the first grade without any problems.

When Jill got off the bus that first evening, she knew she'd hate school forever. She tried all day to ignore the other kids, but she could feel their stares on her back every minute of the day.

Her mother met her at the door and asked her how the day went. She had a tendency to ramble and Jill learned to listen with half of her attention and plan a strategy with the other half.

"Did you like the other kids in your class? They all seemed like wonderful children. I hope you can make lots of friends and I can't wait to meet all the mothers."

Jill already had picked out the girls she wanted for friends, and the ones that she thought were beneath her would soon feel her less than friendly side.

Jill didn't hate her mother, but she didn't think she loved her either. She felt humiliated by her, and even at her age, she set her sights way above the goals her mother had.

While she was in the hospital, the doctors asked her many questions. After that first day, she figured out the answers they wanted to hear. Every time she used her looks and innocence to outsmart them, she loved the feeling of triumph it gave her.

"Jill, hang your dress up and put on your play clothes. Dinner won't be ready for a while. I'm so glad your first day went so well." Her mother brushed a kiss on the top of her head and went downstairs.

Jill took her dress and hung it in the closet with great care. She loved this dress more than any she owned. This dress was the real reason she went to the hospital. The day at the mall when she saw the dress, and she knew she had to have it for the first day of school, was one of the first times she used her tantrums to their fullest height. Jill at six years old was a manipulator, and a good one at that.

Jill's father, Edward, worked in the steel plant in the center of the town. Centerville's main industry was producing steel. More than half of the population worked for The Bethlehem Steel Company.

The wages were not spectacular, but most of the men made enough to afford their bills and a few luxuries. Her mother watched everything they spent and she was proud of the money the two of them had put away for Jill to attend college. It was important to Edward to send his only daughter to school to learn a trade, and hope that she could move away from working in the dirty steel industry.

Jill spotted the dress as soon as they stepped into The Kids Corner Shoppe. She knew her mother usually went to the clearance aisle first, but Jill knew what she wanted and fully intended to get it.

The pale blue dress was hanging on the wall, in a display for the beginning of the school year. The Kids Corner Shoppe had only ordered two of the dresses, because the market for an expensive dress like this one in this town was small.

When Mrs. Buckner saw the price, she instantly told Jill, "Honey, it's just way too much money for one dress. Your father works hard to make the money, and we shouldn't waste it."

Jill hesitated about three seconds before she started a tantrum that shocked her mother. Jill was a headstrong child, but her mother could settle her down most of the time.

Jill didn't mean to hold her breath long enough to pass out, but her determination to have this one dress, was worth what she had to do to make sure it was hanging in her closet before she went to school.

As soon as Jill hit the floor, the attendant, Miss Blevins was at her side. The ambulance arrived quickly and took her to the emergency room. The heart specialist was concerned about Jill's elevated blood pressure, and ran tests. He wanted to make sure that she had no heart abnormalities before he released her.

Jill didn't mind being in the hospital. She kinda liked all the attention. She lost track of the number of nurses and doctors that commented on her beauty. Before this, she had not thought about pretty or ugly much at all. When she heard one of the doctors comment to another one that she would be a beautiful woman some day and could choose any man she wanted, Jill stored it away to use as she grew up.

Jill asked her mother if they could buy the blue dress for the first day of school the first night at the hospital. Her mother didn't want to upset Jill, so she kept telling her that they'd have to wait and see.

"But mommy, I want to be the only one with that pretty dress. I can't go to school without it. I won't go, I won't go."

"Jill, I told you that we can't afford to spend $50.00 on one dress. That's more than I have ever spent on one outfit my entire life. Your father wouldn't be pleased with us, honey. Don't you understand?"

"I don't care, I just want the dress. If you buy me the dress, I promise I'll go to school every day and work hard. You know I can, mommy. I want that dress."

"We'll see about it honey when you get home."

"Mommy, I'm not going home until I get that dress. I'll tell the doctors that you are mean, and they won't let you take me home. Will you buy me that dress please?"

Jill had mastered a look of innocence that usually won her mother over. She laid it on doubly thick; she would do whatever it took to get that dress. Her mind was made up; she wouldn't go to school without it.

The first week, the doctors didn't understand why Jill became light headed every time she stood up. They ran several tests and discovered no medical cause.

The second week, Jill couldn't believe that her mother was being so stubborn. If she would just go get the dress, Jill would quit lying about feeling faint and she could go home.

Her father came to see her one evening and Jill started crying in front of him and told him that she wanted the pretty dress they saw in the store. When he questioned his wife, he told her to go and buy the dress for Jill as a coming home present. The battle had been won. Jill miraculously got better, and went home after the fourteenth day. The dress was there for her first morning of school.

The first grade passed fast and Jill mastered her skill with her teachers, especially the male ones, and all the boys in the school. She learned that beauty goes a long way when you want something.

When Jill was a teenager, she looked at her mother in ways that were more critical. Her mother wasn't an ugly woman, but she was no match for Jill's looks. She tried to improve her mother's tastes in clothes and make-up, but her mother didn't see the significance of worrying all the time about the way you look. Betty Buckner wasn't vain at all, and her looks didn't rule her days.

Jill begged her dad to pay for many beauty seminars at the local malls. Classes about clothing and applying make-up were Jill's favorite pastime. She learned how to bring out all her best features, and Jill was the most beautiful girl in each class. The old saying about beauty on the outside rang true with Jill, she had no beauty at all on the inside. She worried about herself, and applied each new trick on how to get all she wanted.

When Jill got in high school, the boys followed her wherever she went. Most of the girls were jealous of her looks, and consequently Jill didn't have many girlfriends. The plain Jane's in the class became Jill's puppets and waited on her hand and foot.

Many mornings Jill set her alarm for 4:00 a.m. so she could spend forty-five minutes straightening her hair. The process was slow and tedious, but when she was done, it looked spectacular. Then when her hair was done to her satisfaction, she would spend another thirty minutes applying her make-up. It took extra time to cover up the circles under her eyes from the lack of sleep. Unfortunately, it was the price she had to pay to make sure that every person's head turned when she walked by.

At the senior prom, Jill received fifteen invitations for dates. She chose the best-looking boy out of the class for the privilege of going out with her for the evening. The pictures of Jill Buckner and Michael Brinks, the head quarterback, made the front page of the evening paper. The photographer wanted everyone to feast on Jill's beauty, because she was something to behold.

Betty and Edward, Jill's parents were extremely proud of their daughter. For graduation, they gave her a bright red Mustang, and her father recorded her squeals the night they gave it to her.

After Jill graduated from high school, she hadn't formed good study habits, so she wasn't looking forward to continuing her schooling. Nevertheless, she took the money her father and mother saved and enrolled in the local junior college. She applied for courses relating to retail and sales with her electives in beauty and cosmetics. Jill was a natural born celebrity type that loved to be in the spotlight.

One of her girlfriends talked her into auditioning for a play the school was doing and she got the leading role of Marilyn Monroe. Jill had the perfect skin and features of Marilyn Monroe and when she wore the blonde wig over her own dark hair, she was a knockout. She was self-absorbed before the role and soon lost all interest in anyone else's feelings but her own. Jill took the part of selfish beauty to heart and as she swooned in the popularity. Her beautiful face and body was her ticket to gain worldly fame and fortune.

Jill's roommate was Norma Jean Billings. Norma Jean was a petite red haired, sweet kid. Her family had plenty of money, but you couldn't tell it by the way she acted. Norma Jean cared about others and she spent her days enjoying her classes and spending her free time just having innocent fun. Everyone at the dorm liked her and she was often asked how she could stand living with a selfish witch like Jill.

"Oh, you have to overlook her, she wouldn't hurt a fly. She isn't as cold as she seems. Yesterday she asked me about the handicapped girl down the hall. We were talking about carrying her books for the whole week, just to help her out." Norma Jean didn't tell the whole truth, she was the one that wanted to carry her books; she just didn't want everyone to think that Jill was that hateful.

Actually, Norma Jean feared Jill a little. She overheard a conversation between Jill and two other girls, Marsha and Janet. They followed Jill around almost everywhere she went. Norma Jean had wondered about the relationship and hoped that Jill really did care about the two girls. The part of the conversation she heard left little doubt as to why Jill befriended them.

Jill was saying to them, "I told you two the only way that you could walk with me is if you ironed every one of my shirts this week. Now, you bring three of them back not finished and you want me to thank you. Who are you kidding? You have an hour to make sure every one of them is starched and ironed and hanging in my closet, or I find two other idiots to be my pals. You got that?"

Marsha and Janet grabbed the shirts and hurried out the door and down the hall. Norma Jean noticed that they were still Jill's shadows on Friday and she knew that the shirts had been ironed and hung within that hour. Norma Jean backed away from Jill somewhat after the incident but she didn't think that Jill even noticed. For every friend that Jill offended, usually two more lined up to be seen with the "prettiest gal in the school."

Norma Jean made a comment to Jill once about treating people with respect and she didn't care much for Jill's answer.

"I don't have to respect the stupid people's feelings; they kiss the ground I walk on without my asking them to. I can't help if they are the ones with the problem. Wouldn't you want to be seen with me if you were as ugly as they are? I give to them more than they give to me. Such is life!"

Even though Norma Jean had a different circle of friends, she always treated Jill with respect and courtesy.

CHAPTER SEVEN

Jill's attention focused on Kurt Lawson, the leading man in the play. The first time she saw him, her breath caught in her throat. Their roles threw them together, and he couldn't help but notice Jill and her perfect face and body. Kurt wanted to be a sports announcer after he graduated. By the time the first semester was over, the two of them were inseparable. Jill felt she wasn't whole unless she was with Kurt.

During the first half of the school term, Jill and Kurt made three trips home to see her parents. Betty and Edward liked Kurt and hoped to eventually see the two get married and give them a few grandchildren.

Kurt had a selfish side in his character, maybe even a little worse than Jill. The two of them made a great looking couple and other kids flocked around them to be in the "cool" circle.

Kurt's downfall was drugs. He would smoke marijuana whenever he could get it. A few of the boys he knew would get it for him, in exchange for the right to be his best buddy. Jill wasn't aware of his drug habit, and she never touched any drugs or alcohol since they might affect her looks, and nothing was more important than that.

By the last semester of the first year at college, Kurt had advanced to using cocaine. His attitude towards Jill grew more abusive. She was so in love with him that she took his abuse and clung to him more. When school ended, Kurt asked her to marry him and she said yes.

The wedding was a wonderful affair, and the guests all agreed that the two of them were the best-looking bride and groom they'd ever seen.

Kurt and Jill bought a small house next to the college. Kurt wanted to take extra courses in the fall so he could finish early. He had big plans of being on TV as an announcer within a year.

Jill found a job at the nearest mall selling cosmetics in the Macy's Department Store. Jill's training and schooling helped her to advance and she soon earned a promotion to Manager of the Eastern Division. She loved to work with all the new products and she had a natural talent for what the public wanted.

The first year of their marriage flew by quickly. Kurt stayed busy at school with his classes and worked part time for the local station doing some ads for the local merchants. His deep voice on the audio commercials opened up more than one door, and by the end of the next semester, his goal had changed. He wanted to be an actor and told Jill they'd be moving to California within a few months. She wasn't pleased.

"Why would I want to move?" she asked him. "I have a good job and I don't have any desire to live there. What do you think you are going to do? You can't seriously think that you can be a movie star?"

"Yes, I do think I can land a movie contract. How do you think anyone else gets discovered? If I stay here, I sure won't. Besides, you don't think they have big shopping malls in California. You can transfer there and maybe even make more money. Isn't it worth a try? What's holding us here?" Kurt asked.

Jill surprised herself by considering moving for Kurt. For the first time in her life, she actually didn't mind making a sacrifice for someone else. Kurt was the most important thing to her. She didn't want to live her life without him in it. So, within a few months, they made plans to move.

Her mother and father hated to see them move away. Their hopes for grandchildren was rekindled every time they had a visit from Kurt and Jill, and they kept assuring them that they would only wait so long, and then they'd really start hounding them.

For the next few months, life was busy moving, finding a new home, discovering a new part of the world. Jill did get a position with Macy's and all her co-workers were impressed with her knowledge and her beauty. She loved the opportunities to try new products and market each one. The company approached her and proposed a campaign using her face on a new line of make-up. Jill's bloated ego accepted immediately. Within a few months Jill heard about a position with the Golden State Ad Agency. She applied and was accepted immediately. The partners were impressed with her credentials and she settled into her new job with ease.

Kurt spent his days auditioning for small soap opera parts. The competition was fierce, but finally he secured a full time part in a new show, The World At Its Best. Life was very complicated for them both, and within a few months, they grew apart. Kurt's looks drew the girls to him and sometimes he didn't fight too hard to keep them away. His drug use slowed for a while, but one of the main characters in the soap supplied him freely, and it didn't take long for him to crave the cocaine every day.

Jill began to notice the change in Kurt, and after a little snooping, she found the cause. She tried to shame Kurt into quitting for her, and he really did try for a couple of weeks. But the drugs won out and the relationship started to decline. For the first time in her life, Jill cared about something besides her looks. She didn't want to lose Kurt. She loved him in spite of the drug habit and the abuse she suffered. Kurt's personality changed with the cocaine. He was mean and hateful about everything.

Jill spent extra time worrying about her appearance and half her salary on a new wardrobe. Before when she had a difficult problem, she tried to solve it with bribes and promises. But this time she had a lot at stake, her marriage. Jill tried every trick she had to win back Kurt's attention. She played the part of the seductress, and for a few months, Kurt's disposition changed a little and he paid more attention to her.

Jill started feeling a little sick to her stomach in the mornings and she thought she was working too hard and needed to slow down. The sickness grew worse so she made a doctor appointment. The news she heard completely floored her. She was pregnant. Jill didn't have any desire to be a mother. She couldn't remember one thought she had given to any child ever in her entire life. She didn't like children at all.

That afternoon when Kurt came home, she surprised him with a home cooked meal. Everything she sat on the table was Kurt's favorite dishes. Their dinner went well, and afterward she broke the news to him that he would soon be a father. Kurt was shocked and speechless for a few minutes. As the realization of the news sank in, his mood changed. He was overjoyed. The thought of having a son or daughter made him happy and he vowed that he'd never touch the alcohol or drugs again.

Jill considered getting an abortion, and she went so far as to discuss it with her doctor. He suggested therapy to help her marriage and didn't support the idea of abortion. He recommended a therapist and Kurt and Jill met with him for three months every Thursday.

Jill was seven months pregnant and not in the best of humor. She hated what the baby was doing to her figure. Her skin stayed radiant, and she did have a glow, but she still hated carrying the weight of the baby. She barely ate anything because she worried about stretch marks ruining her body. The new baby wasn't a top priority, but she was willing to go through with it for Kurt. She thought it was the one thing that would cement their relationship. As long as she had Kurt's child, he would stay with her.

When she was eight months pregnant, she received a phone call late one evening. It was the local police headquarters. They told her that her husband had an accident and asked if someone could bring her to the station. She told them that she was home alone and she had no one to call. Jill had few friends and no one at all that she could call on for a situation like this. She assured the officer that she was capable of handling the problem by herself. She asked if Kurt was hurt and why if there had been an accident; why not meet them at the hospital. The officer told her that she'd have to come to the station for the details, and asked if she would like a patrol car to pick her up. She told him she was eight months pregnant, and yes, she would like a car to come and get her.

Within fifteen minutes, the patrol car was outside her house. She grabbed her purse and ran out. The officer held the door for her and reassured her that he would take care of her, considering her condition.

They arrived at the station and the officer escorted her to the captain's office. When she entered his office, he recognized her from the magazine campaign pictures his wife was showing him yesterday. He felt sorry for her, but he had to deliver the bad news.

After making sure there was nothing that they could get for her, he told her that Kurt, her husband, had been found in an alley two hours ago. From what the preliminary findings showed, he died from an overdose. Kurt was only thirty-one years old.

Captain Harris asked Jill if she would identify the body. "I'm sorry to ask you that Mrs. Lawson, but we need the next of kin to take care of this. I'll call someone else, his parents, or family members if you would like me to. I hate to ask you do this since you are pregnant."

"There is no one else to call. We moved here from Virginia, and Kurt's parents are both deceased. He didn't have any other family. I will call my parents to fly out here. But right now, we have no family here at all."

"Are you sure you are up to this. Can I call your doctor for you? This is a hard task for anyone to do. From what we can tell, someone beat your husband with a blunt instrument, and may have administered a lethal dose of cocaine in his system. We found the drug next to your husband's body. Did your husband use cocaine, Mrs. Lawson? Do you know of anyone that would want to hurt him? Did he owe someone money?"

Jill hated this. She wanted to scream and never stop. Why would Kurt do this to her? She thought he quit using any drug months ago. He seemed so much better.

Jill took a few moments and then said, "Yes, my husband used cocaine on a regular basis up until a few months ago. He told me he had quit. I don't know of anyone that hated him, or anyone he owed money. I have no idea what happened. At this point, I'm not sure I care. I don't deserve this. I will go and identify his body, if you need me to. Are you sure it is my husband?"

"Ma'am we found his wallet with his other possessions. I'm positive it is your husband from his picture on his driver's license. I wouldn't put you through this if I had any doubt. I'm sorry, but this is procedure. I need someone to claim the body. We'll send it to the morgue for an autopsy. Would you like a few moments before we proceed to the morgue? Would you like some water?"

"Yes, if you don't mind I could use some water. I just want to get this over."

The captain called the desk and asked someone to bring Mrs. Lawson water. He waited until she drank the water and then stood.

"Are you ready to go now?"

"Yes, I'm ready. You said my husband was beaten. Is it bad?"

"Yes, I'm afraid it is. Whoever attacked him, knew what they were doing. From what we have determined so far someone beat your husband and crushed his skull. We can't be sure until we have the autopsy report. Shall we go then?"

He led the way down the corridor and opened the door to the morgue. "Mrs. Lawson if you could wait here in front of this window, I'll let the coroner know we are here. He will bring the body in front of the glass for you to see. Are you sure you are up to this?"

"Yes, Captain, I'm not a child. I can handle this."

The Captain opened the adjoining door and Jill braced herself for what was to come. She thought, "I hate Kurt for this. He lied to me. Now I'll be all alone. It's not fair."

Jill heard the door open and the Captain walked to her and stood beside her. She watched as a man pushed a stretcher covered with a white sheet to the window. Captain Harris looked at her and Jill nodded her head.

The coroner pulled the sheet down from the body, and Jill knew instantly it was Kurt. She could see the damage to his head, but she had no doubt that it was him. She felt her knees buckle and Captain Harris reached out to steady her. He motioned for the sheet to be pulled back over the body and he turned her and started out of the room.

Jill felt the tears welling up in her eyes. She didn't cry often, and wondered if she could get through this. The baby kicked in her stomach and she placed her hand over it and made a little whimper sound. Captain Harris took her back to his office and called for one of the female officers to come and check on her.

"Mrs. Lawson, are you positive that this is your husband's body?"

"Yes sir, I'm positive. Now what do I do? Do you have any idea who did this to him? I want to know. I want whoever did this to the father of my baby to pay. I have money and I want the best attorney to find and prosecute whoever did this right away."

"Mrs. Lawson, let me assure you that whoever did this will be punished severely. I don't know how long the autopsy will take but if you call my office tomorrow I'm sure we should know something by then."

There was a knock at the door and the captain went to see who it was. Officer Kyrsten Attig came into the office and bent to take Mrs. Lawson's pulse. She asked, "How are you doing? Are you having any pain at all? I think you should lie down."

Jill answered quickly, "I don't have to lie down. I'm just pregnant, not sick. I want to leave now. I'll call tomorrow and see if you have found out anything."

Officer Attig continued to count her pulse. She tuned to the Captain when she was done and said, "Mrs. Lawson's pulse is a little high, but I don't think it is an immediate concern."

"Thank you officer. Do you want me to call for a car now to take you home? I can't imagine how much of a strain this is to you. My condolences are with you, and whatever you need, just call me. I'll give you one of my cards." He reached into his drawer and gave her a card.

Jill rose, thanked him, and said, "I appreciate all you've done and please call me as soon as you know anything."

The captain motioned for the officer to take Jill home. When she arrived, she locked the front door, made it as far as the living room sofa, and then collapsed. Her heart would never mend. She lay on the sofa and sobbed. Why did Kurt do this? Did he owe money? Was she going to have to pay it? She finally got up and went into the kitchen to prepare something to eat.

Jill planned to have meat loaf tonight for Kurt's supper. Now what was she going to do? She knew she wouldn't feel like eating for quite some time. She decided to fix it anyway, and got the ingredients ready. She would freeze it to use later.

While the meat loaf was in the oven, she went to take a shower. The baby was kicking hard today. Did he, or she, understand what was going on? Could a child know when they have lost a parent? She couldn't remember any time that the baby had kicked so much. Did it know what was wrong?

She prepared her supper and went into the living room. Usually she ate at the small kitchen table with Kurt, but since he wasn't here, she didn't want to do the normal routine. Her life now wouldn't be normal. How was she going to handle funeral arrangements? She hadn't attended a funeral since she was a child. The last one she remembered going to was a cousin on her father's side. Now she had to bury her husband with help from no one. She would call her parents in the morning and send them money for a plane ticket.

As Jill sat on the sofa, she thought back over her marriage and life with Kurt. He was really the only person she had felt love for in her whole life. She didn't want to go on without him. Why would he leave her all alone? Were the drugs so important to him he gave his life for them? She really had thought he quit a few months ago. But, I guess she and the baby weren't enough for him.

The baby kicked again and Jill felt hatred grow for the thing that she carried inside her. She would rather have lost the baby than Kurt. She didn't want to give birth to something she hated. She would contact her doctor tomorrow and put it up for adoption. Without Kurt, she had no reason to keep it.

As soon as she decided to get rid of the baby, a peace came over her and she just wanted to go to bed and sleep. Tomorrow was going to be a busy day.

CHAPTER EIGHT

Jill was awake before the sun came up. Usually she would jump up and face the day with enthusiasm. She loved her home, her job, her husband, and in general, life had been good. Now, she hated her home, she wasn't sure about her job, and she was determined to rid herself of this baby. She went into the bathroom to brush her teeth after fixing her coffee. She turned sideways in the mirror and was simply disgusted with her protruding stomach. She thought to herself, why would any woman want to be pregnant? She hated it.

For a few seconds she considered trying to kill the baby. "I wonder how someone would go about it. Could I do it without hurting myself? Why am I talking to myself?" she asked aloud. She dismissed the thought for now and went downstairs. The doctor would know who would be willing to take a baby from a woman

51

who just lost her husband. "It's probably done every day," she thought to herself.

She ate a small breakfast and after taking a shower, found the card the Captain gave her and called the station. The officer at the desk told her that the captain wouldn't be in for another hour. She wasn't pleased and told him so. She was used to having things done immediately. She had never been a patient person.

She left her home number and insisted that the captain call her when he came in.

She found her phone directory and called her doctor's office. She got their voice mail, so she left a message for the doctor to call her.

As Jill sat on the sofa, the unfairness of the whole situation became too much for her, and before she knew what she was doing, the pillows from the couch went flying across the room. By the time her anger subsided, she had made a mess of the whole room. There were magazines scattered on the floor, the flower arrangements on her end tables ripped to shreds, and the pictures of her and Kurt smashed to pieces.

Exhausted she collapsed on the floor and she sat and cried for a half hour. Life had taken a wrong turn for her and she really wondered what the next step was. She wasn't usually helpless. All her life she determined to take control of her own destiny and she knew exactly what she wanted from life. Now, look at the mess Kurt left her. He was a coward hiding with his drugs, and putting himself in places he should never have been. Now he was dead. Now he was absolutely no help to her.

Jill went upstairs and fixed her make-up. Even if life was hopeless, she fell back on her old habit of making herself look the best she could. It gave her the confidence to face the day. She picked out a cream-colored two-piece suit to wear. At eight months pregnant, she was a very beautiful woman.

The phone rang and she went to answer it. Captain Harris said, "Mrs. Lawson, I received your message. I did talk with the coroner this morning and he should be able to release your husband's body tomorrow morning. The funeral home you choose can call him and make the necessary arrangements. I haven't had a chance to talk to the officers assigned to this case yet, but as soon as I do, I'll call you with an update. We are ruling your husband's death a homicide."

"So you're telling me that Kurt was murdered? Do you think someone he knew killed him? Are there any clues as to who did this horrible thing to my husband?"

"No, right now I have nothing definite to tell you. The coroner did find cocaine in your husband's system. I'm sure that the officers will follow the evidence and I'll inform you the second I have an update. Is there anything else I can do for you?"

"No, I'll call the funeral home this morning. Since my husband is now gone, I must learn to take of myself. I'll be fine. I have some more phone calls to make and I'll be in touch with you soon."

"Remember if I can do anything else, just call me. I'm so sorry about your husband's death, Mrs. Lawson."

"Thank you, Captain Harris. I will talk to you soon. Good-bye."

After Captain Harris hung up the phone, he thought to himself, "I wouldn't want to cross her. I think she knows how to take of herself."

She waited for a while before she called her parents. Her mother was very upset to hear about Kurt's death. She called Jill's father to the phone and when he heard, he asked if she was alright. "How is the baby doing? You must take care of the baby. It's all you have left of Kurt now."

Jill told her father that the police thought Kurt's death was a homicide and asked that he not tell her mother. She didn't want her to fall apart. She told him she was going to call the airline and book a flight for some time the following day and whenever she had the details, she would call and let them know. Her father assured Jill that they loved her and the baby and they'd wait to hear from her.

Jill shook her head as she hung up the phone. How callous would they think she was when they learned she intended to give away her baby? Would they love her then? Her feelings hadn't changed. She really didn't want this baby at all.

She made the next call to her office. She told her secretary, Carla, what happened and was not in the mood for her shocked reaction. Carla should have expected the cool reception from Mrs. Lawson. She knew her well after working with her for two years. In all that time, she kept her personal feelings well hid. Mrs.

Lawson wasn't an easy woman to work for, but the pay was just too good to give up. She assured her that she would take care of things at her office until she heard from her.

The rest of the staff was shocked to hear of Mr. Lawson's murder. Most of them had met him, and all the women swooned over him, he was so handsome. They felt sorry for Mrs. Lawson, even though most of them didn't personally care for her. She didn't have many friends at the company. Yet, everyone was in awe of her beauty and grace, and her ability to sell the product won their respect.

Jill started a list of people to contact for the funeral. She wasn't sure of the contact person's name for the staff and Kurt's co-workers. She wondered how they would write Kurt out of the script. Maybe they would murder his character. Wouldn't that be ironic?

She tried to call Gary, Kurt's best friend from the show. Gary's wife, Amanda, said she had no idea where he was but assured her she would give him a message as soon as she could. She did tell Jill a number to call for the cast director for the show.

Jill called and listened to another shocked reaction from Kurt's director. No one could believe someone would deliberately hurt Kurt. Jill told him she would call as soon as she knew the arrangements. He thanked her and told her he would fax a copy of the staff and co-workers of Kurt's. It took her another ten minutes to get off the phone.

Then she called her gynecologist, Dr. Jackson, and was told that he was out of the office for the day. The receptionist made her appointment for the following morning to see him. She told Jill if she needed to see someone sooner, all she had to do was call the office and someone would clear an appointment for her, but Jill assured her that she could wait until the following day.

The next phone call would be difficult. She got the phone book to find funeral homes in the area. She knew Kurt had sufficient life insurance, but a thought occurred to her. Would they pay a claim for someone that was murdered? She would have to call the insurance agent and ask him.

She found a funeral home close by and she called them. She wasn't pleased with the lack of professionalism the person on the phone displayed, so she told them she was going to call someone else and hung up.

She scanned down the list and chose another one. The man that answered asked several questions and said, "Mrs. Lawson, I'm James Harkins, and I own the funeral home. I can assure you that our service and prices are the best around. I would be glad to meet with you this morning to discuss the details. May I ask what happened to your husband?"

"I'd rather not go into that just yet, but if I can make an appointment for 12:30 today, I'll give you the details then."

"I'm sorry. I didn't mean to pry. Yes, 12:30 is fine. I'll be expecting you, and thank you for calling."

She still had a while before she had to leave, so she thought she would go through Kurt's clothes to find a suit for him. She went to his closet and just touching his clothing broke her heart. How could she live without him? The memories upset her and she slammed the door to the closet and hurried back downstairs. That job would have to wait. Maybe she would have her father choose Kurt's clothing when he arrived.

The phone rang again and when she answered, it was Captain Harris.

"Mrs. Lawson, I'm sorry to bother you but I need to ask you some questions. Do you know someone named Gary Enfield? Someone discovered his body a few blocks from your husband. I need to know if there is a connection between the two men."

"Yes, my husband worked with Gary on the soap opera TV series. I talked with his wife a short while ago, and she told me that she had no idea where Gary was. Are you telling me that both Kurt and Gary were murdered? I know that Gary supplied my husband with drugs, and they spent a lot of time together. I have no idea if they were together last night. I didn't think to ask Gary's wife if he came home at all last night. I'll give you her number and you can ask her."

"Yes, thank you. I believe the two murders are connected. I appreciate the information. Have you made any arrangements yet? I hope that this doesn't hold up the process with the release of the body. Sometimes when two cases are related, we handle the evidence a little differently. I'll call you with any further information."

The thought of Kurt and Gary both being killed shocked Jill. Her hands shook and her heart raced. She didn't like this one bit. Her life had been neat and orderly. Now it was one complete disaster. What next?

CHAPTER NINE

Jill arrived at the funeral home at 12:15. The receptionist recognized her from the make-up campaign ads and told her how she used the colors Jill recommended. She wanted to ask for her autograph, but she thought it might be offensive under the circumstances. She asked her to have a seat and Mr. Harkins would be ready for her in a few minutes.

Mr. Harkins came down the hall and asked her to follow him to his office. Jill thought the decor was sensitive and decided that she would use this funeral home. He showed her the caskets and she chose one she thought Kurt would have liked.

"Mrs. Lawson, I was wondering if you mind talking about what happened to your husband? You mentioned an accident, and I didn't want to press you over the phone. Where is your husband's body, is it at the hospital? We will need to know so we can handle the transport here to our facility."

"I'm sorry I was short with you over the phone. I just didn't want to repeat all the details over and over to everyone I called. I do like your facility and I would like you to handle all the arrangements and the funeral. I know I will have to accept and deal with what has happened, but I'm not sure I can. My husband was murdered. His body was discovered in an alley last night. According to the police investigation, someone crushed his skull and administered an overdose of cocaine. Actually, my husband's co-worker was also found a short distance away."

Mr. Harkins was indeed shocked. The victims of crimes were hard funerals. Jill continued, "The police suspect that it was a drug deal gone bad. I'm in shock, and as you can see, very pregnant. That isn't a good combination. I apologize for my attitude with you, but I'm sure you understand?"

"Yes, of course. Was your husband badly injured? Do you want a closed casket?"

"The blow to the head did some damage, and when I identified the body at the police station, I wasn't paying a lot of attention to anything. Yes, I do think that a closed casket would be best. I don't want thrill seekers to come just to view the body of someone who was murdered. I shouldn't say that but I'm sure in your line of work, you would agree."

"Yes, I do agree. Do you know if they have cleared his body for release? I presume that he is in the morgue at the police station."

"Yes, I talked to Captain Harris this morning and he told me that he should know for sure how long it will take later today. I told him that you would call him and handle that."

"Yes. That's fine. I'll call him within the hour. Now, do you have clothing for your husband, or do you want us to provide a suit? We do have appropriate clothing, but if you prefer something from your husband's wardrobe, that would be fine."

"I wanted to wait for my father to arrive to help with that. I don't think I can go through Kurt's things. Do I have to do that right away?"

"No, we'll take care of that later. Do you expect a lot of people?"

"Yes, Kurt played in a TV soap opera and had many friends there. I also expect some of his fans may try to attend. I thought of having a small memorial just for the ones that supported his character on the show. Would that be possible?"

"Yes, we can discuss that later. If you would like, I have books with different memorial cards to choose from, and thank you cards. While you look, I'll go collect the papers and be right back."

Jill took the thick books from him, and leafed through the styles. She chose one with the Lord's Prayer on the front. The thank you cards matched and she placed the marker in the appropriate page. When Mr. Harkins came back, she showed him her choices.

"Can I ask you a question, Mr. Harkins? If my husband was indeed murdered, can I collect his insurance? I'll need help when the baby is born." She thought to herself, "Yeah, if only he knew I

57

was thinking of giving up the baby. What would he think of me then?"

"I'm not sure if your husband's insurance specified circumstances that would keep you from filing a claim. I'll call and check with them if you phone here later today and give the receptionist the necessary information. Most insurance companies pay everything except suicide. From what I understand, your husband didn't commit suicide, is that right?"

"Yes, Captain Harris told me the initial findings indicate that my husband's skull was crushed, and that is murder. I'll call later and thank you for your help."

Jill left the funeral home and headed back to her house. Her parents would be staying for a week, so she needed to make a list for groceries and supplies. She also wanted to go to her office for a few hours. She wanted to make sure that nothing pressing interfered with the service and she intended to take a few days leave. Her maternity leave was fast arriving, and she thought she would make sure she could be out of her office for at least six weeks. Especially if she wanted to get rid of this baby and not have to answer so many questions.

When Jill arrived home that evening, she had three messages on her machine. The first one was from Captain Harris stating that they needed nothing else from Kurt's body, and the funeral home had arranged to pick up the body tomorrow morning.

The second one was from her father telling her they would arrive at the airport at 10:00 a.m. the next morning.

The third call was from Amanda Enfield, Gary's wife, crying after hearing the news about her husband.

Jill phoned her father to verify the plane number and arrival time. She told him she was looking forward to seeing them.

She didn't return the other two calls. It had been a long day, and this baby was hard to cope with on top of the stress of what had happened the last two days. As she sat on the sofa to remove her shoes, the extra weight of the baby and the added strain on her muscles got to her. She swore that she would rid herself of this unwanted thing as soon as she could.

Jill fixed a light supper and ate at her desk in the study. She logged on to the internet to browse information about adoption.

Most of the information was for adopting a child. Not too many sites talked about giving your own child up for adoption. The only ones she could find were advising young mothers and teens to consider adoption instead of abortion. Finally, she found a site that gave numbers for attorneys looking for children, so she jotted down the numbers just in case her doctor wouldn't help her.

She turned off the computer and rose to go upstairs to get ready for bed. She found herself waiting for the door to open and glancing at the clock. She hadn't realized she expected Kurt to come home before their regular bedtime. She shook herself vigorously to shake off the emotions, and headed up the stairs.

After taking a shower and brushing her teeth, she settled in the bed. Usually she slept on the left side of the bed, but she moved to the right side where Kurt had slept. She curled his pillow under her head and could smell the fragrance of his after-shave he had always worn. She missed her husband.

CHAPTER TEN

Edward and Betty Buckner stood up to exit the plane after it landed. The ride out to California from Centerville, Virginia was a quiet one. The two didn't talk much; they didn't look forward to what was facing them when they met their only daughter. Kurt had changed Jill. She cared about someone besides herself after she met him. They knew their daughter was self-centered before, and hoped she didn't become depressed again. Maybe the birth of this baby would help her and give her something to look forward to each new day.

Jill was waiting for them and after they loaded their luggage, she drove to her house. It was the first time her parents had been in her home, and they were impressed with it. The house had been designed for an actress, and it was fit for any queen. Jill had grown used to living here, and she watched as her parents marveled over its beauty. The view of the ocean from the back deck was spectacular. Her mother couldn't get over the kitchen and she repeated how if she owned this kitchen she would be cooking twenty-four hours a day at least fifty times.

As soon as Jill got her parents settled, she told them she had an appointment at the doctor. They asked if anything was wrong with the baby and she assured them the baby was fine. She wasn't quite prepared to tell them what she had in mind. That news wouldn't make them happy. All this time they had waited for a grandchild, and they were not going to agree with her giving it to someone else.

Kurt's name hadn't come up in the conversation. "Mom, Dad, I know we need to talk about Kurt, and we will as soon as I get back. Dad, if I show you where Kurt's closet is, would you mind picking out a dark suit, a white shirt, and tie for him. I could not bring myself to do it. I'd appreciate it."

"Yes, I'll do that. Do you want me, or your mother, to go with you to the doctor's office? You have been under a great deal of stress. We wouldn't mind at all."

"No, dad, I'm fine. I won't be gone long and you and mom must be tired. Please make yourself at home while I'm gone. Is there anything special I can get for you?"

"No, dear, I wish you'd let me go with you. I miss taking care of you and our grandchild. Have you had the test done to see if it is a boy or girl? I was going to ask you that last month when you called, but I forgot."

"No, mom, I didn't want to know. Kurt wanted to wait and be surprised. He favored a girl, but he said a boy would work. He would have made a good father."

Jill turned, opened the door, and stepped out on the step before they could see her tears. She waved good-bye and went to her car. She didn't want to cry in front of them.

Jill drove downtown to her doctor's office. She asked the receptionist, "I'm sorry to change your schedule but do you think that I could talk to Dr. Hanna for a few minutes if she's in the office today? I have a personal problem and I think it might be easier to talk to her instead of Dr. Jackson."

"Yes of course Mrs. Lawson. I'll check with her and if you'll have a seat, I'll be right back."

Within fifteen minutes, she was in Dr. Hanna's office. "Mrs. Lawson, how are you doing today? I hope things are going well with the baby. You don't have long to wait until your due date. The receptionist told me that you needed to talk to me. I hope I can help you."

Jill asked, "Dr. Hanna, may I talk candidly about a problem I have? I wanted to meet with you because I thought it would be easier to talk to a woman."

"Of course, you can talk to me about anything that concerns you or your baby. What seems to be troubling you?"

"I'm a blunt person, Dr. Hanna. I have just learned that my husband was murdered and I want to give this baby up for adoption."

Dr. Hanna was speechless. She was used to mother's worrying when the time got closer to delivery, but she didn't expect to hear anything like that.

"Mrs. Lawson, I'm so sorry about your husband. He starred in the soap opera didn't he? I met him several times here in the office."

"Yes, Kurt played in The World At Its Best. He was my world and now I don't know what I'm going to do without him."

"Mrs. Lawson, please sit here and relax for a few minutes. I'll ask one of my partners to take my next few patients. I'll be right back."

Dr. Hanna paged one of the other doctors and asked if he could cover her patients for the next hour. She told him she had an emergency with Mrs. Lawson, and she would fill him in later. He agreed and she thanked him and went back to her own office.

"Mrs. Lawson, can I get you anything? I'm truly sorry about your husband. I can understand the stress and trauma that news of your husband's death has caused. We must be careful for the baby's sake. I wouldn't want anything to bring on premature labor. Have you had any contractions in the last two days?"

"No, I feel fine. The baby is fine. I just don't want it. I want to give it to someone else. I said I'm blunt. If I alarmed you, I'm sorry. I need to know what I can do as far as adoption. Without my husband, I don't want this baby at all."

"Mrs. Lawson, I know you're upset. I know that what you're dealing with isn't easy. I'm sure without your husband you think the baby will remind you of him, but you will find that it also will bring you comfort and delight. You still have a piece of your husband in your baby. This way, he'll remain with you always."

"You don't understand. I can't love a child. The only reason I kept it at all was for Kurt. I have no desire for a child. I don't like children. I have a life for myself and it doesn't include a full time job of looking after a baby. If my husband were alive, I would have tried to raise it for him. I loved him more than I ever imagined I could love anyone. Now I don't have him, and I don't want his child. It is not him."

"Mrs. Lawson, I'm going to prescribe a mild anti-depressant for you. It won't harm the baby and it will help you deal with the ordeal in front of you. I want you to think about what you have said, and I know you can't make a decision like this too soon. Give yourself time to adjust to the grief and I assure you that you will feel differently about the baby by the time it is born. Will you take the medicine if I give it to you?"

"I don't need medicine to know what I want. My due date is three and a half weeks away and I don't want to wait until the last minute."

"Mrs. Lawson, your body changes so much when you are pregnant. Your emotions are off balance."

"Dr. Hanna, I won't change my mind. Does this office have access to adoption agencies that they could recommend? Will you get the information for me, or do I have to go to someone else? I want my baby to go to someone who is responsible. I'm going to be busy in the next few weeks. My parents have flown in from the east, and will be staying for a week. I'll make another appointment for a few days from now."

Jill stood up to leave. The matter had been settled in her mind. She didn't need time or medication to know what she wanted. And, she didn't need someone else telling her to keep a baby she didn't want.

"Mrs. Lawson, please don't leave until you are calm. I'll give you some medication now to help you if you'll let me. I'm responsible for you and your baby and I won't allow you to leave if you mean to harm your baby or yourself. Would you consider checking into the hospital for a few days so we can administer medication to help you through this and monitor the baby at the same time?"

"No, Dr. Hanna I told you that my husband is dead and I have arrangements to make and my parents are in town and I must stay with them."

"But, are you going to be alright? Do you promise that you won't make any decisions about your baby until next week when we can see each other?"

"Yes, I know I have the three weeks to research the best agency to use. I don't intend to harm myself. I can't imagine my life without my husband, but I won't be a coward like he was and end my life because of my own selfishness."

"I'm going to write a prescription for you and I want you to take them until you come back. Okay?"

"Yes, I'll take the medicine if I feel I can't cope. I promise. And thank you for making time for me today."

Jill walked to the receptionist's desk and scheduled an appointment for the following week. She left the office and made a stop at the grocery store on the way home. She wanted to make something easy for her and her parents for supper. She picked up three steaks, bought potato salad, and fresh green beans to go with them. She didn't feel like cooking or eating, but she knew life must move on. At this point what choice did she have?

When she got back to her house, she was tired. Her mother met her at the door and hugged her. She tried to hug her back, but she didn't have the strength to pretend today. She didn't feel a bond with her mother, or her father. She knew it was her own fault since they had shown her plenty of love all her life. She liked her parents, but had never bonded with them the way a daughter should. The only person she ever loved was gone now. But since her parents had flown out to be with her, she wanted to be hospitable to them.

Her mother helped her to make supper and they were sitting down to eat when the phone rang. Jill answered it and was sorry she did when she heard Amanda Enfield's voice.

"Jill, I'm glad I finally reached you. I'm sure by now you heard that Gary was found dead not too far from Kurt. Did you know where they were going that night? I don't remember Gary telling me anything about the two of them going anywhere, do you?"

"No, Amanda, I don't remember Kurt mentioning that he was

going with Gary that night. I have no idea who would want my husband dead. Do you?"

"No, I can't live without Gary. What are we going to do now? Have you talked with the police? I had to go to the station and I asked them a lot of questions, but they had no answers for me. They have no idea what happened. I'll never believe that anyone would want to hurt either of them. I think it was a robbery gone badly. Why would anyone want to kill our husbands? It has to be someone that they didn't know."

"Amanda, I hate to run. My parents are here and I need to talk with them and eat. Can I call you back later?"

"Sure, I'm sorry to interrupt. I'm sorry about Kurt."

"I'm sorry about Gary too. Neither of them deserved to die like potheads on the street. Do you know if Gary was still using drugs? The police said it may have been a bad drug deal."

"I thought Gary quit when Kurt did. I can't believe that the two of them would sacrifice everything just to get high. I know Kurt was looking forward to the baby, and I'm sorry about that too. You will have to raise your child by yourself."

"Amanda I don't mean to sound callous, but I can take care of myself."

"I'll let you go. Please, call me later."

She hung up the phone and went back to the table.

"Are you alright, dear? Who was on the phone, you look upset. Come and sit down and I'll serve the food."

Mr. Buckner pulled Jill's chair out and helped her to scoot back to the table.

"Thank you mom. That was Amanda Enfield. Her husband was also killed and she was asking if I heard any news yet. I told her I would call her later."

"Oh I feel so bad for you two girls. Do you mind telling your father and me what happened to Kurt? Was it a mugging or robbery? I can't imagine someone wanting to hurt Kurt."

"No, mom. Kurt was not mugged. Someone crushed his skull. The Captain seems to think that it could be drug related. Kurt had drugs in his system. I don't want you to think badly of him, but he did have a drug problem for a while. I thought he quit when he found out that we were expecting a baby. I'm not sure of the details yet, but I do know that for whatever reason, my husband is dead. I'm not sure what I'm going to do now. I have things I need to think about."

"Honey, are you worried about money? Your dad and I can help with your expenses if you need us to. This house has to be expensive. Jill you could sell this house and move back to Virginia with us. You and the baby can start over and we can help you."

"I appreciate your concern, mom. I don't have to worry about money. My job pays me well, and I know Kurt had good life insurance. Hopefully they will pay if someone is murdered. I'll be fine. I don't want to move back east. I love this house, and my life is here."

"Okay, Jill. We're here for whatever you need."

Jill started clearing the dishes and both her parents rose to help her. They carried the dishes to the kitchen, and after they finished, they went to the back deck to enjoy the view.

The next morning, Jill asked her dad if he would mind taking Kurt's clothing to the funeral home. He told her he'd be glad to do it. While he was gone, Jill went through their safe and found the insurance papers. She called Mr. Harkins and gave him the information. He promised to call as soon as he found out anything.

After her father returned, the three of them decided to go out to eat that evening. Jill wanted to show them some of the town, and she needed to get out of the house for a while. The restaurant was nice and the meal with her parents was relaxing. Jill had to admit she did miss them a little and she was grateful for their help with what life had dealt her.

Jill woke the next morning with a terrible headache. She had two glasses of white wine with dinner the night before. Her mother gave her a concerned look and glanced at her stomach and the baby, but the look Jill gave her back kept her silent. The last thing on Jill's mind was the alcohol might hurt the "precious baby." What about her? She didn't much care, and if she'd been by herself, she would certainly have gotten wasted. The anger she felt against Kurt hit her full force as she climbed out of bed.

What was she to do now without him? What was he doing in that alley anyhow? How was she supposed to explain to all their friends and co-workers what happened to him? The weight of what she had to look forward to was too heavy right now.

While she was brushing her teeth, another thought occurred to her. What was she going to tell everyone? Was it better to tell them the truth, or make up lies so she wouldn't have to answer their questions, and put up with their pity for her for being stupid enough to marry such a jerk? She would figure it out later; right now, she just wanted a cup of strong black coffee.

Her father was sitting at the kitchen table when she went downstairs. He said, "Good morning, honey. Did you sleep all right? The baby is so big, I'm sure it is hard for you to rest. Can I make breakfast for you?"

"No, dad, I just want coffee. My head is killing me. I don't want to hear about this baby either right now. What was I thinking to let myself get pregnant?" She quickly thought to herself that for now she just needed to keep her mouth closed about the baby. If she did decide to give it away, she'd wait until her parents were back home to tell them. She didn't need them arguing with her about it now.

She sat down and thanked her father for the coffee. "Is mom still asleep? I think she really enjoyed the restaurant last night. It's our favorite place to eat." As soon as the words were out of her mouth, she realized what she said.

"Jill, I'm so sorry about Kurt. It doesn't seem possible that he's gone. I'll do my best to help you through this. Your mother and I loved Kurt. We'll miss him too."

Her father rose and stood behind her chair and kissed the top of her head. It reminded her of when she was little; he had a habit of kissing her head almost every time he left the room. "I'll go and see if your mother is up yet. Do you have to go anywhere this morning?"

"No, I need to call Captain Harris and asked if they found out anything new. And I have to call Mr. Harkins at the funeral home about Kurt's life insurance."

"Do you want me to handle that? I can go down to the funeral home myself and talk to Mr. Harkins. I'll take the papers with me and if he has any questions, I can help him. Do you mind if I do that?"

"No, dad, I don't mind. I appreciate your help."

After her father left the room, Jill laid her head on the table and cried. She didn't want to handle Kurt's life insurance. She wanted him to come back home, be with her, and take care of her.

CHAPTER ELEVEN

When Jill's father, Edward arrived at the funeral home around 10:00 a.m., Mr. Harkins took him into the office.

"Mr. Buckner, I'm glad to meet you. How's your daughter today? She gave me the information I needed and I'm glad to tell you that the insurance company assured me that your daughter will be able to collect the full amount on your son-in law's policy. There were no restrictions. You can tell Mrs. Lawson that she needs to sign these papers and take them to the notary. She'll receive her husband's life insurance in about three weeks. Are there any other questions that I can help with?"

"I appreciate your help so much. I know my daughter is worried about keeping her home and caring for the baby. I can't think of anything else. The clothing that I brought for Kurt was okay?"

"Yes, the suit was fine. Do you have any idea how many people that you and your family expect for the viewing? I suggest that you have the viewing of the body an hour before the service. I spoke to your daughter briefly and we discussed a closed casket. Your daughter, and you and your wife may privately view the body before the service."

"I don't know how many Jill expects. I'm sure that the people that Kurt and Jill worked with every day will certainly want to attend. We live in Virginia, and this actually is the first time we have been to our daughter's home."

"I'd like to talk to your daughter by tomorrow afternoon. I'll ask her about it then. We need to discuss the songs, and the minister. Did your daughter attend a church in this area?"

"No, I don't think they did. Do you have someone you could suggest for us? I'm not familiar at all with this area, and I'm not sure if Jill has thought about it yet?"

"Yes, I have the names of several ministers that we recommend. I'll call her later with the ones I think she'd like."

"If that's all then, I'll have my daughter call you soon."

Mr. Buckner headed back to his daughter's house. He felt better knowing that there were no problems with the life insurance company, and he'd rest easier knowing that his daughter and her child wouldn't have to worry about money. When he arrived at the house, his wife met him at the door and told him that Jill was lying down.

"She didn't feel well, so I told her to take a nap, and that I'd fix lunch and call her in a little while. I hope she doesn't have any problems with this child; the stress she's under isn't good. How did it go with Mr. Harkins? Did he find out about the life insurance? I worry about Jill and the baby living in this big house. It must be expensive to pay for of all this. I love it here though, don't you? I would love to wake up every morning to the sound of the ocean. I know Jill loves this home and she wouldn't want to leave it."

"Yes, Mr. Harkins assured me that there would be no problems with the life insurance. Jill told me that Kurt had an excellent policy. I'm glad he took the time to invest in a good policy. We won't have to worry about our daughter or her child."

They heard Jill stirring upstairs and her mother went into the kitchen to start the tuna for lunch. As she was fixing the coffee, Jill came down the stairs.

"Dad, you are home. Did Mr. Harkins have any answers for us?"

"Yes, he told me that Kurt's policy had no restrictions, and you would receive your benefits in about three weeks. I did go over the papers with him, and I think all you need to do is go to a notary and sign them. I'll take you whenever you want to go. Do you know where the closest one is?"

"I'll jump on the internet and find the closest one, and I'll take advantage of you taking me everywhere if you don't mind. My feet and legs ache from carrying this baby."

"I'm glad to be able to help. Your mother is making lunch. Do you need anything done before we eat?"

"No, I'm fine. Why don't we sit on the back deck and soak up the warm sun until lunch is ready."

Around 2:00 Jill told her parents she needed to go to her office for about an hour. She wanted to make sure everything was taken care of so she could take off a few more days.

A few weeks ago, Jill's manager approached her about a campaign that included cosmetics for pregnant women and the meeting was scheduled for this afternoon. They wanted to use Jill as their model, and introduce a new line of cosmetics for new mothers. The natural glow in Jill's skin enhanced her beauty and she was flattered they asked her. It was the only advantage to being pregnant she had found so far.

She still wanted to do the photo shoot, but she wasn't sure what her manager would think if she did it so soon after her husband's death. Jill's image was almost more important to her than her looks, almost! What would people think if she did a photo shoot the same week she buried her husband.

Jill thought about how to have the manager ask her to do the shoot in a way that wouldn't make her look like a selfish wife. She wanted this campaign. As she rode the elevator up to the tenth floor, she reminded herself to show grief, before she showed excitement for this job.

Sam Wheeler, her manager, was waiting in her office. He was glancing through the shots of Jill from her last photo shoot. "She sure is one beautiful lady," he said as he looked over a few of the photos. "I wouldn't mind having her on my arm."

Sam heard Jill speaking to her receptionist and he went to the door. "Jill I wasn't sure that you would come today. I just heard about your husband's murder. If you want to postpone this, we can. Let me say up front that if you want to bow out of this campaign, you can do that too. I understand you have a lot on your plate right now."

"Sam, how are you today? I thought about calling you to cancel, but I know you've put a lot of effort into this, and I would have felt bad. I need something to look forward to, and I think that I'd love to continue with this if we can. I'm going to miss Kurt every day, but I think he would want me to stay busy. Besides, without him, the baby and I may need the money."

"Oh, I never thought of that aspect of it. If you need us to help you with your financial situation, I'm sure we could advance the money to you. I think you're perfect for this shoot. Being pregnant has made you more beautiful. I'm sorry, should I say that to you?"

"What's wrong with a man giving a woman a compliment?"

"Well, now that you are a single woman, oh that was a stupid thing to say. I'm so sorry. I've never known when to keep my mouth shut."

"No Sam I appreciate the compliment. I know that you meant it as just a compliment. No matter where my life is right now, I still like to think I look good. Please don't feel bad. And, I do think that this might be the perfect time for me to have something to look forward to. And, my baby is due in three weeks, so we need to hurry. I could sit home and cry over Kurt, but he'd still be gone."

Jill forced a few tears to flow, though she really was going to miss Kurt. But he was gone and she had to start worrying about herself. After all, he was the idiot that let himself get involved with drugs and got his skull crushed. So, in a way, he didn't even deserve her tears.

"Do you have time to hear a few of my ideas now? I worked on this a few hours last night. I'll wait until later if you like. I'm excited about you doing this, and after the success from the last one, I think it's good for the company. As a matter of fact, I think I could get you more money than you got the last time."

Jill almost jumped for joy but she caught herself and remembered she was supposed to be in mourning.

Jill knew the campaign was good. She also knew how much profit that the company made from her face on the magazine covers. It's not every day that you get your picture in a magazine. She was proud of where she was, and she wouldn't lose it or look back, not for Kurt, not for her parents, and certainly not for this baby.

She listened in awe as Sam showed her his ideas. He was good at what he did, and she got excited with him.

"Would you think badly of me if I did this photo shoot now? I wouldn't want people to talk, but I'll do whatever you say. I've learned to ignore people's comments about me."

"No Jill, I'd admire you for your courage. Most women would give up if their husbands died. I know my own wife would. I admire your strength and I'm sure your husband would agree."

"Thank you Sam. I have some time before I need to be home, and if you want to go over this, I'd love to hear your ideas."

The two of them poured over the photographs for another hour. Jill noticed the time, and told Sam that she needed to do some work on the computer, and she didn't want to stay late. The ideas that Sam showed her were things she'd never seen before. She was positive that the campaign would go well. She couldn't wait to get started.

Jill left after spending forty-five minutes catching up. She needed to stop at the police station before she went home.

Captain Harris was surprised to see her. "Mrs. Lawson, how are you today? I do have a report on your husband's death. Would you like to go over it now, or is there someone you can call to be with you?"

"No, it's just me now. I'm fine. I need to hear what happened to Kurt."

The report stated that witnesses saw Kurt and Gary the afternoon of the murder at a local hangout called The Roadside Café. One of the customers asked Kurt for his autograph. The two men had been drinking all afternoon, and Kurt told the young girl to leave him alone. The girl's brother took offense to Kurt's remarks and grabbed him by the collar. Kurt got angry and told the man, "What makes you think that I care about a hag like your sister? I could have any girl I want, and sorry but it ain't her!"

The whole place was laughing at his sister and her friends as they ran out of the café. The man told Kurt that he would be waiting for him and he had better watch his back, and then he left the café.

The detectives were able to get a description, and had located the girl. She said that her brother wasn't home, and she had not seen him since she had left the café. When they asked her if she thought her brother had anything to do with the murders, she said absolutely not. Willy, her brother, would never hurt anyone. He did run off at the mouth a lot, but she'd never known him to carry out his threats.

"A warrant has been issued to question Willy Barnes and according to the file; a lead on his whereabouts came in about an hour ago."

Jill was stunned to think that someone could've killed Kurt for making fun of an ugly girl. She knew Kurt was capable of saying such a thing, but surely the brother wasn't stupid enough to hunt Kurt down and kill him.

Jill asked Captain Harris to call her at home if he learned anything else. She headed home; it had been a long day.

Her parents had already eaten by the time she arrived home. Her mother fixed her a plate and heated it in the microwave. Jill ate a few bites and thanked her mother for going to the trouble, but assured her she wasn't hungry.

A call came in from Captain Harris around 7:00 p.m. that Willy Barnes had been located and was at the station for questioning. He promised that he would call her the next morning if they were pressing charges against him. Jill asked him to keep it quiet that Kurt may have been murdered for such a ridiculous reason as making fun of an ugly girl. She didn't want that news to spread.

Jill had a hard time sleeping that night. The baby was growing and it was more difficult to get comfortable. Up until this point, the baby she was carrying didn't enter into her mind very often. She hadn't gained a lot of weight, and her life was pretty much the same. Now, she had to contend with the constant moving and kicking that the baby did and it was beginning to be a bother. Actually, when she thought of the baby late that night, she felt no love whatsoever. Jill felt nothing at all. She certainly didn't feel the maternal instincts that most mothers felt.

CHAPTER TWELVE

Jill woke the next morning with another severe headache. She thought about calling Dr. Hanna for medication. Then she thought to herself, why should I worry about taking pain medication that might hurt a baby that I don't even want or care about?

She went to the medicine cabinet in her bathroom, shook a

Vicodin out of the bottle, reached for the water, and swallowed the pill. She couldn't wait until the pain medicine took away the pain in her head. She dressed and headed downstairs. As she entered the kitchen, she heard her mother and father on the deck. She poured her coffee and joined them.

"Good morning sweetheart," her father said. "How are you and my grand baby today?"

"I'm alright Dad. I have a terrible headache again, but I took some pills and it should subside soon. You two are up early."

"Your mother loves to sit and look at the ocean. I wish we could afford a place like this one to retire in. This is beautiful scenery."

"I loved it here the first time I saw it. I'm glad that Kurt and I bought this house. It is quite beautiful, isn't it?

"Yes, it is. Do you want eggs and sausage for breakfast?" her mother asked.

"I might eat the eggs, but sausage gives me indigestion. You don't have to bother for me. I have to go out in a little while and I could grab something while I'm out. You and Dad can eat whatever you want. Make yourselves at home."

Jill sat with her parents enjoying the sound of the water for a while. The phone rang and she rose to answer it.

"Hello, Yes Captain Harris. Is there any news?"

"Mrs. Lawson, I met with the detectives on your husband's case this morning. I understand that Willy Barnes did finally confess to murdering your husband and his friend Gary. Willy got angry over a comment that your husband made to his sister. He followed the two men into the alley, and didn't mean to hit your husband hard, but he wanted him to apologize to his sister. Unfortunately, the blow was fatal. Gary took off running and Willy thought he had to stop him or he'd tell what happened. Mr. Barnes tried to cover up the murders by injecting drugs into their systems to make it look like an over dose."

"So you are telling me that Kurt was killed because he wouldn't apologize for a remark he made to a girl he didn't even know? How ridiculous is that? Are you positive that's what happened? What will happen to Mr. Barnes? Is he going to jail for life?"

"Mrs. Lawson that decision will be up to a jury. I'm sure that the confession will seal his fate in court. I don't think you have to worry about Mr. Barnes. When he's convicted he'll never see the light of day again for a double homicide."

"Captain Harris, I'd appreciate if you keep this quiet. I don't want people to know that my husband was murdered for a joke that he said about an insignificant ugly girl. I'd rather it be told that he died of an overdose."

"Mrs. Lawson, I have no intentions of spreading facts about the case to the media. But someone might leak the information."

"I'm serious. I don't want this to go any further. It's no one's business except mine what my husband was doing."

"Mrs. Lawson you have my word that this department won't talk to any of the press. I understand that your husband was in a popular soap opera. There again, I can't control how the media reacts to his murder. I imagine that it will be front page news."

"If I have anything to say about it, I'll request that it isn't published. I'll talk to Kurt's P.R. man. He's used to keeping rumors out of the press. Is there anything else?"

"No, I'll be in touch in the next few days with any further developments. I'm sorry about your husband. I hope that you and your baby take care."

"Thank you Captain. I'll talk to you in a few days."

Jill went back to the deck. When her parents asked about the call, she didn't tell them the details of the murder. She told them that Captain Harris had arrested a man named Willy Barnes, who had confessed to killing Kurt and Gary. Her mother came to hug her but hesitated when Jill didn't make a move toward her. Mrs. Buckner could read her daughter well, and she knew that this wasn't the time to hug her. Some things don't change.

"Dad, I found a notary downtown. Would you mind driving me there? I'd like to go into the office for a few hours. You and mom can stay in town and have lunch on me."

"Jill, we don't want to take your money. You paid our way out here, and you need to save money for the baby."

"Mom, Kurt's life insurance is more than enough for me. I'm going to continue working. In fact, the company has started another campaign using me as a model for mothers-to-be and it pays very well."

"Okay, we'd love to go with you. We can walk around the shops until you are ready to come home."

Jill told them she was going to shower and get ready and they could leave in about an hour.

Her mother and father dropped her at her office after finishing the paperwork at the notary. Jill was anxious to meet with Sam to start the photo shoot. She couldn't wait to see the layouts.

Sam took her straight to make-up and he was astonished at the radiance the camera picked up from Jill. She was certainly one of the most beautiful women he'd ever seen. She had a quality of being untouchable, and the camera intensified the feeling. It was going to be magnificent when they were finished. He was surprised of the stamina Jill showed. Most pregnant women got a little emotional, but Jill didn't complain once.

After two hours, the cameraman assured Sam that he had plenty of photos. Sam told Jill that the proofs would be ready for her approval within four days. She thanked him and went back to her office.

Jill's secretary, Carla, asked her if she minded if the office sent flowers to the funeral home. She knew Jill well enough to know that if she didn't get her permission, she'd have to suffer for several days. She'd been on the chopping block too many times and she tried to avoid it whenever possible.

Jill said, "Why would you have to ask me such a silly question? You know it would be an honor to accept flowers from everyone in Kurt's memory. Yes, tell everyone I would love that."

As Jill shut her door to the office, Carla breathed a sigh of relief. Now she could tell the office they could send flowers. She grew tired of making excuses for Mrs. Lawson. People didn't understand how difficult that woman really was.

Jill flipped through her messages and opened several boxes of sample foundations, eye shadow, and lip-gloss that a major client wanted her to model. Some of the colors she thought were too old for her, and she boxed them up to give to her mother. She knew her mother enjoyed receiving packages from her, and Jill kept her supplied with free samples. Jill knew her mother wore some of the make-up, but all these years it hadn't sank in how to bring out her best qualities, and hide her flaws. She guessed it was just too late for her mother. What a shame. Women should worry twenty-four hours a day what they looked like. To Jill it was a mystery that not every woman had the drive that she did.

At 2:00 p.m., she called her father and told him she could leave anytime. She said she would meet him downstairs in twenty minutes.

Jill went into the study after she arrived home to call the funeral home. She discussed arrangements, the choice of the casket, the minister, and details of the service. They decided the service would be in three days and the announcement would be in the paper the following day.

Jill glanced up in the middle of her phone conversation and saw a picture of her and Kurt on the desk. She didn't think it was bragging, after all the truth is just the truth, they were two good-looking people. She doubted that she'd ever meet another man that she could care about as much as she had cared for Kurt.

The next two days she took her parents to a few places she thought they would enjoy. They loved California and its people. The three of them enjoyed each other's company and their relationship seemed to grow closer.

The day of the funeral, as Jill was deciding which outfit to wear, her mother knocked on her door. When her mother stepped inside Jill's walk-in-closet, she was flabbergasted. She couldn't imagine choosing one outfit from the hundreds that hung on the racks. It would take her all day long just to look through them all. And the shoes! Where did one woman find so many different shoes? Betty owned six pair; she had brought two pair with her.

Betty asked Jill if she had a necklace she could borrow for the day. Jill said, "Of course, mother. Would you like gold or silver? I keep them in a locked cabinet down the hall. Give me one second to get this dress on and I'll help you choose something."

"I'll go and check on your father. Just give me a holler when you get ready."

Betty helped her husband tie his tie and followed him down the stairs to the kitchen. She started the coffee and poured the orange juice. She heard Jill call her to say she was ready to show her the jewelry. Betty went upstairs and went with her daughter to the jewelry case. When Jill unlocked the cases, her mother was speechless, and said, "Jill I've never seen so much jewelry in my life. How can you decide which one to wear?"

Jill's mother chose a simple silver locket and promised that she would give it back as soon as the funeral was over. "Mom, since you like it, I want you to keep it. And I was thinking I would like Dad to go through Kurt's things and pick whatever he would like to have. Kurt owned some nice clothing and I think Dad could wear some of it. Do you think he would want to do that?"

"I'll ask him, honey. I think your father would be pleased that you asked. You look so lovely in that dress. You are a beautiful child, Jill. I hope your baby looks like you. You have made your father and me proud of you. I'm so sorry that Kurt is gone. I can't imagine life without your father. I want you to know that if you need us, we are only a phone call away."

She reached over to hug Jill and was surprised when she felt her hug back. Usually Jill didn't like to be touched, but she knew what her daughter was going through was very tough on her.

Mother and daughter went down the steps together and shared fixing the eggs and toast. They all three chattered as they ate.

After cleaning up, Jill went to the study to call her office. She checked with Carla to see if there were any messages. A lot of co-workers and friends had called and assured her that if she needed anything to call them.

They left for the funeral home at 10:00. Jill dreaded seeing Kurt's body for the last time more than she had dreaded anything else in her life. The unfairness of it all was weighing heavy on her heart.

Mr. Harkins met them and escorted the three of them to the viewing parlor. He raised the lid to the casket and stepped back to give them privacy. Jill stood still and couldn't will her feet to move. She felt her father's arm on her shoulder and her mother's arm slip around her waist. Within a few moments, she stiffened her back and pushed everything else aside and took the few steps toward the casket.

As Jill approached the casket, she could see a form inside. She lowered her gaze and her eyes settled on the face of the man who used to be her husband. As tears formed in her eyes, she reached for the body and put her hand on his arm. It was cold and stiff; there was no sign of life. Jill pulled her hand back and as she backed away, she could feel the old Jill take over. She vowed that she'd never put her trust in anyone ever again.

Jill told herself that she didn't need one single person in her life. She was the only one that mattered. At the same time she was silently making promises to herself, the baby moved inside her and kicked stronger than it had ever done before. She put her hand on her stomach and under her breath cursed the baby she was carrying. A hatred for the life that Kurt created inside of her consumed her. She had no desire for a baby. She would get rid of it as soon as she could.

Jill walked to Mr. Harkins and told him she needed to sit down. He took her to the main parlor and asked if there was anything he could get for her. She looked pale and unsteady and he didn't want her to faint and hurt herself or the baby.

"Are you alright, Mrs. Lawson? Would you like some water?"

"Yes, I would appreciate it, thank you."

Mr. Harkins left and returned in a few minutes with a glass of cool water. Jill drank most of it and assured him that she felt much better. Her parents joined her and the people started filing in a few minutes later. Jill wiped the tears and stood to greet everyone and thank them for coming.

The service lasted two and half-hours. Jill was surprised at the number of people that came. She didn't realize that Kurt had known so many people. And from the tone of the comments, most of them genuinely liked him.

When they reached the graveside, Jill was very quiet. The baby kicked inside her stomach while she stood and looked down at the casket holding her dead husband. She whispered softly so no one could hear, "I will never love this child. I don't want anything that would remind me of a dead husband."

Her mother asked her if she was okay. She nodded her head yes. She turned and walked slowly away from the grave, headed to the car, and waited for her father and mother. She just wanted to go home and forget all this had ever happened.

Jill walked in the door to her home, and went straight upstairs, and her parents heard her door shut. They changed and sat on the deck discussing how they could help their daughter and grandchild through this tragedy.

"Edward what can we do to help Jill. She's been better the last week than she's been for years. I actually thought that this might bring us together. I want to love her, and I can't wait for our grandchild."

"Now Betty, you can't live her life for her. We've always known that Jill wasn't like the other children. She's always been self-centered. Yes, I did see a change in her for a while. I enjoyed this Jill more than the one we usually deal with."

"But we can't go home and leave her like this. What are parents for if they can't help their child when they are hurting? I'll stay with her for a while, if she'll allow me to. I want to be here when the baby is born."

"Honey, don't get your hopes up. You know that Jill doesn't want anyone fussing over her. She's the kind that can take of herself. I'm not sure that you staying here would be a good idea. I think that in order to deal with our daughter, we need to do it from a distance. If you stay, you know she'll start the same things she started before. Do you think you can live through that again?"

"But I love her. I do want to help her. I think she'll need help with the baby. I'm her mother and I'm afraid of what kind of mother she'll be. It would be nice if she'd drop all the baggage and be normal. Loving her is quite difficult. I hope the baby isn't like that. I sometimes wonder if Jill can be a mother."

Her husband looked at her with a surprised look. "Why would you say that? She's your daughter, and loving her child may come natural for her.

"I hope so. I used to pray that Jill would never have her own child. I was afraid for her future children. Jill is in no way ready for motherhood. I don't know if she ever will be."

The next day Jill came downstairs around 10:00. Her mother stood to hug her but Jill backed away from her. "Jill, are you alright? Please let us help you honey. Your dad and I will stay a while if you want us to. We've no idea what you are feeling, but we love you and will do anything to help you."

"Mom, I'm sorry. I don't mind if you and Dad want to stay a few days. You are welcome to enjoy the scenery; the ocean is beautiful, isn't it? I'm grateful to Kurt for finding this home. It's the only good thing he ever did. Now, I have to get used to being alone. I'll get through this. I won't let him ruin me."

"Honey, you have your baby to look forward to. When he or she is born, you won't be alone. Aren't you anxious to meet your child?"

"Dad, the less we say about this baby, the better. I regret getting pregnant. Right now, it's only a complication in my life. The one thing I don't need is more complications. Did you and mom have breakfast yet?"

"Yes, your mother made us French toast. She saved two pieces for you to heat. Do you want me to get them for you?"

"No, I'll get them. Do you want more coffee? Is this your cup?"

Jill headed towards the coffeemaker, and her mother excused herself to go upstairs to take a shower.

Her father said, "Yes, I'd love coffee. Do you have plans for today? Your mom and I thought we could go for a walk on the beach. Do you want to come with us?"

"No, I want to catch up on some paperwork I brought home. Did I tell you that the agency is using me in a series of cosmetics for new mothers? We did a photo shoot two days ago and my manager was pleased with the shots. The ads should hit the magazines in a few weeks. I loved the new line of maternity clothing I modeled. I wish I could wear some of them after the baby is born, some of the outfits were divine."

"Your mother was telling me about it. I'm proud of you Jill. You're a beautiful woman, and I know our granddaughter will be beautiful too."

"What, you have an inside scoop on knowing the sex of your grandchild before I give birth?"

"No, I just have a feeling it will be a girl. I can't wait to meet her."

Her father hesitated before continuing, "Your mother mentioned staying until the baby is born if you want her to. I told her that I could survive at home by myself if she wants to stay for a while. Do you think you would like her to be here with you?"

"Right now I would like to be alone. I handle stress better by myself. I don't think I will be fit to be around for some time. It's going to be a big adjustment living without Kurt. I appreciate the thought, but I don't want to hurt her feelings. Can you tell her for me?"

"Yes, I'll tell her. We'll head back home tomorrow. If you need us to come back at any time, we're only a phone call away. Do you promise to call if you need us?"

"Yes, dad I promise. I wish things could be different. While Kurt was alive, he'd have loved for you and mom to see our home. He was proud of this place. He often said he couldn't imagine that an old country boy like him could afford a home like this."

Her parents left for their walk and Jill headed to the study to work. She couldn't concentrate and soon gave up and put the paperwork away. She called Sam to ask how the photos turned out.

"From what I have seen so far, it's the best shoot the company has done. I have to pass on that the cameraman sends his thanks. He told me that with a model like you, the work is easy. Your face doesn't need any touching up. Jill, I'm sorry about Kurt's death. The service was wonderful. Do you have any idea when you are coming back to the office? The baby is due in a few weeks, isn't it?"

"Thank you Sam. Women don't ever get tired of hearing how beautiful they are. Yes, the baby is due in three weeks. I was telling my dad this morning that I'm almost sad that I have to give up the maternity wardrobe. Some of the pieces were exquisite. I'll have to hire the agency to design more outfits for me after the baby is born. I love the work they do. You should've seen my mother's face when she entered my closet. My mother has twenty outfits, and she only wears half of those. I keep telling her that women can't have too many clothes. And, she was flabbergasted when I told her that you need a separate pair of shoes for each outfit. She shares a closet with my father. I can remember when I was little; I had to fake a heart attack just to get a new dress." Jill thought back to the fit she threw about her first new dress for school.

"Oh, I can just imagine your mother's expression when she saw your ten thousand pair of shoes. My wife used to say the same thing, and believe me, my bank account suffered every time she headed out the door to find the "perfect" dress. That's one reason why she is my ex-wife, I couldn't afford her."

"Yeah, with the money you make, you could buy any woman a new wardrobe. But us women have to look gorgeous, it just ain't right not to."

"You do a good job in the gorgeous department. I'm amazed at your beauty, and I wasn't disappointed at how the camera loved you and I can't wait for you to see the finished proofs. Will you be coming in tomorrow? I should have most of them on the wall for you to see."

"I think I can come in after 1:00. My folks are leaving tomorrow. I was just about to call to book their flight home, and I'll let you know if I have to change the time. So I will see you then."

"Okay, let me know if 1:00 doesn't work. I'll look forward to seeing you."

Jill called the airlines next and booked a flight for her parents at 8:00 a.m. She headed out the door to find them on the beach. The sun was bright, but a slight breeze blowing made it bearable. Her parents were sitting in the sand, she joined them, and they admired the view.

"I booked your flight for tomorrow morning at 8:00 a.m. and would like to take you out to dinner tonight for being here with me through Kurt's service. I love the Steak House Restaurant and swear that their bread is the best in the world. Is 6:00 this evening alright?"

"You don't have to spend money on us, Jill. You need to save it for the baby. You may need it."

"Mom, I can afford it. Please, let's go and enjoy. I want to do it."

"That's fine then. I don't think I brought anything fancy enough to wear. I'm not used to the way people dress here. Their clothes are beautiful. All the ladies back home wouldn't believe how different California is."

"Can I give you one of my outfits to wear? I have designer suits that I don't wear any more. I know a perfect one for you. When we head back I'll show you."

"I look forward to it."

The three of them stayed for another hour admiring the water and the peacefulness. Jill sat on the sand and remembered several times that she and Kurt were out at night watching the sunset. She had to quit thinking about him, it hurt too much.

The outfit she chose fit her mother perfectly. It took ten years off her age and she even talked her mother into letting her use a little make-up on her. She gave several bags of cosmetics for her to take home, and her mother assured her that the girls in her bridge club would swoon over the selection.

The dinner went well and the three of them ended the evening on a somber note. It had been a difficult week.

The next morning she did hug her parents as they left to board the plane. It surprised Jill to find that she'd miss her parents after they were gone. It was a strange feeling to think of anyone besides herself, and she wished again that Kurt could have been with them.

CHAPTER THIRTEEN

Jill met Sam at 1:00 and she was thrilled with the photos. She had to admit, even if it seemed conceited, she was the most beautiful woman she knew. The first set was mostly head shots but when she started flipping through the next set, her pregnant stomach disgusted her. She told Sam that she didn't want any of the photos that showed her below her waist. He reminded her that the whole theme behind this campaign was new mothers. He didn't want to upset her, but insisted that the client wanted a pregnant model for its new line of cosmetics.

Jill shook her head and laughed a silly laugh. "Sorry Sam, you know how vain women are. I don't know any woman who thinks she looks good with her huge stomach sticking out in her pictures. I guess I have to swallow my pride and be happy to be chosen "Pretty Mommy".

Sam put his arm around her shoulders and said, "Believe me Jill; I can't imagine anyone looking at these photos of you and calling you just "Pretty Mommy." You look great pregnant. Your stomach isn't even that big. My wife got big as an elephant with my son. She really did stick out. I felt sorry for her carrying all that weight around for the last three months. She never did get her figure back. I can tell you that you don't look like a fat mommy."

"Thanks Sam. I needed to hear that."

"Now, let's take a break. I heard that the cafeteria has a new flavored coffee, and you gotta try it."

"Okay, let me meet you there in a few minutes. We mommies have to hit the bathrooms more than usual."

"Okay, I'll put these proofs away and meet you in the cafeteria."

Jill headed for the ladies room. One of the women she worked with met her in the hall and said how sorry she was to hear about Kurt.

"All the office is buzzing over the new line for mommies. I hear that the management is well pleased with the line and congratulations are in order. I loved your last shoot. My husband still takes the magazines out and drools over your pictures. Good luck on your new baby."

Jill thanked her and made her way down the hall. Three more people stopped her to say how sorry they were to hear about her husband's death. She started to get depressed and when she finally got to the ladies room, tears were flowing when she thought about Kurt. She determined to forget him, straightened her back, and swore under her breath again how she would survive. Kurt had left her and he didn't deserve her tears.

By the time she was on her way to the cafeteria, the old selfish Jill had taken over once again. The only way to survive in life was to think of yourself, and let everyone else do the same. It was her world, and she would worry about good ole Jill, no one else did.

The next morning after she woke up, it dawned on her that Dr. Hanna had not called her back about the adoption information. She made herself a note to call her on her lunch break.

Jill wanted to make sure she had options, and time was running out. The baby was due in fourteen days. Sam called her that morning at her office. He asked if he could meet with her in a half hour. When he arrived, he was excited. He told her that the management wanted to offer her another assignment. Since she was popular after her first two layouts, they wanted her to do a third one with her and her baby.

"Jill, your face has sold more products for our clients than anyone else has. They want me to assure them that you will give this company exclusive rights to use you again. You are a gold mine. Your face is becoming a household fixture. You can't pick up a magazine or watch the TV for an hour without seeing your face. The figures show that the new mother line has exceeded their projections. So what do you say? Are you up to you and baby giving it a go as soon as you recover?"

"What if it's a boy? Wouldn't a girl be better? I don't know Sam. I'm not sure if I want a baby layout. What does a baby have to do with women's cosmetics?"

"Jill, you don't understand. With your looks, most women will connect with you when you have your own baby. The idea is even when you are a new mother, and busier than ever, you still need to work on your face. Every woman wants to look good. And, you are a perfect goal for any woman. If our cosmetics line makes them look more like you, than it will sell the product. And if you look as good with a baby as you do now, than I rest my case."

All this extra attention appealed to the selfish streak in Jill. She loved to hear that she was beautiful. It made her more self-centered and fed the old habits in her soul.

Jill found herself wondering if the baby could be an asset. If she gave it up for adoption, what would that do to her image? She wasn't naïve enough to believe that people would feel the same way if they found out she gave her own child away. Was she willing to take that chance? She needed to do some more thinking about what she was going to do.

"Let me think about all that. You don't give a girl a chance to rest at all, do you? How soon do they need to know? They don't think I would go somewhere else, do they? What do they want to offer?"

"I think they'd offer you all that you asked for. I'm telling you Jill, your last photo shoot did well. The line we advertised with your face is selling well beyond their hopes. You have a face all women want. You can probably name your price, and if you sign an exclusive contract, I'd be grateful. I'll get the details for you soon if you want me to. I can assure you they don't want to risk losing you. When are you starting your maternity leave?"

"I feel so good that I may keep coming in to the office until I start labor. I've had no problems so far. I'll think about everything you said, and I'll let you know. I'm glad that I'm staying busy. I need work right now. I don't know what I'd do without it."

"As soon as you make up your mind, let me know. I'll draw up the contract and take your offer to the board as soon as I can. It would be nice to have it taken care of before the baby comes. Will you call me soon?"

"Yes, let me have a couple of days to think about it. I promise you'll be the first one I call."

That evening at home Jill fought with herself as to what she should do. This baby wasn't even real to her. So far, it had benefited her career. There wasn't one moment when she had thought she couldn't wait to hold and cuddle her own flesh and blood. It was an extension of her husband now that he was gone, but that didn't interest her either. Right now, the only thing she could think of that it was good for her career. In her mind, she knew that if she were to give it away, it would definitely hurt her image. All those little mommies that looked up to her would hate her. All the people that bowed to her would be shocked. She would lose everything that mattered to her. At the end of her day, she loved the worship from the world more than anything.

Jill reminded herself she was the envy of most women. And, as soon as she gave birth to this burdensome baby, most men would once again lust after her. Was she willing to give all that up for a kid? Couldn't she keep it and treat it as a pet? You have a dog or cat and feed it and it doesn't need much more than that. Really, would it change her life so much? She had enough money to hire someone full time to do all the nasty deeds one did for babies. She could keep it and still reap the benefits without having any of the downfalls of being a mommy, couldn't she?

"Wow, this might not be as bad as I thought. I could have the best of both worlds. I could keep my old beautiful self, and play the role of good mommy at the same time. Yeah, I think that would work. I'm glad all that is settled."

She was so relieved she wanted to celebrate. She went into the kitchen and made herself a tall, cold, chocolate milkshake. She didn't splurge very often because her figure was much more important than food. In this case, since it was such a significant decision, she would throw caution to the wind. "I will call Sam tomorrow and make my demands. Look out world, here comes Jill Lawson and her newborn baby!"

CHAPTER FOURTEEN

Jill woke early on Monday looking forward to the day. She had a meeting with Sam and the company sponsors to discuss a contract for her next series for "Mommies and Babies." Over the past few years, Jill had developed a business savvy about obtaining many perks before signing a contract. She'd dealt with enough CEO's to know that the money wasn't an obstacle to get what you wanted. Since this would be her third series, she now had leverage.

As she was selecting an outfit for the day, she came across one of Kurt's shirts in between two of hers. When she picked up the dry cleaning, she had missed putting it away in his closet. She carried it to the bed and lay down holding it in her arms. She missed having a husband to wake up to every morning. She missed having Kurt to talk to. He would have been glad to hear that the company wanted to feature her and the baby in a new ad. She only spent a few minutes thinking of him before the anger took hold. She hated him for leaving her. She threw the shirt in the floor and went to climb in the shower. She walked over the shirt on her way downstairs and thought she would leave it for the cleaning lady. She hoped she threw it in the trash.

On the way to the office, Jill started to get excited again. She was looking forward to the new ads. Keeping busy was the thing she needed now. She didn't need to mourn any more. She was still alive, and nothing was going to get in her way again. She knew what she wanted, and felt secure in her future.

Sam was waiting in her office with her favorite mocha drink. She smiled sweetly at him as he handed it to her and bowed. She liked Sam. He was okay looking, not as handsome as Kurt had been, but not bad. She felt no attraction for him, but she enjoyed his company. It had only been weeks since she lost her husband,

and she didn't need any complications with any man right now.

Sam started reading her the details on the list of things she had told him she wanted included in this next campaign.

Jill told him she wouldn't settle for less than $250,000.00 for exclusive rights. She wanted half of the wardrobe after the shooting was over. She wanted to have the right to choose the outfits for her baby because she hated the typical blue and pink outfits. From what she could remember of the babies she had bothered to look at, the outfits were boring. She hoped they would go for the new ideas she had been playing with. She could see her baby, if it was a girl, in silk outfits and she had sketches she wanted to show them.

Sam assured her that most of her demands would be met. He didn't see anyone objecting to what she was asking. The money that they could make from using her face was unbelievable. Right now, some major competitors would give a lot of money to hire Jill Lawson. In order to keep her, Sam wanted them to give her whatever she wanted.

All rose as Jill entered the room. The meeting started and it was easy for Sam to secure Jill's demands almost without any hold-ups. Everything Jill wanted was included. The salary and perks didn't seem extreme to anyone.

Next, they discussed the possibility of whether the baby would be a boy or girl. One of the young executives had great input for a baby boy. His ideas were fresh and new and everyone was interested in what he had to say. Jill showed the sketches she had drawn for girl's outfits, and everyone seemed thrilled with them. The meeting lasted an hour and Jill's head was swimming with excitement as she left.

Sam said, "Congratulations to you Jill. I'm well pleased with how that meeting went. I'm so glad that I get to work with you again. You should be proud; it's not every day that a woman receives that much attention. Now, you have to go to lunch with me so we can celebrate. I won't take no for an answer. You pick the place."

"Thanks, Sam. I couldn't have done this without you. I too feel privileged to be able to work with you again. The last shoot was great. I'd love to go to lunch. Let's try the new place around the corner. I've heard rave reviews from all the girls in the office. I haven't had time to try them yet. Is that alright?"

"That's fine. I'll pick you up at 11:45. And Jill thanks again. I'll see you in a little while then."

"I'll be ready. I want to work on some more sketches to show the committee when we meet again next week. I'm glad they liked my ideas."

"They liked them because they were excellent. You have a good eye for fashion trends. Just don't work too hard."

She waved to Sam and headed for her office. She got involved in her new drawings and she didn't realize that so much time had passed when she heard Sam speaking to her secretary. She glanced at her clock and saw that it was 11:35.

Jill went into the restroom, to touch up her make-up, grabbed her purse, and met Sam at the door. The restaurant was packed but they were shown to their table quickly. The food was delicious and the atmosphere was quiet. Jill was glad she had accepted the lunch invitation.

When they got back to the office, Jill noticed her back was starting to ache. She thought sitting in the chair so long while she worked on the drawings was to blame. She decided to stroll around the grounds to ease the ache. The weather was nice and cool and walking helped her to feel better.

When she got back to the office, she worked another two hours, and decided to stop for the day and go home early. She buzzed her secretary and told her she was leaving at 2:00 if nothing was pressing, and after her secretary told her that her day was free, she walked to the elevator. On the way down to the parking garage, she felt the backache returning, and couldn't wait to get home and put her feet up and take a break.

As soon as she got in the door at home, she kicked off her heels and after fixing a glass of ice tea, sat down and propped her feet up. The day had been a good one. With Kurt's life insurance and now her advance from her contract, she had no financial worry at all. She was proud of how far she had come. She decided to call her parents and check on them.

"Hi, mom, it's Jill. I wanted to call and see how you and Dad were doing. How's the weather there?"

"It's really a beautiful fall day here in Virginia. The leaves are turning and the mums are blooming. How are you and the baby doing?"

"I have a slight backache today that I can't seem to shake. I wanted to tell you and Dad that I signed a contract today for an ad campaign for me, and the baby. They want to feature both of us. Isn't that great?"

"Yes, Jill that is wonderful. Our grandchild will be famous and everyone will fall in love with him or her I'm sure. Have you had any bleeding today? Maybe your back is telling you that labor is getting closer. I remember with you I had a backache for two days. What does your doctor say?"

"I didn't call them yet. I have an appointment on Wednesday. I'll put up with it until then. Did you get my package I sent you? I put extra lipstick in the box for your friends. I know they enjoy trying the samples. Tell them I want them to let me know which colors they like. I think the next ad campaign I work on will be for older women. I know most of them will be pleased to be guinea pigs."

"Yes, it'll make their day if I tell them that you need their opinion. I didn't get it yet, maybe tomorrow. I'll call and let you know. And, if you have any pains, call me as soon as you do. Do you want me to come out and be there with you?"

"Actually Mom, I think I'll be fine. It's only labor. I plan to have an epidural and I'll feel no pain. I'm not due for another week, but I'll let you know as soon as something happens. Tell Dad I said Hello, and I'll talk to you soon."

Jill fixed a light supper and sat down to watch a movie. The evenings were lonely without Kurt. She handled it good when she was busy, but in the quiet hours, she missed him. She went to bed early and was in her office by 8:00 the next day.

Sam called her before lunch to ask her if she had time to meet with the designers for final fittings for five of the outfits for the first photo shoot. The people joked with Jill about how huge her stomach was. They told her that she'd never fit into a normal size 3 again, but they would go ahead and make them that size anyway. Jill knew they were kidding and promised them that she would be into a size 3 within three weeks after giving birth to this baby.

The fabric and colors matched Jill to a tee. The team worked well together and they told Sam they'd have the finished products in a few days.

Jill sat in her office after they left and felt good about her future. She loved the attention, and she especially loved the beautiful clothing. The only thing standing in her way now was this baby. It had been awful quiet the last few days. She hadn't felt it kick much since the day at the grave site. A new thought hit her. What would she do if something were wrong with this baby? Where was she going to get another baby to use for the campaign? She had an appointment at the doctor tomorrow and she would insist that the doctor made sure that this baby was fine.

She was early for her appointment the next day at the gynecologist. She immediately told Dr. Hanna that she needed to make sure this baby was fine. "The baby hasn't kicked for a while."

Dr. Hanna listened to the heartbeat, and let Jill listen. "The baby's doing fine. New mothers worry about their babies, but things seem to be fine."

Jill didn't tell her the reason she needed this baby to be okay. She didn't think she'd think well of her if she told her she needed a perfect baby to take pictures with her.

"Mrs. Lawson have you reconsidered what we discussed about adoption the last time you were here?"

"Oh, that. No, I'm fine. I think you were right. It was the stress of losing my husband, but now I'm looking forward to having my baby. I apologize for the things I said that day. I don't know what came over me."

"No, don't apologize. We deal with new mothers and hormones every day. I'm so sorry about your husband. Are you going to grief counseling? I can recommend a good group for you."

"No, I have a lot of support from my friends so everything is looking up. As soon as I have this baby, my life will be complete. Thank you for your concern."

"If you need to talk, call me anytime. Please, take care of yourself Mrs. Lawson. Maybe I'll be on duty when you deliver."

"Oh, that would be nice. I certainly will call you if I need to. Thank you again."

Jill felt a smirk cross her face after she left the office. She fooled the good doctor again. She didn't intend to fall in love with this baby. She'd use it just like she used everyone else in her life. That is as long as it benefited her.

The next few days she kept busy. She stayed at the office as long as she could so she didn't have to spend the long nights at home. Maybe she would look for someone interesting. She needed someone to spend evenings with her.

Sunday morning she woke to find her bed was soaked. She knew that her water broke, so she called Dr. Hanna to ask what she should do. Dr, Hanna said, "As long as you aren't having any pains, you can take your time and prepare to go to the hospital for the epidural. I'll notify the hospital you'll arrive in the next two hours."

Jill showered, packed her bag, and called a cab. The driver was anxious to reach the hospital and kept saying that he didn't want a baby born in his cab. Jill told him she wasn't having much pain and he relaxed.

The nurses met her at the door and wheeled her to the fourth floor. The attendant started an IV and monitored the baby's heartbeat. Within the hour, her pains started and the doctor arrived and administered the epidural. Jill told her she didn't want to feel any pain, and Dr. Hanna told her she that the drug worked well with most patients.

Jill's labor lasted about five and a half hours. Her daughter was born early that evening. The nurse laid the baby on Jill's stomach and she thought that the baby favored Kurt more than her. She spent just a few minutes wondering what he would have thought of their daughter. One of the nurses asked her what she was going to name the baby. Jill had no idea. She hadn't thought about it. She told herself to listen and the first girl's name she heard, she would claim the name.

As the team was washing the baby, one of the girls dropped a towel on the floor. The other nurse said, "What's the matter Annie? You got the dropsy's today?"

So, that was how she found her daughter's name. The nurse's name was Annie and Annie it should be. It was good enough for her. She wanted to make her mother happy, so she chose to use her mother's middle name, which was Mae.

Annie Mae Lawson had arrived in the world. Heaven help this

poor child.

By the next afternoon, Jill's room was full of flowers and candy after the hospital's staff leaked that Jill was there. The people she worked with and ones that worked with Kurt sent flowers to the new baby girl.

Jill shook her head every time one of the nurses commented on how beautiful the little one was. They all said that Annie was one of the prettiest babies that had ever been born at this hospital. Jill hadn't taken much time to look at her. The nurses were so taken by her that they didn't mind feeding her, or changing her, or holding her, and cooing to her. They didn't notice that the mother worried more about her hair than she did her own daughter.

Annie was a good baby. It was as though she knew she wasn't supposed to make noise and she didn't cry at all. Jill may have thought twice about giving her away if she had, and maybe Annie knew this.

Jill called the agency she had decided to use and arranged for the full time nurse to move in the next day. She had hired the agency to prepare the nursery with all the necessary things. Money was no problem, she instructed them to get the best of everything. After all, she had to worry about her image. People were going to visit and she wanted them to think she gave her daughter the best of everything. What a nice mother!

The visitors that evening were enthralled with Annie's beauty and sweet personality. The women commented on how content Annie was and they couldn't resist hugging and kissing her.

Jill and Annie made the journey home the next day. The nurse met the cab and took the baby straight to the nursery. Nurse Hazel Waters was a strict woman, which met with Jill's approval. A lot of others wanted this job and the excellent pay, but Jill needed someone as cold as she was, and Miss Hazel seemed like the best choice.

Annie's life began with a strict regiment. No one held her, no one talked to her, only when it was time for her to eat. The stream of visitors didn't last long. Most people felt awkward around Nurse Hazel. They cut their hugs short, and didn't coo too loud. It was as though they were afraid that Nurse Hazel would punish them for showing love to the beautiful little baby girl.

Jill recovered from giving birth quickly. The weekly trips to the gym had helped her to keep her figure. She couldn't wait to get back in that size 3. She thought maybe that she could get down to a size 2 if she worked hard. It gave her something to look forward to.

She went into the nursery the first day and asked Nurse Hazel if she had what she needed. Hazel said she had everything. Jill told her that she had opened an account at the neighboring department store for whatever supplies she needed. Hazel thanked her and said that was fine, she would only purchase what she needed for the baby. Jill hadn't returned to the nursery since then. Even cold hearted Nurse Hazel wondered about this woman. But, she had been hired to care for the baby's needs; she hadn't been hired to judge the mother. The money was good, and the apartment was very comfortable.

The routine went smoothly. Jill had absolutely no contact with Annie. Nurse Hazel fed her every four hours. In between times, she laid her in the crib.

The living quarters included the biggest TV that Hazel ever saw. The old western movies she loved were on all day and all night.

After the third week, Jill started going into the office a few hours a day. The wardrobes for the photo shoots were finished and Jill was thrilled when she saw them. She approved of all but one dark pantsuit. She argued with one of the team members that it would make her look drab and boring. To prove her point she put the jacket on and asked him to take her photo, develop it, and meet back with the team as soon as possible.

When the photo was finished, the whole team agreed that Jill was right. Even the one that had argued with her in the first place acquired a new respect for Jill's perception of what was best for the ads. Jill asked to have the suit done again in a cream-colored silk, and accent it with a pale yellow scarf. The outfit was just the right look for the mascara ad the company wanted. Jill was pleased with the outcome, and went home that day in a great mood.

When Jill entered her home, she heard the baby crying from the nursery. It was the first time she heard her daughter's cry. She thought about going into the nursery but she heard the nurse talking to the baby, so she went to pour herself a drink instead. She liked to unwind and relax on the deck after the long day at the office. Her evenings were her own personal time, she didn't even think about holding Annie and getting to know her.

Nurse Hazel came out to the deck and asked to speak to her. She told her that she thought that Annie had an infected eye.

Jill got on the phone and asked if the pediatrician could see her daughter immediately. The next photo shoot was in a few days and she wanted to make sure it wasn't serious. The doctor's office worked her in and she told Hazel to prepare the baby. Jill tried to hold the baby in the doctor's office, thinking of her image again, but she didn't do well with her and handed her back to Hazel. Jill knew she had to learn how to hold the baby between now and the photo shoot, she couldn't have Hazel stand in for her then.

The doctor prescribed eye drops and reassured her that Annie would be fine. He told her that the eyes are the fastest healing part of the body. Jill breathed a sigh of relief and the doctor really thought she was worried about her daughter.

When they got back home, Jill told Hazel that she'd like to have Annie brought to her at 6:00. She told her that she needed to stop being afraid of holding her own baby. Hazel thought to herself, it wasn't a matter of being afraid but she thought that Jill didn't even care about her own daughter. But, she was the one that paid her, so she kept her opinion to herself.

At 6:00 on the dot, she carried Annie into the sitting room. She put Annie on Jill's lap and she sat for a few minutes. Annie looked up at Jill, but she felt no connection whatsoever to this child. She just hoped that she could fake it and get through the upcoming days without making a fool of herself. The whole ad campaign was centered on a mommy and a baby. Without Annie, she didn't have the job. She didn't think that the crew would want to sit and wait for a baby who threw a fit every time her mother held her.

For the next few days, at 6:00 p.m., Jill held Annie for fifteen minutes. Annie didn't cry, and she didn't squirm. She calmly lay in Jill's lap. Jill didn't touch her, or hug her. She just let her sit in her lap. Hazel stood a few feet away in case they had problems. After a few days of practicing, Jill grew confident that she could hold Annie long enough to take the photos. She would keep Nurse Hazel very close just in case there was a problem.

The day came when the crew was ready for the baby. Everything was ready when Hazel arrived with Annie. When she carried her into the office, all of the team gathered around her. They were thrilled with the baby. They thought she was as photogenic as her mother was. They couldn't believe their luck. They'd been afraid that they might have to photograph an ugly baby. Annie had the demeanor of a perfect, content, sweet baby the whole time. They couldn't have searched for a better model. Annie was quiet and didn't cry at all, even when Jill held her for the photos.

Jill and Annie instantly became the perfect "Mommy and Baby". The ad campaign went great. The photos portrayed a mother and child that bonded so well together, they seemed to be one person. The agency was pleased and astonished as the numbers showed that they had a gold mine in Jill, and now her baby. They scheduled another shoot in the spring and started planning for it with enthusiasm.

CHAPTER FIFTEEN

Things went fine for the first six months after Annie was born. Jill left every morning trusting her care to Nurse Hazel. Jill received a promotion to consultant for the company's biggest account. Her manager just loved her input on what appealed to the average woman, and he wanted her to have a hand in planning their biggest advertisements. Jill loved the extra responsibility and she thrived on the excitement.

One day after she arrived home and had sit with her evening cocktail to relax, Nurse Hazel came into the living room and asked to speak to her. "Is there a problem with the baby?"

"No, ma'am. I wanted to let you know that I received a phone call earlier today that my father is gravely ill. My family lives in Greece, and I'll be handing in my resignation. I'd like to be with him for his last few months. I'll be leaving in two weeks, and I'd be glad to help you find a replacement. I've enjoyed working for you and Annie. I hate to leave, but I have to see my father before he dies. I'm so sorry for the inconvenience it will cause you."

"Yes, it certainly is an inconvenience. I'm very pleased with your work, and I can offer you a raise, if that's the problem. I really wish you would stay, and I don't want to have to start all over again with someone else. You know the rules here, and you have followed them well."

Hazel had expected Mrs. Lawson to react this way. She had not taken part at all in her baby's care and she didn't expect that would change.

"Mrs. Lawson, I appreciate the compliment. I don't want more money. I must see my father. His doctors have found prostate cancer and they have given him only months to live. I can't put it off. I must leave immediately. I'd never forgive myself for not seeing him. I'll start the interviews for my replacement as soon as possible. I have contacted the agency and I actually have three prospects already. If you'd like me too, I'll interview them first and if I think they are appropriate for the job, I'll recommend them."

"This is so bothersome. Are you sure you won't stay? I don't have time for this now."

"No, Mrs. Lawson, I'll be leaving in two weeks. I've booked my flight already and have started packing my things."

"Very well, just interview the women and let me know which ones I can trust with the care of my daughter. I don't have to remind you that I pay well, and I expect certain things. I want someone that is prepared to take full responsibility for her. You'll let me know then?"

"Yes, ma'am. I'll start tomorrow and I'll do my best to find the right person. Thank you."

Jill was aggravated and upset. She liked things to run smoothly. She didn't want to bother with this problem of her daughter's nurse. She was too busy and had too many other things on her mind. "Oh well," she thought, "I'll leave it up to Hazel to find someone. Considering the price I pay, how hard will it be to hire another nurse? I'm sure there are many women that would love to take her job."

Three days later, Hazel approached Jill again and asked if she would like to set up appointments for the following evening to interview the two nurses she thought she should consider.

"Yes, I suppose if I must. Have you found them fit for the job?"

"Yes. The two I've chosen will take good care of Annie. I'll have the first one come at 6:00 tomorrow evening. I'll allow an hour and have the second one here at 7:00."

"Fine, I'll see them tomorrow then."

The next evening Camille Roberts arrived promptly at 6:00. Hazel escorted her to the living room where Mrs.Lawson was waiting. Jill asked her to have a seat on the sofa.

"Have you brought your references with you? I'm sure Nurse Hazel has told you what I expect and what the salary is. Now, what are the ages of the children you worked with last?"

"I did bring my references, and I've worked with children from birth until twelve years old. The last home I was in, the father's employer transferred him to Mississippi, and I didn't want to move with them."

"Would you make this a permanent position?"

"Oh, yes. I'd stay until your daughter reaches eighteen, if that's what you require. I understand that there are living quarters here."

"Yes, your living quarters are beside the nursery. You have your own kitchen, bathroom, and sitting room. You'll prepare everything my daughter needs there. Remember you'll be required to be with my daughter full time."

"And your daughter is six months old?"

"Yes, and you'll be required to take full responsibility for her. I expect you to be with her day and night. I must remind you that I pay well, and I don't like complications."

"That's fine. I'm prepared to take full responsibility for your child. I've discussed the requirements with Miss Waters at length and I understand what you require of a nurse. I'd be able to start immediately."

Jill spent another few minutes talking to her and said she'd be in touch as soon as she made a decision.

The second woman arrived ten minutes early. Her name was Mimi Langley. She didn't appeal to Jill from the moment she met her, and she didn't waste much time with her. She conducted a short interview and told her she would let her know.

After the women left, she discussed the two nurses with Hazel. They both agreed that Camille was the best choice. Jill told Hazel to call her the next day and have her spend the next week with her and make sure she knew what to do when Hazel left.

Jill went to the Vintage Shoppe the next day on her lunch hour and purchased a beautiful silk scarf for Hazel. She hated to lose her and wanted to give a gift to show that she was pleased with the job she did with Annie.

CHAPTER SIXTEEN

Nurse Camille bonded with Annie from the first moment she picked her up. She knew from what Hazel told her that Mrs. Lawson never came into the nursery. She could hold Annie as much as she wanted. Annie eyes got brighter when she sang to her. Camille had never been married, and had no children of her own. This to her was the next best thing, and she was paid to love a child. What better job could a woman have?

When the spring arrived, Camille took Annie for a walk almost every day. She spent the time telling her about the new world she would discover as she grew. Their days were joyful and happy.

Jill went to ask Camille what size clothing her daughter wore so she could start on the sketches for their next scheduled photo shoot. She knew Annie was nine months old, but she had no idea what size she wore. When she entered the nursery, Camille was down on the floor on her hands and knees building a house with blocks. Camille was surprised to see Mrs. Lawson, and stood up when she came into the room.

"Mrs. Lawson, I'm sorry. I didn't hear you. What can we do for you? Annie's glad to see you, see she's smiling at you."

Jill glanced down at Annie and was surprised to see how much she'd grown. She marveled at how she was beginning to look just like her. She really was a beautiful baby. Her first thought was that Sam would be ecstatic to photograph her.

"Camille, I need to know what size clothing my daughter wears. We're going to do an ad campaign for a Mother and Daughter clothing line, and I need to start on her wardrobe."

Camille was speechless for a few seconds. She was shocked of how heartless Mrs. Lawson sounded, and she wondered how a mother could have a child and not want to love her. A thought struck her that she had never heard her call her daughter by her name. She wondered if she even knew her name.

"Of course, Mrs. Lawson, I'll get one of her outfits for you. I purchased this dress a few days ago, and I don't think that Annie will grow much between now and then."

"Thank you, Camille. I'll take this with me, if you don't mind. I'll let you know the dates of the photo shoot. I'll need you to bring the baby to my office on that date. We should only need her for three days." Jill walked out of the room without looking at Annie again.

Camille sat back down beside Annie and made a silent promise that she would love her twice as much to make up for the love she missed from her own mother.

Jill worked long hours on the preparations for the upcoming campaign and she wanted to design several of the outfits featured in the shoot. She thought if the company liked her work, she'd try to open her own line of women's clothing. The first dress was beautiful and the matching one for Annie was so gorgeous she just knew that mothers wouldn't be able to resist them. Jill felt as though she finally found what she wanted to do with the rest of her career. She enjoyed designing more than modeling.

When Jill showed Sam the outfits, he was thrilled. He kept telling her that he knew she had an insight into exactly what women wanted, and this just proved he was right. He couldn't wait to get started.

Jill told Camille that she needed her to bring Annie to her office the following week. "I want you to take Annie to the hairdresser on Monday. I made prior arrangements and they knew exactly how I want Annie's hair done."

Camille assured her that she would have Annie to the appointment on time.

On Tuesday morning, Camille bathed Annie and made sure she was extra pretty. It didn't take much work since she had inherited her mother's beauty. When she arrived at Mrs. Lawson's office, she was impressed with the décor and the authority that Jill had earned for herself. Annie watched everyone and seemed fascinated with the hustle and bustle. She sat quietly and everyone commented on how well behaved she was.

The photos turned out to be spectacular. Annie was a natural and it seemed as though she knew as soon as her mother held her that she was expected to pose and sit perfectly still. The camera crew kept telling Jill that Annie was the best model that they'd ever dealt with. Jill smiled and acted like she was the perfect mother, and she in turn deserved a perfect child. Camille sat on the sideline and thought to herself, what they would say if they knew how Mrs. Lawson really treated her own daughter.

The next three days were busy ones, and Annie and Camille were glad to stay at home and play after it was over. They soon got back into their routine and life went on that way for the next several months.

Jill's reputation as a superb model and designer grew by leaps and bounds after the ads hit the stands. The agency could hardly keep up with the inquiries for Jill's designs and the cosmetics sales did more than the company had projected. Jill's self-esteem also grew. She loved the adoration and thrived on the notoriety. Life for her was satisfying. She couldn't have asked for anything more.

When Annie turned two years old, Camille got sick. She noticed a lump in her right breast, and the doctors discovered she had breast cancer. When she reported to Jill that she had to schedule chemotherapy four times a week, she cried for herself and for Annie. There was no way she could care for Annie full time and she told her she would hand in her resignation by the end of the week.

Jill was angry. "Now is the not the best time for this. I simply don't have time to hire another nurse. I can't spare the time off work right now. You'll have to do it. I want you to contact the employment agency and start interviews immediately. Make sure they know that I do expect full time care. I can't spare time for a child, and I do not want to worry about it. Am I clear?"

"Yes, Mrs. Lawson you are very clear. I'll call tomorrow and as soon as I find the right person, I'll have her meet with you."

"Thank you Camille, I'm so glad that you understand. I appreciate the job you have done with my daughter. I'm pleased that she is so well behaved. I hate to lose you. And I do wish you the best of health."

"Thank you, Mrs. Lawson. I love Annie and this job hasn't been work to me, but I have had fun and I wish I could stay. I'll never forget her."

"Well, you'll have to forget her, I'm afraid. I won't change my mind once you leave. It's not fair on your replacement if I tell them that you will come back after you are well. So, when you leave, you leave for good."

"Yes, I understand. But, I can't care for Annie full time if I'm sick. I must relinquish her care to someone else."

"Well, that is all. Let me know as soon as you find someone."

Camille walked back to the nursery and Annie looked up from the pile of toys she was playing with, and greeted her with a big smile. Camille wished she could take this poor child with her when she left. Who would love her now?

Camille contacted the agency and interviewed twenty-two people the first week. They told her that they were running out of applicants, and the ones that had sent to her with the best of the lot. Most of the women were so cold, and Camille didn't like any of them. How could they not love Annie? Even if it was a job, how could they resist connecting with such a sweet innocent little girl?

The agency sent three more people to interview, with the sad news that these were the last three they had. Camille knew she had to pick the one soon. It wasn't going to be easy; she didn't feel comfortable giving the total care of Annie to any of them. She loved Annie as if she were her own child. She had spent the last year and a half, twenty-four hours a day with her and she hated to leave. Her health was getting worse by the day, and she knew she had to start the chemo immediately. The cancer would kill her and she had to try to fight to save her life.

Finally, she settled on the best two of the women she had interviewed. She asked Jill if she could bring them back for her to meet them.

The first woman's name was Harriet Mason. Camille liked the way she held Annie and talked to her non-stop. The second one, Nadine Shoemaker, was as qualified as the first, but she didn't have the same personality. Camille preferred the friendly one.

Jill didn't waste too much time with the interviews. She wanted to get the matter settled with the least amount of effort. She liked Harriet better, but she thought she was too nice. After all, she was hiring a nurse, not a playmate.

Camille escorted the women out, and came back to ask Mrs. Lawson which one she wanted her to contact. After a few minutes of discussion, they chose Harriet.

"Camille, take care of the details with her for me. I'll leave it to you to make sure that Harriet does understand that I don't want to be bothered with the daily care. I don't wish to be involved unless it is an emergency. Can you do that?"

"Yes, Mrs. Lawson. I'll make sure that Nurse Harriet understands the situation fully. I wish I could stay with Annie. I've grown to love the child. I'll miss her."

"Very well Camille. I'd like to extend to you a month's salary for your dedication to my daughter, and for your health care. I hope you're well soon."

"Thank you, ma'am. I appreciate the extra money. I can use it to help with my chemo. My parents are helping me pay most of it. The doctors are optimistic with treatment I can get better."

"I'll have your check waiting for you the day you leave."

Camille turned to leave and felt her hands shake with anger. She didn't know when she had met a colder person than Jill. How could she not want to bond with her own daughter? I feel sorry for Annie if she ever has to depend on her mother, she thought to herself as she headed back to the nursery.

The next two weeks she spent training Nurse Harriet. Annie seemed to like her, but she looked at Camille with sadness as though she knew she wouldn't see her again. It broke Camille's heart the day she left and had to trust a stranger with the care of the little girl she had grown to think of her own. It's just not fair that a biological mother can give birth to a child, but not automatically love that child. Unfortunately, mothers can make the choice to love, ignore, or even hate their own children.

Nurse Harriet was excellent with Annie. It took a few weeks for the two of them to feel comfortable with each other. By the end of the first month, they laughed and played with ease.

Jill's workload doubled after the clothing line was so successful. She looked forward to each day, and spent more time at the office than she did at home. One day she came home early with a sinus headache, and she heard Annie's laughter coming from the playground. After she fixed herself a drink, she walked around the backyard garden and found Nurse Harriet pushing Annie on the swing. Jill stood and watched them for a few minutes until Harriet looked up and saw her.

"Mrs. Lawson, you're home early. I'm sorry, were we making too much noise?"

"No, I wanted some air. I had to leave work because of my sinus headache. I'm going to sit out for a while and try to lie down before dinner. Do you know if the cook is coming early tonight? I would like to change the menu to something lighter. Can you call him for me?"

"Yes, certainly I'll try to call him. I don't think it'll be a problem. I'll tell him you are not feeling well, and I'm sure he can change the meal for you."

"Thank you Harriet. How's my daughter doing these days?"

Harriet picked Annie up off the swing and walked towards Jill.

"Annie, it's your mother. She came home early today. Would you like to hold her, Mrs. Lawson?"

"No, I don't trust myself with her. I'll sit over on the bench. Please don't mind me. Continue with whatever you normally do."

Harriet and Annie went to play in the sand box and Harriet noticed Jill walking back to the house after about a half an hour. She wondered why Mrs. Lawson never held Annie. Actually, come to think of it, she had never even seen her in the same room with Annie. Harriet had been caring for Annie for months, and in all that time, Mrs. Lawson hadn't hugged or smiled at her own child.

CHAPTER SEVENTEEN

Sam called Jill on Wednesday, and asked if she was busy after lunch. He wanted to meet with her to discuss an idea the management had ran by him.

"Sure, for you Sam I'd cancel everything. I look forward to the break. I can't seem to be able to finish this piece I'm working on. The front of the dress just doesn't suit me, and I need to get away from it for a while."

"I will see you at 1:30 then."

"Okay. See you then."

She cleared her desk after lunch and took a few minutes to sit on her balcony and wait for Sam. She heard him knock on her door, and she yelled for him to come out to the balcony. He had brought her a latte and she thanked him and told him to sit and enjoy the beautiful view from twenty-three stories in the air.

"Jill, how are you? I swear you get more beautiful every time I see you. I'm still waiting for you to go out to dinner with me. We'd make a smashing couple."

"Sam, you never change. I keep telling you that someday a good woman will snap you up, and believe me when I tell you I'm not a good woman. How've you been?"

"I've been busy as usual. I wanted to talk with you about some of the things the company has been working on. I saw the numbers this morning on your cosmetic and clothing line. They are holding steady and the management is very pleased with your work. I think they are going to offer you a chance to model with your daughter again."

"I didn't realize that there was a shoot scheduled. I'd love a chance to model some of the new designs I've been working on."

"The Christmas holiday shoot has several spots open, and I think they'll approach you with a proposal in the next few weeks. I was looking over the last set of photos we did with you and your daughter, and I love them. Both of you photograph so well, and your daughter is just the sweetest little girl."

"Yes, she is sweet. I swear she grows every day. Before I know it, she'll be in school. Oh, I hated school. I hope she does better than I did."

"I'm surprised that you hated school. I'd think that every boy in the place would have wanted to sit next to you."

"Yeah, I guess they did. But you know it gets old having everyone you know scrambling to get close to you. I hated the stupid girls. They were all so jealous, and the boys acted like fools most of the time. I'm glad I grew up. Adult men act a little more mature. Anyway, enough about that. What else is new?"

"I did want to tell you about a new idea being thrown around. I think the company is going to open a day care here at the office. I was asked to sit in on the meeting last week, and they want every employee to bring their children into the office. And, since you are in the spotlight, you'll probably be asked to set the standard for everyone else. Is your daughter in daycare now?"

"No, I have a full time nurse sitting with her. I'm completely satisfied with the arrangement, and I don't want to bring her to the office every day. I hope you talked them out of the idea."

"No, it is too late. An article is coming out at the end of the month about how our company is devoting their resources to help all the employees have a better working relationship, and how keeping your child close to you helps you be more content in your working environment."

"To me I think it's a ridiculous idea. Who would want their child beside them all day? You would never get any work done. I pay well to have someone with my child, and I get my free time. It's a perfect arrangement. I really don't want to change it."

"Jill, you have been, and will be again, featured as the perfect mother. You and your daughter are the examples. I'm sure they will want to photograph you with your child for future issues."

"I don't care about that. I'm content with the way it is now. I can be the perfect mother and have a full time nurse."

"I hope you understand that it's not a request, I think it would be mandatory for you. I would be thrilled to have my children with me. I have two boys, and I don't see them nearly enough. And I'm sure that you miss your daughter every day. Just think if you could have her here right down the hall. If you get a few minutes, you could go and sit with her. Wouldn't that be great?"

Jill stopped herself from blowing her stack. The last thing she wanted was to have her child hanging around her neck all day every day. She had one thing to protect here, and that was her image. Her whole life had been built on image, and she didn't want to blow that now. Why couldn't things go on just as they had been?

"I'll think about it, okay. Now, let me show you my latest designs. They are just to die for. I especially love the lingerie line I started. I think it will do well. Let's go in and I'll get some of them."

Sam was impressed with Jill's new lingerie line. "Jill, I love the black silk robe. I'd give my right arm to see you model that one. Can we make a date and see if you look as good in it as I think you would?"

"Sure Sam, I'll put that on my list of things to do. What about this beige set? Do you think it's too revealing? I'm not sure about it. I think I'll redesign this one. I think men like to leave some things to the imagination. I know it added to the excitement with Kurt. It's been a while since I thought about him. I still miss him."

"I'm sorry Jill. I shouldn't say what I do to you. I know the way you lost Kurt was awful. I'm just kidding with you, but I really do think you are the most beautiful woman I ever saw."

Jill smiled at him and went to hug Sam. "I love you Sam, just not in that way."

"I know. I have to get out of here. I have a meeting in an hour and I want to check a few details between now and then. I'll get back to you on the nursery and the details, okay?"

"Yes, that's fine. I'll see you soon then. Maybe we can do dinner one evening, if you promise not to think of it as a date. I need male companionship. I need someone to spend time with."

"That sounds like a plan. Let me know what night."

"I will."

After Sam left, Jill started on the changes to the beige lingerie. She was so engrossed in it that she didn't know two hours had passed until her secretary buzzed her to say it was time for the staff meeting. She grabbed her papers, raced out the door, and slipped inside just as the door closed.

The upcoming holiday shoots were the main topic of the meeting. They discussed different layouts and they asked Jill if she would be able to do a shoot with her daughter. According to the feedback, the public was anxious to see them again.

The wardrobes for the Christmas season looked fantastic already. Their biggest client was introducing a new facial line and Jill was excited to play a big part in the advertisements. The nursery idea didn't come up, and Jill didn't think about it at all until three weeks later when Sam called and told her that the construction of the nursery wing was under way. Jill was perturbed at the aggravation of the whole thing. She had a nurse for her kid; she didn't need to bring her in here.

That night after she got home, Jill fixed herself a drink and decided to stop by the nursery to see how Harriet was doing with her child. She knew she would be going on three years old now, and she couldn't remember the last time she had spent more than two seconds with her. She thought back to a few months ago when she asked Harriet to bring her out to the dining room while they ate. Another thought hit Jill. She didn't remember ever calling her by name. It was as though Annie was a ghost, not a daughter. Jill couldn't recall one time that she thought of her and a mental picture came into her mind. She had absolutely no mother skills whatsoever. At that thought, Jill shook her head slightly as if to say, "So be it."

She knocked on the door to the nursery and heard nothing so she opened the door. No one was in the room. She went into the sitting room and still saw no one. She went to the back of the house and headed out to the patio. She heard a child's giggles as she rounded the corner.

Nurse Harriet saw her coming and stopped the swing. She told her, "Annie honey, look it is your mother."

"Hi, Annie, how are you? I wanted to check and see how big you're getting. I need to work on our holiday wardrobe and I don't want to make the clothing too small."

Harriet thought to herself, she came out here to see what size clothing her daughter wears now, what a shame. For one second I thought that maybe she came to see Annie. "She certainly is growing isn't she? I'll get you one of her outfits when we return inside. How are you today, Mrs. Lawson? It is a gorgeous day, isn't it?"

"Yes, it is. I don't know her size. I think the date for the shoot won't be for another month and a half, do you think she will grow much by then?"

"No, Annie won't grow much in that time. Children usually grow slow at three years old. I loved the last photographs of the two of you. You certainly are beautiful, Mrs. Lawson. I have a feeling that Annie will be beautiful also, just like her mother. I haven't seen a photo of her father, does she look like him?"

"She has a few of Kurt's features. He was a good-looking man. I'll show you what he looked like if you would like. I put all his pictures away after he was killed. I didn't want to look at them."

"I'm sorry. I didn't mean to pry. I didn't realize that your husband died. I didn't want to intrude so I never asked. You are very young to be raising a daughter on your own. And, might I add, you have done well. I'm sure he would have been proud of what you have accomplished."

"I really don't care if he would be proud or not. He was murdered and not in a nice way. I don't speak of him anymore."

"I'm sorry. I didn't mean to be intrusive. I apologize."

"No don't worry about it, you didn't know. Anyway, I'll talk to you later. I'm going to go in and take a nice hot bath and relax."

"Yes, of course. Annie and I will stay out a while longer."

Jill turned and headed back to the house. She didn't glance at Annie again, it seemed like Annie was Harriet's child, not hers. She had dismissed her daughter just like she had dismissed her dead husband.

CHAPTER EIGHTEEN

Jill couldn't remember ever being so busy. Her lingerie line was doing fantastic. She wanted to work on evening wear next for the holidays. She could visualize the dresses and outfits in her mind, now she needed to make them a reality. The new fabrics were easy to work with and women wanted clothing that was easy to care for. Her designs fitted the normal woman and were affordable.

Jill spent little time at home, and Harriet and Annie grew closer every day. Annie's laughter filled the home and Harriet loved her. They walked to the park every day and visited the zoo next door. Annie had learned the names of all the animals and she loved the monkeys best. They visited them so often Harriet could swear that they lined up and waited for her and Annie to arrive. The littlest one had a white spot in the middle of his forehead and Annie called him Spot. Harriet laughed and laughed when she thought of Spot the monkey. She told Annie if they owned their own home she would buy her one of each of the animals.

One night Mrs. Lawson came and told Harriet that she wanted to bring four of the outfits she had made for Annie home for her to try them on. "I'll need you to bring Annie to the office next Thursday for two hours. Sam wants to see her and make sure he has the right size stools. Then the following week, I'll need her there for at least three days. If everything goes well, we should be done in that time."

"I'll make sure I mark it on the calendar. Mrs. Lawson, could I ask you a favor. I'm going to visit my family in three weeks, and I'd like to take Annie with me."

"Where does your family live? I don't remember you talking about them."

"My family lives in Constantine. It's only an hour's drive from here. I'd like to leave on Friday night and spend the weekend with my sister. We'd be home by Monday evening, if it's alright."

"I don't know, Harriet. I never thought about Annie leaving for days. I'm not sure I'm comfortable with the idea. If I say no, what will you do?"

"I guess I could leave her with someone else until I get back. I have a friend that we spend time with that would love to stay here with Annie while I'm gone. I'd rather take her with me. My family was looking forward to meeting her."

"May I remind you dear that Annie is my child not yours. It seems like you might have forgotten that little fact. I have the say over her."

"Mrs. Lawson, believe me, I know whose child Annie is. I assumed that you would rather I take her with me. I assumed wrong."

"Let me think about it for a while. I'll let you know."

Jill turned her back and walked away. Harriet felt foolish. She did assume that Mrs. Lawson wouldn't care one bit if she took Annie for three months, as long as it didn't interfere with her life. She knew it was a power play. Annie wasn't an object to argue over. She was a sweet innocent child who had no idea that Jill was her real mother, not Harriet. She loved Harriet and had no idea who Jill was, and why should she? In her first three years of life, she had not spent one day with her mother.

Jill called Harriet to the study the next morning. She told her, "I'm going to let Annie go with you. I don't have the time to worry about this right now."

"Thank you, Mrs. Lawson. I'll enjoy showing her off to my family. Your daughter is a wonderful child. And let me say, if I may, that I don't think she is my child. I do love her, but I know this is my job. I wouldn't want to hurt Annie in any way, and if I sounded presumptuous, I'm sorry. I'll take good care of her."

"I hope you do. You are excused."

Harriet went back to the nursery and told Annie the news. "Annie, we are going on a trip. I want you to meet my family and they will love you."

"What is a trip?"

"Oh you silly girl, I told you about the trip. We'll be going on a big bus. We'll ride on the bus for a while, and then I'll show you where I grew up. Would you like that?"

Annie clapped her hands together, bobbed her head up and down, and squealed with joy. What a happy child, Harriet thought.

Harriet and Annie spent the next three weeks packing and planning for their trip. Harriet's family loved Annie. Annie was a happy little girl and she was exhausted when they arrived back home.

CHAPTER NINETEEN

Jill was excited about the photo shoot for two reasons. First of all she loved seeing her face in print, and she couldn't wait to see if her hard work on the new designs would be well received by the public. She spent ninety-nine percent of her day thinking about herself. She made a note to remind Harriet that she'd have to take Annie to the hairdresser and make sure that all her nails were done and her hair was perfect. It was imperative that Annie looked like the "perfect daughter", since Jill was portrayed as the "perfect mother".

Harriet assured her that she had spent a lot of time telling the regular girl how important is was for Annie to have extra time allotted for their visit. The Majesty Salon that handled all of Jill's needs was well aware of how important Jill and her acquaintances were. They were paid well to cater to the beautiful models that were regular customers. Harriet felt so out of place when she took Annie for her appointments, she didn't travel in the same circle as all the beautiful women that surrounded her when she was there.

The holiday issue was one of the most important of the year. The sponsors worked most of the year for the Christmas season. The cosmetic agencies presented their new colors and shades and the clothing industry showed off the glitter and glamor awaiting the women in the stores.

Jill's new position and new designs were featured in most of the ads and she was nervous. She knew that if this holiday season was successful, she'd really be a household name and known by the world.

The day for the photo shoot arrived and Harriet made sure that Annie was bathed and ready early. When they got to Jill's office the chatter began and Annie was the bright spot of their day. Jill played the part of devoted mother quite well, and Harriet took a back seat in the show. Jill asked her to follow them to the photo studio and she was fascinated watching as Sam photographed mother and daughter. Harriet found herself admiring Jill's beauty and wished to herself that she was as beautiful on the inside.

After they were finished, Jill handed Annie back to Harriet and kissed the top of her head before she headed back to the office. "Mommy will see you at home, sweetheart," she said as she hurried out the door. Harriet told Annie, "Say goodbye to your mother, Annie." Annie said, "Goodbye, mommy."

Harriet shook her head as she rode the elevator down to the lobby. She wondered what Mrs. Lawson's co-workers would think of her if they knew how little mommy and daughter knew each other.

The following week it took a few hours longer than expected to finish the layout but Annie was a trooper through it all. She didn't cry or act up once. Annie loved the attention and she was a natural in front of the camera. Harriet wondered what she would grow up to be, maybe a famous actress. She hoped that Annie would keep her personality and that fame wouldn't turn her into what her mother was.

After the photos were all done, Sam called Jill the following week and asked if she wanted to see some of the prints. Jill went to his studio and she couldn't contain her enthusiasm when she saw the photos. Sam was one of the best and he had captured her and Annie better than she had imagined. Jill knew that the season would surpass any other that the agency had done. She was confident that they had never had anyone to match Jill and Annie. Jill's ego was even more inflated after hearing Sam's praise.

She left Sam's office flying high on a cloud. The agency also wanted to make a deal for her holiday evening wear, and the lingerie line was doing better than expected. Jill was proud of how far she had come from the small town girl she started out as. She'd love to have the opportunity to hear what the ordinary people from her home town were saying about her now.

The only down side to the contentment Jill was riding on was that a week later Sam brought up the nursery at the office idea. He told her that the staff had been hired and he hoped that she could bring Annie as the first child to be enrolled. He didn't notice the agitation on Jill's face as he went on about the expense the company had gone to. He told her he needed her to take the forms to fill out and hoped she could return them to him in two days.

Jill hesitated as her mind tried to think of an excuse she could use. What in the world was she to do? How could she gracefully exclude her daughter from this office daycare? She couldn't come up with a thing so she reached out and took the forms. "I'll see what I can do."

On the way back to her office she was definitely perturbed. She snapped at her secretary to bring her a hot coffee and slammed her door. Carla had no idea what Mrs. Lawson was upset about, but she knew that she had to make an excellent cup of coffee and do it quick. She entered the office and sat the coffee on the desk and asked, "Will there be anything else, Mrs. Lawson."

"Yes, I need the latest charts on the sale of the black sequin evening gown. Maybe that will cheer me up."

"I'll find the chart and be right back." Carla knew where the chart was and was able to take it back in the office to Jill in five minutes. She hoped that the latest figures showing that the dress was outselling the competition would put Mrs. Lawson in a better mood. Carla laid the chart down on her desk and softly closed the door. She held her breath for a few minutes and was relieved when the intercom was silent. She knew her boss well enough to know that good sales numbers could reach her more than most anything.

When she was ready to leave Jill put the forms for the daycare in her bag and left the office. She told herself that she'd put Sam off as long as she could with the excuse that she forgot them. It worked for three days until he brought her new forms and told her that he'd wait until she finished them. Jill didn't like being put on the spot, but she started on the forms, and was finished with them in fifteen minutes. She handed them back to Sam and he grinned and told her that he had to take them to the daycare office and he would see her later.

"What am I supposed to do now," she thought. "The last thing I need is to have the hassle of a child I hardly know being here all day long."

The next day the staff had a meeting at 1:00. Jill received a lot of compliments on her designs and actually got three orders for her red sequin two-piece suit. The ladies all said they wanted to wear it to the annual Christmas party and laughed at the thought of all three suits being alike. The fact that they'd be dressed the same didn't matter. Jill's reputation had grown and they were thrilled just to have a designer label.

The president of the company, Dan Colby, took over and told the group that there were several things he needed to bring to their attention. "First I want to talk a few minutes about the year-end bonuses. The company's sales numbers have surpassed any year in the history of our company, and I credit it to your hard work. I compliment Sam and Jill on the excellent photo layouts. Each of you can expect a nice bonus at the end of the year."

Next he discussed the spring layout and hoped that the response would continue to grow for their products and sales accounts.

"I want to bring to your attention the new day care facility that will be finished by the middle of next week. I congratulate the first active member, Jill Lawson, and her daughter Annie. I'm so glad that you are able to join in this venture, Jill. Since you and your daughter represent our company so well, I'm glad that it is you that took the honors of being the first parent to participate. Thank you Jill for making sure that you got your correct papers in place before next week."

Jill was shocked to know that she was to be the first one on the list of the employees. She remembered Sam telling her that the company was pushing for her to take part in this venture. She found herself speaking before she thought, "Excuse me, Mr. Colby. I'm not sure that I'll be using the day care a lot because I have an efficient nanny for my daughter. I may bring her in part time."

"I'm sorry Mrs. Lawson. I was under the impression that since you and your daughter are the "perfect mommy and daughter" that you would no longer need a nanny. Sam led me to believe that you were anxious to enroll in our program. Believe me when I tell you that the company has invested a lot of publicity to make this happen. Since we used this theme for your campaigns, the audience will be expecting you to set the example. Is there a problem with the facility? Do we not have the necessary equipment for your daughter's comfort?"

"No sir. I must say that from what I have seen the facility is efficient and exactly what any parent would want for their children. It is just that I'm not sure that I have the time to spend with my daughter here, I have so many different projects started right now."

"Mrs. Lawson I'm going to be blunt, I don't have to tell you that our company is already planning to do the next layout with you and your daughter in this daycare atmosphere. It has been proven that a parent that can spend time with their children during the day is a more satisfied employee. Sam and I have already booked the next issue of the magazine featuring parents spending more quality time with their children. I hope you'll let your nanny go and take advantage of this opportunity that a lot of parents would love to have. My mother never had anyone else watching me. If I had children that were pre-school age, I'd have them here with me in an instant. Can we count on you to represent us again?"

Jill was angry but she remembered what her motto had been for most of her life, it is all about image. She quickly pushed the anger aside and said, "Yes, you can count on me. My daughter Annie will be here when the facility opens. And thank you sir for giving me the chance to once again represent all of you here."

"Very well then, I think that's all I have for today. Shall we adjourn and please all of you join me for coffee and dessert at the café next door and we'll celebrate all our good fortunes."

The staff gathered their things and hurried back to their desks to close up for the day. Jill was fuming inside but she smiled as everyone passed her. She lingered in the conference room hoping that she wasn't being missed. She had no desire to join the group at the café.

Sam motioned for her to hurry and called out that he'd wait for her by the elevator. She had no choice but to drop her things back at her office and head towards the elevator. The pasted smile on her face masked the turmoil running around in her head. She kept repeating in her mind, "It's all about image. Remember Jill, that's what got you where you are now. You must maintain the image."

CHAPTER TWENTY

On the way home Jill was pre-occupied and almost missed the exit to head home. She had no idea what to do about her situation. Her daughter had been an asset to her career without being a bother. She had absolutely no desire to take a child to work. She loved her job, and she was good at it. How dare Mr. Colby demand that she get rid of her nanny. What business what is of his whether she had someone to raise her daughter, it didn't affect him in any way.

On the other hand, what was she without the company? Her image had never been tainted before, and she didn't plan on letting it happen over something as insignificant as her daughter. Her career was secure from her own hard work. It had nothing whatsoever to do with having a perfect relationship with her child. "Oh well, I guess I can play the part for a little while until Mr. Colby forgets about the whole issue, and then I'll give the responsibility of a child back to the person who really wants it, and that ain't me."

When she got home Jill removed her jacket and shoes and headed to the kitchen for a refreshing cold drink. She needed to buzz Harriet and get this over. She pushed the intercom. "Harriet will you please meet me in the study as soon as you can."

"Yes, of course, Mrs. Lawson. And should I bring Annie?"

"No, I need to talk to you and I don't want to bother with her. This will only take a few minutes. Can't you pen her up or something while we speak?"

"I'll turn on the TV and put the gate at the door. I'll be there in ten minutes."

Jill walked to the study and turned on her PC. She wanted to finish a drawing of a wedding dress she was working on before next week's staff meeting. She was totally involved in the drawing and was startled when Harriet spoke.

"Mrs. Lawson, I'm sorry. I didn't mean to startle you. You wanted to talk to me about something?"

"Yes, I need to tell you some bad news. I'm going to let you go. I'm not pleased about it, but I have no choice. I'll be taking Annie to work every day to the daycare my company has offered. My boss is insisting that I set the example for the other employees, and that is more important than anything. I will of course pay you a substantial severance pay. I'm expected to take Annie in as soon as next week, so I'll no longer need you here. I'm sorry, and I hope you won't be too upset."

"Mrs. Lawson, how are you going to watch Annie in the evenings? Would you like me to take just evening hours? I'll gladly take the cut in pay and maybe find another part time position. I'm so close to Annie, and I wouldn't want to leave her suddenly. I'm afraid it will affect her."

"May I remind you that you are only the baby sitter? You don't have to bother yourself with the care of my daughter. I'm telling you that I no longer require your service and I expect you to be packed by the end of next week. I'll certainly provide a good reference for you, and you should have no problem finding another position. I'm sure that there are others that could use a full time nanny. If I hear of any one I will let you know."

Jill turned and walked up the stairs to take a shower. Harriet didn't move for some time and finally got over the shock long enough to turn and head back to the nursery. "Where in the world will this child end up if she depends on her mother for her care?" she asked herself.

After her shower, Jill went down to the kitchen to prepare a sandwich from the delicious roast beef her cook left from the day before. She took her sandwich and headed to the living room to watch the fashion channel. She wanted to see the latest designs being shown by her competition. Within minutes she was totally engrossed in the show and had forgotten all about Annie and Harriet.

Back in the nursery, Harriet asked Annie to come and sit with her while they watched a new cartoon show she had promised Annie she could watch. The whole time the show was playing she found herself rubbing Annie's hair and wishing she could run away and hide with her. It would be the hardest thing she ever did to walk away from this child. She really did fear for her safety. Annie was only three years old, and got into everything she could. How was someone like Mrs. Lawson going to watch a curious toddler when all she cared about was herself? Did she dare leave Annie with her?

The next two days were busy ones for Jill. Her wedding dress design was giving her a fit, and she was growing frustrated with it. She knew what she wanted but it didn't look the same on paper as it did in her mind. She may have to change it back to the original idea, but she didn't want to sacrifice the special detail she wanted it to have. She decided to take a break and walked to the elevator to head downstairs to the lounge for a salad. On the way she met Sam.

"Hey beautiful lady, how are you? I haven't seen you for a couple of days. Whatever you are working on must be important."

"Yes, I'm trying to finalize my new wedding dress for the staff meeting, and I'm running in to a few glitches. I want the bodice to be outlined with small white pearls, but they are too heavy and are pulling the neck line too low. I thought I would take a break for a late lunch and hopefully the afternoon will be better. How are you doing?"

"I'm great. I lined up a few interviews with three new sponsors, and by the way I wanted to ask if you were interested in a few modeling shots for a new ad we may be obtaining for new furniture for children. The company wants a new image and I can't think of a better spokesperson than you to represent it. I realize you are going in a hundred different directions, but I really think I can sell you and Annie to them with hardly any effort. What do you think?"

"Sam, you know I would love to have the exposure. I'm not sure I can find the time. Let me see how this dress ends up and I'll get back to you."

"Sure, just let me know. By the way is Annie excited about coming here in a few days?"

"Yes she is. When I told her she squealed with delight. You know how little ones are, they get so excited."

"I'm looking forward to seeing her again. I'll be making time just to visit the daycare so I can play with her. She sure is a beauty."

Sam got off on the second floor and waved as the door closed. "Yeah right she was excited," she thought. "I have no idea what that daughter of mine is excited about, nor do I really care."

Jill made her way to the salad bar and as she ate, she mulled over the problem neckline, and when the solution came to her as how to fix it, she hurried back to her office.

Jill worked non-stop for almost two hours. When she stood up her neck was stiff and her hand was cramped from drawing. She was pleased with her progress and decided to put it away until the next morning. She'd come in a little early and knew that the new neckline would look perfect on the dress. She wanted to stop on the way home and pick up a few things, and she made a mental note to check with Harriet about what supplies she would need for her daughter.

Jill arrived home around 6:30 pm and as she walked up the walk noticed that the house looked unusually dark. She headed for the kitchen to put the groceries away and afterward she went to the nursery and knocked on the closed door. There was no answer so she opened the door and turned on the light. The front room looked bare. The tables were empty, the last time she was in this part of the room the tables had been cluttered with all the toys and supplies for Annie. She walked to the next room, and noticed that it too was bare. It looked as though no one had been here for a while. She headed to the back where Harriet's bedroom was. Jill opened up a few drawers in the closest dresser and discovered that they were empty. She went to the closet and wasn't surprised to find them empty as well.

"Harriet, are you here?" she asked. "I need to speak with you right away." Jill waited a few seconds for a response and the silence of the room disquieted her. She turned and went to each of the rooms opening the doors and calling for Harriet.

After searching for another ten minutes, Jill figured that Harriet was gone, and she must have taken Annie with her. The last time they spoke, Jill told her to find a new job. Now what had this stupid woman done? Had she taken Annie with her? What in the world would make her think that she could get away with this? Did she not know who she was up against? Jill had good friends in high places and she felt sorry for Harriet when she found her.

Jill got the phone and called her lawyer, Ned Barrows. She told him what she thought Harriet had done, and he told her to call 911 and report it as a kidnapping right away. "It will take me thirty minutes to get to your home, and if the police arrive before I do give them a description of your daughter, and find a picture of her, and the nanny. If you have them ready for them, the alert will go out quicker, and hopefully we'll find the two of them before she gets too far away with your daughter. I'll be right there, and please don't worry Mrs. Lawson, we will find them."

Jill dialed 911 and told the dispatcher what had happened. She went to find pictures of Annie and Harriet before they arrived. She walked back to the nursery and realized that she wouldn't find a picture there, because Harriet had taken everything. Jill stopped in her tracks and thought to herself, "Where am I going to get a picture of either of them. I've never taken a picture of my child."

She scurried to the corner cabinet and pulled out all the papers and scattered them on the floor. She knew she needed an excuse for not having her picture of her daughter, so she'd tell the police that Harriet had taken all the photo albums with her so that Jill wouldn't be able to give a photo to identify her.

Within a few minutes she heard the door bell and asked the two uniformed police officers to come to the living room. They introduced themselves as Officer Templeton, and Officer Davis. They asked her to have a seat and to give them a detailed statement about what she discovered when she arrived home. She told them she had called her lawyer and would like to wait for him. Within a few minutes the doorbell rang again, and it was Mr. Barrows.

He told Jill to answer all the questions to the best of her ability and the more she remembered, the quicker they could find her daughter.

Jill remembered to tear up while she was giving her statement and several times she told the officers that she needed a few minutes. They asked her why she thought that Nurse Harriet took Annie and left.

"I know she was upset. I told her that I was going to have to let her go. My company has started a daycare, and I no longer needed her. I was going to pay her well and give her a good reference. I know she has family, but I don't remember where she said they were from."

Officer Davis asked, "Mrs. Lawson did Miss Mason own a vehicle? Did she have friends that live close by? We'll need a list of the people she saw on a regular basis. And would you please get a recent photo of Miss Mason and your daughter. We'll need to have these things quickly if we intend to stop her from leaving the city with your daughter."

"Oh, you're going to have to excuse me. My mind just won't work when I'm so upset. I noticed minutes before you arrived that the cabinet where I keep all the photos was opened and all the papers were thrown on the floor. I hope that Harriet didn't take all of the photos, what will we do then?"

Jill walked in the next room and showed them the mess on the floor. She stooped down and began looking through all the papers, and said, "I don't see one photo album here. She must have taken them with her. I'm so sorry. I kept all the photos in this cabinet. My mother hated to dust, so I never bought frames. I guess women follow the footsteps of their mother. I don't have one picture of my daughter. What am I going to do if I never get her back? She had no right to take her. Please tell me that you can find them."

"Mrs. Lawson, please have a seat before you fall down. I'm sorry that you have to go through this."

"Oh wait, I do have a picture of my daughter." Jill remembered that she had copies of the latest magazine featuring her and Annie. She went to the desk and opened them to a picture of the two of them. She relished the expression on the officer's faces when she showed it to them.

"Mrs. Lawson may I say that your daughter is beautiful, just like her mother. We'll put this out on the airwaves immediately. We need to have as much information as possible in order to catch Miss Mason. Did she own a car?"

"No, she always called a cab or walked whenever she went out. I always told her to have whatever my daughter needed delivered. She would take my daughter to the park every day, but it is very close so they loved the walk. I can call the agency that referred Harriet to me and see if they knew of any close friends she may have had. I can't remember her speaking of anyone often."

"We're going to put a bulletin on the air and hopefully someone has seen them. I'd like to see your daughter's bedroom if you don't mind."

"Yes, of course, it's down the hall to the left. I provided a unit for the nanny to have privacy while she lived here. The nursery and the sitting room are there."

"Thank you. Are you going to be okay? Is there someone you can call to come and stay with you?"

Jill could think of no one except Sam that would make the effort to comfort her. She didn't really want to call him, but she thought maybe he would come if she asked him. "I'll call a close friend of mine. I hate to bother him, but I'm not sure I can do this all alone." She went to the phone and dialed Sam's number.

Officer Davis and Officer Templeton went towards the nursery. When Sam answered, Jill said, "Sam, I'm so sorry to bother you. I have a crisis and I hoped that I could cry on your shoulder. My nanny has run away with my daughter. I have the police here now and I just needed to hear someone's voice. I'm sorry Sam. I shouldn't have laid on this on you. Forgive me, and I'll let you go."

"Jill, don't be silly. I'm glad you called. Give me your address and I'll come right over. Do you have any idea where they went? Do the police think she has done this before? Harriet seemed so capable when she had Annie at the studio."

Jill hurriedly gave the address to Sam and assured him that she would be fine until he got there. As she was hanging up the phone, the officers came back to the room. "Mrs. Lawson, did you notice anything unusual about Miss Mason in the last few days? Did she seem upset or edgy about anything?"

"She was upset with me. I'm taking my daughter to work with me, and I didn't need her anymore. She didn't take that news well. I know she had grown fond of my daughter, but I never expected this. I told her that she was the nanny, and she had no rights to my daughter." As soon as Jill said the words, she regretted them. She didn't want these police officers to think that her household had any conflict. She, after all, was the perfect mother, and played the part well.

"We're going to put out a bulletin to the cab companies and the bus stations. If Miss Mason had plans to leave the area, someone must have seen her. Will you excuse us for a few minutes? We're going to our cruiser, and we will be right back."

Shortly after they left the doorbell rang. Sam hugged her as soon as she opened the door. "Jill, are you okay? Did the officers find out anything yet? I can't believe that Harriet would take Annie. Are you sure they didn't go somewhere just to visit? Maybe you forgot or Harriet thought that she told you."

"Harriet took all her clothes and all my daughter's things too. She knew exactly what she was doing. Since I'm taking Annie to work with me I told her that I didn't need her anymore, she got angry and wanted to make me suffer. I promised that I would pay here extra, and give her a good reference. Why would she do this Sam?"

Sam approached Jill and held her and laid her head on his shoulder. Jill took advantage of the feeling. It had been a long time since a man had held her, and it made her think of Kurt. This upset her and she did have tears in her eyes when she thought of how she needed him now. Sam held her for a few more minutes and when there was a knock on the door, he went to open it. Officer Davis and Officer Templeton asked if they could come in.

"Mrs. Lawson, we were able to determine that a woman and a small female child matching your daughter's description were seen boarding a bus this afternoon. From what I understand, everyone was so impressed with your daughter's beauty that she left an impression on the employees. We have a destination and asked the station where she is to get off to apprehend her and the child. If we find them, we'll call you immediately. In the meantime, we'll broadcast the description to all our officers. Ma'am we'll be back in touch as soon as we can. If you need us, here's my card. Call the number on there, and you'll be dispatched directly to us."

Mr. Barrows thanked the officers for their help and said whenever they needed Mrs. Lawson to come to the station, he would come with her. He told Jill to call him if anything changed and assured her that he would call her in the morning.

Jill thanked both of the officers when they left. Sam asked her if she wanted some coffee, and headed towards the kitchen. It was 7:30 pm and she remembered that she hadn't had anything at all to eat. She asked Sam, "Sam would you like a sandwich. I haven't had anything since lunch, and my stomach is empty. I'll fix us something."

"Whatever you need, I'll do it Jill. I want you to sit down. Can I fix it for you?"

"I'm fine. I need to do something. I hate just waiting around. It gets on my nerves more than anything. I'm so used to doing for myself; I can't sit still while someone else waits on me."

"Can I at least make the coffee? I need something to do too. Just show me where everything is."

Jill showed him where she kept the coffee and pot, and took everything she needed for the sandwiches to the counter.

"Jill, do you have family here that you can call. I don't want to intrude. I'll stay if you want. I can't imagine how Harriet thinks she can get away with your child. Unfortunately, her reputation is ruined and she'll never get another job with children. She seemed to be so good with Annie. I noticed that her demeanor was so loving with her. I hope that they can pick her up at the next bus stop and you can have Annie back in a few hours. I don't know what I would do if someone took one of my kids. I'm afraid I would hurt whoever did it."

"I'm in shock I guess. I know when I see Annie again, I will hold on to her tighter from now on. I feel sorry for Miss Harriet after this stunt. I'll see that she gets prosecuted to the fullest extent for this awful thing she has done to me." Jill remembered to show emotion and Sam hugged her again, and waited until she had calmed down.

They sit at the counter and ate and talked about the latest campaign that both of them were working on. Sam told her that he was excited about a few projects he wanted to tackle and Jill brought him up to date on her latest ideas for her fashion designs.

The phone rang and Jill rose to go and answer it. "I'm so glad you found my daughter, and yes I'll be right there."

Sam waited until she hung up the phone and said, "Jill I knew that Annie would be back home. Do you want me to drive you?"

"Sam, I hate to ask you, but I would love the help. They caught Harriet at the station sixty miles north of here. I want to go and get my daughter. Do you have the time to go with me?"

"Yes, of course I'll go. I'll gladly drive you. Are you ready now?"

"Yes, let me grab my purse and my coat. I'll be right back."

Within ten minutes they were on the road, and Jill could feel the anger building. How dare a person like Harriet take something that belonged to her? She had every intention of making her sorry she crossed Jill Lawson.

CHAPTER TWENTY-ONE

Jill and Sam arrived at the bus station where they were holding Harriet and Annie within an hour. The officers met them and took them back the hall to the conference room.

Officer John Black asked them to have a seat, and assured Jill that her daughter was safe and she could see her in a few minutes.

"We have arrested Miss Mason and we'll be charging her with kidnapping. As soon as I ask you a few questions, I'll need you to identify her as the one who was in your employ as a nanny for your daughter. I must ask you to refrain from speaking to her, and I assure you that we have everything under control. I just saw your daughter a few moments ago, and the female officer with her is completely enthralled by her. Your daughter has been checked out and seems to be fine. I'll let you see for yourself, and if you want we can transport her to the nearest hospital. Miss Mason has made a statement and I'll discuss the details with you after you see your daughter."

He motioned for one of the officers to show Jill to the room where Annie was waiting. As the door opened the officer thought she saw a twinge of fear on the little girl's face when she saw her mother. She spoke to her, "Annie, your mother is here. She was worried about you and now you can go home with her shortly."

Jill walked over to Annie and sat beside her in the chair. "Honey, are you okay? Mommy was worried about you. Now I'm here, and we'll be going home."

"But, mommy where is Nurse Harriet? Is she okay too? The policeman told me that I can't see her. I want her to go with us. They asked me if she hurt me, why would they think that she would hurt me. I love her."

Jill was agitated at the mess that Harriet had made for her. She had to watch her actions because she wouldn't want anyone to know that she was a complete stranger to her daughter. Annie knew she was her mother, but she had never been alone with her. An awkward remark could prove to be a problem for her. The last thing she needed was to throw suspicion off Harriet onto herself.

She asked Annie if she was hurt in any way, and told her that she had to go talk to the policeman, and then they would go home. Annie sat quietly and wanted to cry for Harriet but didn't want to upset her mother.

Jill walked down the hall and told Officer Black that she wanted to press charges against Harriet, and then she wanted to take her daughter home.

Officer Black motioned for her to go back to the conference table and asked if he could record their conversation.

"I don't understand Officer Black. I'm not the guilty one. My nanny kidnapped my daughter, and I want to press charges and have her taken to jail immediately. I trusted her with my daughter's full time care, and now she has done this. What else do you need to know?"

"Mrs. Lawson, Miss Mason is concerned about your daughter's safety and care if she is alone with you. She said she took Annie for her own protection. Is that true? Did she discuss your daughter's safety with you?"

"I have no idea what she's talking about. Do I look like the kind of person that wouldn't take care of my own child? Believe me, she was more of a threat to her then I am. What do I have to do to be sure that she won't harm my child again?"

"So you are saying that you have a good relationship with your daughter? I may ask our psychiatrist to talk to Miss Mason. She made accusations against you."

"I won't stand here and defend myself against a woman who kidnapped my daughter. Believe me, whatever she tells you is a lie. I want to take my child home, and I don't want Miss Mason to ever come near me or my daughter again. If necessary, I'll have my lawyer call you tomorrow, and you can deal with him. Now am I free to go?"

"As soon as I check with the paramedics that your daughter is okay, you may take her home. I'd appreciate it if you would go to the police barracks tomorrow and make an official statement. We are going to book Miss Mason on attempted kidnapping charges, and I apologize for the trauma and stress of waiting here tonight. I know you're anxious to see your daughter."

"Yes, Officer Black I'm tired and I'll go to the station tomorrow. Will you tell your officers that I'm grateful for their help? I could have lost my daughter forever."

Jill went over to Annie and reached for her hand. Annie climbed down off her chair and took her mother's hand and followed her out to the waiting room. She noticed Sam and remembered him from her mommy's office. "Annie, are you okay? Your mother and I are so glad you are safe and I'll take you both home. How about we stop on the way for ice cream, would you like that?"

"Am I allowed to have ice cream now? I love ice cream. It's my favorite food of all."

"Annie you are such a sweetheart. I could take you home and make you my little girl. I have a daughter, but she is thirteen now. Are you ready to go Jill?"

"Yes, I'm more than ready to get away from here. The next time I see Miss Mason I hope it'll be in court." Jill started towards the door without even thinking about Annie. When she was almost to the door, she turned and looked for Sam. She remembered that she had to act the part of a mother, and she held her hand out to Annie, and waited for her to join her.

Sam followed them to his car and opened the back door for Annie to get in. He turned to Jill and asked, "Does Annie have her car seat with her? I forgot about getting one from your house before we left. We can't take her without one."

"I have no idea about that. What are we going to do now?"

"I'll go and ask if Harriet brought one, and maybe they have one here at the bus station we can borrow. I'll be right back."

Sam walked back to the bus station. Jill had no clue how to react around Annie. She stood beside the car and avoided looking at her. She was relieved to see Sam heading toward them with a car seat in his hand. She couldn't wait until they got home.

"Okay Miss Annie, we'll get you fixed up in no time. It's been a while since I had to do this, but I think I can figure it out." In no time he had the seat in place and Annie buckled in and ready to go. "There you go partner, let's go get that ice cream."

"Thanks, Sam. I don't know what I'd have done without you. You saved my life. I forgot what it was like to have someone to help me. I like the feeling though."

"Thank you ma'am, I'm happy to help two of the most beautiful ladies in the whole world. I can be your knight in shining armor, right Annie?"

"I guess so. I don't know what that is."

"A knight is someone that rescues damsels in distress. Oh, that's a little above your head. Let me see, a knight is someone that takes pretty little girls for ice cream."

"Oh, okay. Can I have chocolate ice cream?"

"Sure after the night you have had, you can have whatever you want."

Jill said, "Don't you think it is a little late for ice cream? I think we should go home."

"Jill, don't worry so much, right Annie. We need to celebrate. You found your daughter, and she's just fine, so let's get some ice cream, okay?"

"That's fine. I guess we do deserve something after all this aggravation."

"So onward we go to the ice cream store."

Jill glanced at Sam and was surprised at this side of him. She knew he had two children but she assumed that he paid to have them taken care of like she did. She forced herself to smile at him and hoped that this day would improve and not get any worse than it already had.

Sam remembered seeing a small shop on the drive up. He glanced in the rear view mirror and smiled at Annie. She smiled back and waved to him.

Within fifteen minutes they saw the small shop and the three of them went inside and ordered three large cones. Jill couldn't remember the last time she had an ice cream cone. She ate very little and waited on the other two to finish. Sam and Annie were having a ball, the more they ate, the messier they both got. Sam didn't seem to mind that Annie had ice cream all over her face, and went to the counter and asked for more towels to clean her up. They laughed with each other and as Jill watched the two of them she was agitated and finally insisted that she was tired and that they needed to head home.

Annie fell asleep within fifteen minutes. Jill thanked Sam and told him that she really appreciated having him along with her. She told him that she was surprised by what Harriet had done and that she worried several times since she hired her that she was a little too close to Annie.

"I had to keep telling her that Annie was my daughter, and not hers. I never dreamed that she would go this far. I blame myself for not paying closer attention. I will demand that she be put behind bars to keep her from harming another child. I hope this doesn't affect my daughter, I just want her to be a normal happy little girl." Jill thought she was doing a good job acting like a concerned mother, and congratulated herself on how fast she could adapt.

"Jill, I'm sure that Annie is a normal child. I don't think at her age that she understands the consequences or the danger she could have been in. I liked Harriet, and I thought she did a wonderful job with Annie. I feel sorry for her if she can't have her own child, but she should've known better than to try to take yours. I agree that she should be kept away from children if she has a problem letting go of the child when she's no longer in charge of their care. I'm glad that the authorities caught her before she got too far away."

When they arrived at the house, Sam carried Annie in and tucked her in her bed. He thanked Jill again for letting him help, and promised to call her the next day. It was late, and Jill just wanted to go to bed. She turned the light out in Annie's bedroom and headed to her own room. As soon as her head hit the pillow Jill was asleep, it had been a long day.

The next morning Jill was startled when she heard the door open to her bedroom. She sat up and for a few seconds her heart raced with fear. She wasn't used to someone else opening her door, and she never once thought of Annie. She held her breath as the door slowly opened and was relieved when she saw Annie's face as she peered into the room.

"What do you think you're doing? Why are you in my room?"

"I'm sorry. I can't find Harriet, and I'm hungry."

Jill took a few seconds to collect her thoughts and remembered what happened the night before. Her anger was again kindled against Harriet and the trouble she had created. Jill understood why she had wanted to run with Annie, but she was not stupid enough to let anyone else know the lifestyle that they had at this house. She really believed that Harriet was protecting Annie and in a twisted way she almost wished that she could have let her have Annie. But, how was she going to explain to everyone that her child had been taken and as a mother she had not pulled out all the stops to bring her back. Again she had to maintain the image of a perfect mother and had a perfect home life for her only child.

She told Annie to go downstairs and wait for her while she took a shower and then they would talk. "Turn on your TV or whatever you do and I'll deal with you then."

Annie pulled the door closed and went down the steps to the nursery. She climbed on the sofa and got the remote and pushed the button. Harriet had already programmed the Disney Channel for Annie, and she sat and watched the cartoons for the next hour.

Jill took her time going downstairs. She went to the kitchen to make her morning coffee. She heard the TV and went into the nursery and asked Annie, "What do you eat for breakfast?"

Annie said, "Harriet says I can have cereal if I drink my juice with it."

"Do you know where the cereal is? Can you come and show me and I'll let you have some."

Annie followed her mother to the kitchen and pointed to the cupboard the cereal was in, and went to sit at the table. "No, I'm not fixing it, you do it yourself."

Annie stopped and turned back to where Jill was standing and took the box of cereal from her. She went to the corner of the room and pulled the step stool to the cabinet where she could get herself a bowl. Then she went to the drawer to get a spoon, and to the refrigerator to get the milk. She carried everything to the kitchen table and poured the cereal and the milk on it. She carefully took the milk back, and closed the cereal box and returned it to the cupboard. She passed Jill as she went back towards the table.

"Hopefully you can take care of yourself, because I certainly don't plan on waiting on you like Harriet did. I'm going to the study; make sure you clean up your mess."

Jill poured her coffee and took it to her desk in the study. She logged into the computer and found the latest outfit she was designing. Within minutes she was involved in her work.

Annie finished her cereal and took the bowl to the sink to wash it out and put it in the dishwasher. She got a towel and wiped the table, pushed in her chair, and went back to the nursery. She climbed on the couch, and turned the TV on and waited for her mother to come for her.

Jill worked for over an hour and when she glanced at the clock, she thought she would take a break. She usually had a fruit salad for breakfast which Andre, the cook, prepared for her. Jill was surprised to hear the TV as she went towards the kitchen. It took a few seconds for it to register that Annie was in the house with her.

She really didn't want to bother with her, but she headed that way and looked in the doorway. She saw Annie on the sofa, and she assumed that she was fine, so she went to get her salad. Jill had no intentions of letting a child complicate or disrupt her life.

CHAPTER TWENTY-TWO

Jill called the office and told her secretary that she would be in later. She didn't go into a lot of detail with Carla. She assured Mrs. Lawson that her morning appointments would wait. After Jill hung up the phone, she walked to the nursery and found Annie sleeping on the sofa. She went over and nudged her on the shoulder and as Annie's eyes opened she told her, "You have to get up and get dressed. I'm going to my office and I have to take you with me after what Harriet pulled. I don't want any whining, just get dressed. And don't take too long."

Jill slammed the door and went to her own room to get dressed. She spent a half hour doing her hair and make-up and finally went downstairs. As she headed towards the study she saw Annie sitting on the kitchen stool. "Are you ready to go?"

"Yes, I dressed myself. Where are we going and is Harriet going to be there too?"

Jill was instantly angry. She put her finger in front of Annie just inches from her face. "No, you will never see Harriet again, not that I care. From now on you are with me, and I expect your behavior to be beyond reproach. I won't put up with any crying or whining. I demand that you call me Mother. And I don't want to know you are around when it's just you and me. If I smile at you in front of someone, I want you to smile back at me and make them think that we are both happy."

Annie looked at her mother and nodded her head that she understood. She didn't understand all of it, but she did understand the look radiating from her mother. It was a look that told her that she must do as she was told. She missed Nurse Harriet and felt a loss of the smiling face she had spent every day with. This woman she knew as Mother was not smiling, and Annie felt fear. She accepted the fact that her mother wouldn't take care of her like all the others had done. She knew, even at four years old, that she must listen to her mother and if she didn't listen, she would be sorry.

Jill gathered her papers, her keys, her coffee cup, and headed for the front door. She turned to nod for Annie to follow and noticed that she didn't have any shoes on. Jill got mad and threw all the stuff in her hands on the counter. She headed for Annie and saw her recoil as she reached for her. Jill managed to grab her arm and spin her around.

"What's the matter with you, you stupid girl? Where are your shoes? Do I have to tell you everything? Get upstairs and find your shoes. And brush the top of your hair, it's sticking out. And, you have one minute. I'm going to put these things in the car and when I come back I expect you to look decent."

Jill let go of Annie's arm and when she did Annie fell to the floor. Jill glared down at her for a few seconds and then turned and went out.

Annie jumped up and ran to the closet to find her shoes. She chose the shiny black ones and quickly grabbed her socks. She had her shoes and socks on in just a few seconds and then she ran to her bathroom and stood on her tiptoes to brush her hair. She hoped that it was good enough and she ran to the front door. She stood at the door as her heart beat faster and waited for the front door to open. Jill opened the door and grabbed her arm again and shoved Annie out to the sidewalk. She locked the front door and turned around and took her by the arm and pulled her to the car door. She opened it and walked around to the driver's door and got in the front seat.

When Jill glanced in the mirror, she saw that Annie was still standing outside the car. "Get in. I'm in a hurry. Well!"

Annie scurried up in the car seat and reached for the door handle to shut the car door. It was so heavy that she could barely close it. She didn't know exactly how to fasten the belt in the car seat, but she tried to put it in the lock like she had seen Harriet do it. She heard it click as the car backed out of the driveway. This was the introduction that Annie got to life alone with her mother. She never made a sound as the car sped up the highway. Annie stared out the window and wondered what she had done to make her mother so angry. No one had ever treated her so coldly, but she knew that no one would be with her to take care of her, and she learned a hard lesson that morning, and that was that her mother owned her but didn't love her like Harriet had.

They were about five miles from their destination when Jill turned the rear view mirror towards the back seat so she could see Annie. "I hope you understand what I said to you earlier. I want you to call me Mother. When we get to the agency, I'll take you to the daycare. I'll come and see you at lunchtime, if I can spare a few minutes. Everyone will be watching us and we will make them believe that we adore each other, understand? My job and my reputation is on the line and I dare you to mess up. I'll punish you if you don't do as I say. Now, put a big smile on your face and keep it there the rest of the day."

Jill glared at Annie until she nodded her head. She took the last few seconds to fluff her hair and check her lip gloss. Jill pulled into the parking lot and parked in her allotted space. She got out and went around to the back door and waited for Annie to unhook her seat belt. Annie's hands were shaking and she couldn't get the latch undone. She glanced up at her mother with a look of sorrow, and Jill finally reached in to unhook the seat belt. Annie was stunned when she felt her mother grab her arm and pinch so hard that it brought tears to her eyes. "Listen, I meant what I said. Make sure you do as I say and you'll be fine, got it?"

"Yes, Mother." Annie climbed out of the seat and stepped out of the car. Jill reached for her hand and led Annie to the door. As the automatic door opened, Jill pasted a smile on her face and gave the impression of the world's happiest mother as they entered the lobby. Every one of the staff ran to meet them. Annie was the center of attention for the next few minutes.

One of the girls spotted the red mark on Annie's arm and asked, "Honey what happened to you?"

"Sweetheart, did you bump your arm getting out of the car? Let Mommy see it. Oh, Annie I hope it doesn't hurt too much. We'll get the girls to put something on it when we get upstairs." Jill reached for Annie's hand and they went down the hall to the elevator.

The door opened and they got on the elevator. Since they were the only ones on it, Jill turned to Annie and said, "That was a good girl. I'm glad you didn't say anything about what I did to you. Don't ever tell anyone that I punish you. That is to always stay between us, do you understand?"

Annie answered quietly, "Yes, Mother. I understand. I won't tell, I promise."

"Okay then as long as you do as I say, we'll get along fine. Now, smile nicely for the girls and try to behave today."

When the door to the elevator opened, Jill and Annie were both smiling and the daycare attendants never would have suspected that as a mother Jill was hateful and mean. All they saw was the pretty mother and daughter that had made the company so much money.

All the girls came running towards Annie. They were excited to be able to watch after her all day in the daycare. Most of them were younger than Jill, and they had so much energy and wanted to keep the children occupied and looked forward to their job.

Annie smiled at them and when Joyce, the head assistant took her hand. "Honey, tell your mother bye." Annie turned and said, "Bye Mother, I hope I will see you later today."

"Bye, sweetheart. Now girls, don't spoil her too much. She has to go home with me and I don't spoil her at home. "

"Don't worry Mrs. Lawson. We'll take good care of her. We have a lot of things planned for the children and I know they'll enjoy it."

"Oh, I was just joking. I spoil Annie too. She's just so adorable, don't you think."

"Yes, she's so beautiful and she looks like a miniature of her mother. But we really will take care of her, so don't you worry about her."

"Okay, Annie. I'll see you at lunch."

Jill turned and walked to the elevator and waved as the door closed. She was by herself as she rode up to the next floor where her office was. She shook her head and chuckled. "People just have no idea how much I don't want a daughter. If only they knew!"

When the door opened and Jill stepped into the hallway, she put on the fake smile and completely put Annie out of her mind. "Out of my sight, and out of my mind," she thought.

Annie held on to Joyce's hand and followed her to a giant room at the end of the hall. Annie could see a dark haired boy from the door way. He was sitting on the floor putting a puzzle together. "Annie, this is James. He'll be here everyday too. I hope you'll be good friends. James, this is Annie. Can you say hello to her?"

James stood up and held out his hand to Annie. She reached back and shook his hand and he said, "Hi, Annie. My name is James, and I like to play with soldiers, do you?"

"No, I don't have any soldiers. But I like to play with puzzles. Harriet and me put a puzzle together every day."

"Who is Harriet, your mother? My mother's name is Linda. My dad's name is James too. What's your dad's name?"

Annie didn't know what to say. She had never seen her father, and really she hadn't even thought about a father. She never missed what she never had.

"I don't have a dad, only my mother. Harriet was my nanny. She left with the police, and Mother says I'll never see her again."

"What do you mean you don't have a dad? Everybody has a dad. Did he leave you?"

"No, he was never there. I never did have a dad. Mother said he died. I didn't ask her what happened to him."

James didn't spend too much time analyzing what Annie told him. He grabbed her hand and pulled her down to the floor. "Let's finish this, and then we'll play whatever you want."

Annie picked up the pieces and started putting them in place. Neither child thought too much about anything but the puzzle.

"Okay, I guess the two of you will be fine for a little while. I have to fill out some papers for Annie. James, will you show Annie where the rest of the things are while I go do the papers? I will only be a few minutes."

"Yes, but can we finish the puzzle first?"

"Yes, yell for me if you need me, I'll be in the office right over there, okay?"

Both children looked up and nodded their heads. Joyce headed for the office and Annie concentrated on the puzzle. The first day at daycare was not as bad as she thought it would be. She glanced over at James and he looked up and smiled at her. She smiled back and Annie was glad she was here.

Jill was working on a new pant suit design when she heard voices in the outer office. She looked up from the monitor and saw a young girl talking to her secretary. She went to her door and realized that it must be lunch time and she was supposed to visit Annie in the daycare. That was the idea behind management providing a place for your child so you could spend time with them.

She hurried out and said to the girl, "Oh my, is it lunch already? I lost track of time. How did it go this morning? Was Annie a good girl?"

"Mrs. Lawson, I wish all children were as behaved as Annie. She's just an angel. I wanted to know if you will be eating lunch with her today. We order for the children and if the parents are coming, we order extra. "

"Of course I'll eat with her. After all, isn't she here so I can spend my free time with her?"

Jill told her secretary that she would be in the daycare facility if she needed her and she headed to the elevator. The young girl fell in step beside her.

"Mrs. Lawson, Annie is so intelligent for four years old. She picks up things so easily."

"My nanny taught her well. That's one reason why I hired full time staff because I didn't have enough time to make sure that she had the opportunity to learn since I work. I just loved the last one, Harriet, but I had to let her go when they told me that it was so important for Annie to come here with me. Did you know that we are going to do a photo shoot right in the day care? Yes, I'm glad that I can see her more now. And thank you for the compliment. What's your name?"

"I'm Cari. I work here part time for the summer. My mom works in the advertising department and she got my job here. I love children, and I think I want to be a teacher after I graduate. I'm not sure if I want to do that or become a doctor. I'm leaning more towards being a teacher. I want to teach fourth grade. That was my best year, and I adored Mrs. Grove, my fourth grade teacher. I learned so much from her and I want to help others learn."

"That's so sweet Cari. I hope Annie likes school when she gets older. I've been so busy I haven't taken the time to even read to her. I used to do it every night. Her favorite book is Alice in Wonderland. I love your shoes by the way. Would you be interested in modeling outfits for me? I have my own clothing line and I'm looking for someone about your size to model for me. I could talk to Sam about it if you would like. Before I leave today, will you write down your mother's name and department and I'll see if we can get you some work with me. Would you like that?"

"Are you joking, I would love that. I admire you so much. I would give anything to be as beautiful as you are someday. And Annie will be too when she is older. I'll make sure that I get all the information for you before I leave today. Thank you, Mrs. Lawson. I can't wait."

"I'm always glad to help other young girls. I know when I was your age my mother didn't want to hear about my career in modeling. But she is proud of me today, and I'm sure your mother will be too. Now, let's go and see Annie."

Annie looked up as Jill and Cari came into the room.

"Annie, your mother's going to eat with us today. Do the two of you want chicken or beef? I'll go put in the order."

"I think we'll have the chicken."

"I'll be back with your meals in about fifteen minutes. You can sit anywhere you like Mrs. Lawson."

Jill sat down in a chair next to Annie. After Cari left the room she leaned down and whispered to Annie, "I hope you have behaved yourself today. You do know that everything you say and do is a reflection on me. I don't want to hear a bad report from any of these girls. Remember what I told you, you smile at me and call me mother. Is that clear?"

"Yes, mother. I like it here and I met a new friend named James. We put puzzles together."

"Just do as I say and you will be fine."

Cari came back and asked, "What would the two of you like to drink? We have hot tea or coffee and cola or juice."

"I will take water please, and for Annie, she drinks only milk.

We have to keep her bones healthy."

"Okay, I'll be right back with your lunch."

Jill was anxious to get back to work. This crap of playing good mommy was holding her up when she had better things to do, but she smiled and hid her impatience.

After they ate, Jill told Annie loud enough for the others to hear, "Sweetheart, I have work to do so I'll be back at 4:00 to pick you up to go home. Have a good afternoon and I'll see you soon."

"Yes, mother I'll be good. And thank you for having lunch with me." Annie tried her best to act exactly like a little girl should act. She had never done much play acting but at four years old she was beginning to understand that she had a role to play, and if she didn't play, her mother would punish her.

Jill smiled down at her and turned to leave. Annie stood up and when she did, the tray slid off the table and spilled all over the floor. Instantly Annie looked up at her mother with a worried look. "What did you do that for you clumsy idiot?"

Jill grabbed Annie's arm and spun her around and would have slapped her, but she remembered where she was and instead hugged her. She saw Cari hurrying out to the table and she was so glad that she'd caught herself in time.

"Oh, don't worry about it Mrs. Lawson. Annie probably hit the tray with her arm. I'll clean it up in no time. Are you leaving so soon?"

"I have several things I need to do in my office and I'll be back to pick up Annie at 4:00."

"We'll have fun this afternoon. We have several movies that we can watch and I'll take good care of her."

"I'll see you at 4:00 then, Annie please apologize for the mess you made. I'm sorry Cari. I would stay to help, but I have to run."

"Mrs. Lawson that's what I get paid for. Annie didn't mean it."

Jill headed back to her office and thought to herself, "I know one little devil that is going to be sorry when we get home."

Cari and Annie had a fun afternoon. At 3:30 they started to clean up and wait for Jill to pick her up. Jill was a few minutes late and Cari hugged Annie when she left and assured her that she was looking forward to the next day.

Jill held Annie's hand all the way to the elevator. As soon as the door closed she turned to Annie and slapped her across the face. Annie was completely shocked and the tears flowed instantly.

"I told you not to embarrass me. You're so stupid you're going to make me regret the day I had you. Now, when we get home we'll deal with this matter."

The few seconds before the elevator opened she firmly said, "Wipe that stupid look off your face and dry your eyes."

Annie tried to wipe her face and hoped that when the door opened she was prepared to do whatever her mother would approve of. She licked her fingers and rubbed her cheeks and tried her best to smile when the door to the elevator swung open. As the two of them walked to the front door Annie heard several voices saying good night to them and she hung her head and followed her mother to the car.

Jill opened the back door and walked around to her door and got in. Annie climbed into the car seat and buckled herself in and reached to pull the car door closed. Her world had changed. Little happy Annie had been replaced by a scared confused four year old girl. No one had ever treated her this way, was this normal for mothers to do? On the way home she worried about what was in store for her as she remembered her mother telling her that her punishment would come when they got home.

Jill parked the car in the garage and got out. She picked up her briefcase and went to the adjoining door to the house. Annie waited a few seconds and reached to unbuckle the belt. Her hands were shaking and it took several tries before she got it. She climbed off the seat and opened the back door. Slowly she got out of the car and closed the door. She walked the few steps and was a several feet away when she heard her mother yell.

"What are you waiting for? Get in here now!"

Annie hurried into the house and stood in front of her mother. Jill put her finger close to her face and pointed, "You are going to your room and I don't want to hear one sound from you until tomorrow morning. I expect you to be dressed and waiting by the door when I get ready to leave. I'm not happy with your performance today and we'll see about tomorrow. Now, get out of my sight."

She turned around and walked away. Annie knew that in order

to be safe she should turn and run to her room. She wanted to ask what she had done wrong, but she was afraid of being slapped again, so she hung her head and slowly walked to her room. She went inside and softly closed the door behind her. She went to the bed and climbed up, took off her shoes, and lay down.

Her face still stung where her mother had slapped her, and she had tears again when she remembered. She lay for a long time and finally got up and went into the bathroom. She'd hung her pajamas on the back of the door that morning and she went to the closet and got a washcloth and like a zombie washed up, brushed her teeth, combed her hair, and went back to the bed. She pulled the covers down and reached for her doll, Betsy, that she slept with every night.

"I wish Harriet was back. I don't like my mommy. I hope you can hear me Nurse Harriet, and if you do, will you please come back." She hugged her doll and turned on her side and after a while she fell asleep.

Jill took off her shoes and changed into sweats and went to the kitchen. She prepared herself a salad and some sliced apples. When she was finished, she carried it into the study and ate her dinner. She worked on her computer for an hour and then headed up to her room. After showering she got in bed and turned on the TV. She watched the 11:00 news, and turned off the light, snuggled down into her king size bed and went to sleep. Jill hadn't thought of Annie once the whole evening. It was as though Annie didn't even exist.

Annie woke the next morning and as she opened her eyes she hoped that she still had time to get up and get dressed before her mother got angry again. She jumped out of bed and hurried to wash up and brushed her teeth. She slowly opened her door and crept to the kitchen. She listened for a full minute for sounds from her mother's room. She heard nothing so she went to the cupboard to get the cereal. Her stomach growled from hunger because she hadn't had dinner the night before. She hoped she could eat two bowls of cereal before her mother came down. Annie worried that her mother would be mad again today, and she probably wouldn't get dinner tonight either.

Annie poured the cereal and milk and hopped onto the chair to eat. She ate the first bowl as quickly as she could and poured the second bowl. She was almost finished with it when she heard her mother's door open. She slurped the last bit of milk out of the bowl and ran to the sink to rinse the bowl. She wiped the table off and was sitting in the chair when her mother entered the kitchen.

Jill barely glanced at Annie and went to the coffee maker to start her morning coffee. She brushed past Annie as she reached for the napkins on the table. Jill placed her silverware at the head of the table and went to the refrigerator. She took out the blueberry muffins the cook had made the day before, and grabbed a plate. She placed the muffin in the microwave to heat it. When the buzzer sounded, she walked back towards the table.

She brushed closer to Annie and in order not to be in her mother's way Annie pulled her feet underneath her. Jill turned and this time her leg touched the chair and deliberately moved it. Annie didn't understand why her mother was being so mean. She hoped that she hadn't done anything to upset her mother already and she dared to even take a breath. Jill poured her coffee and walked back to the table. Slowly she cut her muffin and buttered it. She ignored Annie while she enjoyed the muffin licking her fingers after each bite.

Annie was glad she'd taken time to eat the cereal and thought that if her mother had come down earlier, her stomach would have growled louder from her hunger. She made sure that she kept her head down and didn't make eye contact with her mother. This was the next step in the humiliation that would unfortunately become the standard treatment at breakfast in the Lawson house.

CHAPTER TWENTY-THREE

Jill finally spoke to Annie. "You have five minutes until we leave. Please wear something so I won't be embarrassed by you. Make sure you comb that hair, it is sticking out everywhere. What are you waiting for?"

Annie climbed off the chair and ran to her room. She was scared of being hit, but she was glad that she at least had time to eat. She pulled an outfit off the hanger and slipped the shirt over her head. The button caught in her hair and she couldn't get it undone. She pulled as hard as she could but the more she twisted the worse it tangled. She sat down on the floor and tried her best to free her hair from around the stupid button, but it wouldn't come lose. What in the world was she going to do?

After several minutes, Annie heard the door open. She couldn't see, but she figured it was her mother. She felt the pull as Jill grabbed the shirt and said, "What in heaven's name are you doing? I told you to hurry up. What did you do?"

"My hair is caught in the button and I can't get it out. I'm sorry mother, I tried to hurry. Please don't be mad."

Annie felt the kick to her back and doubled over in pain. She cried out and then felt her hair being pulled out by the roots. She still couldn't see anything with the shirt wrapped around her head, but she tried to raise her body as her mother pulled on her hair.

Finally she heard her mother say, "Good grief what did you do? How can one idiot girl get so tangled? I'm going to have to cut your hair. I've got to go and you're making me late. You know this won't go unpunished, don't you?"

Annie heard her mother's footsteps walking away and tried again to free herself. She pulled with all her might and the tears fell as the pain of ripping her hair out by the roots got the best of her.

Jill came back to the room mumbling about the stupid child she was given, and then Annie felt the shirt give way. Jill dropped the shirt in her lap and turned to leave and said, "Now you only have three minutes. Don't make me wait or you'll be doubly sorry."

Annie looked down in her lap. A big chunk of hair was twisted around the top of the button. She reached her hand up to her head and felt a bald spot. She couldn't worry about it now she had to hurry.

She ran to find another shirt and pulled it over her head and hurried to grab her shoes and socks from under the bed. She put them on in record time, and flew to the bathroom mirror. She grabbed a brush and did her best to smooth her hair down. The bald spot stuck out like a sore thumb. She licked her fingers and tried to smooth the rest of her hair over the spot. Then she heard her mother calling, "Annie time is up. Get out here now."

Annie ran to the door and slid past her mother's legs and ran to the car. She opened the back door and got up into her car seat as quick as she could, buckled her belt and closed the door. She was just turning around in her seat when she felt a sharp pain on her arm. She glanced up and saw her mother holding a small sharp knife. "How does that feel? Every time I have to tell you more than once to hurry, that is what you get."

Annie grabbed her arm as her mother closed her door and started the car. She reached up to get the Kleenex that her mother held out to her. "Clean the blood off, and lick it if you have to, but make sure you have none on you when we get to the office."

Annie squeezed her arm and held back tears. She knew if she cried it would be worse for her. She hoped that she would look presentable when they got out of the car. Her lip quivered several times, but she gritted her teeth and kept her head down as not to make contact with her mother in the mirror.

She finally felt the car stop and waited for the front car door to open. She reached down to unlock her seat belt and climbed out. She stepped out on the pavement and walked to the front of the car where her mother stood with her hand out. Annie put her hand in Jill's, and they walked into the lobby. Jill kept her moving until they reached the elevator.

After the door closed Jill snatched her hand away. "You'll stay in my office with me today. I'll tell everyone that you're not feeling well. If anyone asks about your hair, tell them that you cut it yourself and that you're sorry. Make sure you don't tell anyone what I did, do you understand?"

"Yes, mother. I'm sorry."

"And you are also stupid and ugly. Look at your hair. When I wished for a daughter, I didn't want one as stupid or as ugly as a dog, but I got you."

The elevator opened and she followed her mother to her office. She stood in the middle of the doorway and finally she heard her mother say, "Hey, go sit in the corner and be quiet while I'm on the phone."

Annie went to the corner and sat down on the floor. She heard her mother talking to someone and said, "Annie isn't feeling well today and will be staying in the office with me. I'll come down and get lunch. Okay, if you don't mind you can bring some books to her. That's fine. Yes, I'll tell her."

Jill never said a word to Annie after she got off the phone. When they heard a knock on the door, Jill gave a look that told Annie she had to watch what she said.

"Here you go Mrs. Lawson. I brought plenty for Annie. Is she feeling better?" Cari turned and saw Annie in the floor and bent down to touch her hair. "Oh my goodness, what happened to your hair?"

"She was playing with scissors and cut her own hair. I told her that she shouldn't have done it, but I'd never punish her for something so little. It'll grow back and kids must be kids, right? I just hope she feels better tomorrow."

"Oh Annie, why'd you do that to your beautiful hair, you silly goose? Here are some books for you. I hope you feel better tomorrow and I'll see you then, okay? Thanks, Mrs. Lawson. Call me at lunch and I'll bring Annie's tray to her if she feels like eating. Bye, Annie. See you tomorrow."

Annie waited until the door closed and looked over at her mother. Jill had already dismissed her out of her mind and was busy with her computer. Annie reached for a book and lay down on the floor and curled in a ball. Her head hurt and her arm hurt, and she didn't understand. When she thought about a mother, she remembered Harriet and how kind she was. She remembered laughing and playing with her, and she wanted her back. She didn't understand why her mother hated her, and why she wanted to hurt her. But she did know one thing even at her early age, no one was going to help her, and if she said one word against her mother, she would be sorry.

The day was finally over. Annie slept in the corner a big part of the day. She smiled at Cari when she brought her lunch. But as soon as the door closed, her mother took her tray and ate all of it. She didn't say anything; she just took it and ate it. Annie got nothing.

When they left for the day, Annie smiled and waved to everyone

145

at the office. After they got home she followed her mother in the door and went straight to her room. She turned on the TV and eventually she heard her mother's footsteps outside her door. She held her breath and when she heard them walk away she wondered what her mother had wanted.

After waiting for minutes, Annie crawled off the bed and slowly peeked out the door. On the floor there was a plate with a slice of bread with peanut butter on it. Beside the plate was a glass of water. Annie picked up the plate and carried it to the bed. She slowly ate the bread and drank the water. She inched out the hallway and when she thought the coast was clear, she hurried to the sink and rinsed the plate and the cup, and put them in the dishwasher. She ran back to her room and when she got sleepy, she turned out the light and slept.

She was startled the next morning by someone pulling her hair. She heard a voice say, "Get up and get dressed. Don't give me a reason to punish you."

Annie took as little time as she could to get dressed. She ran to the front door and was waiting when her mother came and pushed her out the door. She climbed in the car seat and they headed to the office. This morning she got nothing to eat, but she didn't open her mouth.

As they entered the elevator and her mother let go of her hand, she didn't get slapped so she stayed quiet. She followed her mother to her office, listened to the phone conversation of how she still was not feeling well, and then lay down on the floor.

At lunch time, a girl she hadn't seen yet brought her tray. This time Jill left the sandwich and one of the cookies for her. Annie was hungry so she ate it and stayed quiet the rest of the day. They left the office and arrived home and went though the same routine. Jill left her a half of slice of bread with butter, and a small glass of water. Annie ate it and again slept when she got tired.

The next morning she opened her eyes and it was still dark. Annie jumped out of her bed and ran to the door. She had no idea what time it was, but she wanted to make sure she was ready so her mother couldn't hurt her again. She stood at her door for a long time and listened for any sounds that would mean her mother was already up. She heard none, so she tiptoed to the kitchen.

She went to the refrigerator and pulled on the door. The light came on, and scared her and she shut the door and ran back to her room. She was so hungry but she was afraid that the light would wake her mother. She got up on her bed and waited.

Finally, she again tiptoed to the kitchen, opened the door, and grabbed the first thing she saw. She ran back to her room and hid in the corner. When she opened her hand, she had an apple. Slowly she ate it and put the core in the trash can. She wanted a drink but was afraid to go out to the kitchen again so she went to the bathroom and climbed on the sink and turned on the faucet. She stuck her head under the running water and drank until she had enough. She decided to get dressed and then turned on the TV.

When she heard her mother in the hall, she was dressed and ready to go. Jill opened her door and Annie shuffled to stand beside the door. Jill opened it and Annie walked quietly to the car and buckled herself in the car seat.

Annie spent another day in the corner, but she did stay awake and looked at the books this time. At lunch, Jill left the milk for Annie, and ate the food. Annie was glad she had stolen the apple that morning.

Some days Jill let Annie go to the classroom. She warned Annie all the way to work, on the elevator, and every second she could that if she told anyone, she would be sorry.

Annie hid her confusion the best she could. She tried to talk with the girls at the daycare like she had before, but they thought she was still not feeling well so they didn't think too much of the fact that she was so quiet.

One day she tripped on the way out to the car, and she got a whack on the back of head before she could stand up.

Another day, Jill reached back and cut her arm, just for a warning she said. Annie took the Kleenex and wiped the blood and licked her arm clean before they went into the office. She told the girls that she fell and cut herself the night before playing on the swing. It sounded believable and the girls didn't ask again.

This went on for a few months. Annie tried not to get in her mother's way but sometimes she would be too slow. Jill would hurt her just for a reminder some days.

In the first four months after Harriet left, Annie never got a whole meal. Jill made sure that she fed her enough that no one would suspect that her child was going hungry, but there were never any special items. Annie got used to waiting for the meal to be placed outside her door. She ate what little she got, and took her dishes to the kitchen as soon as she finished. The weekends were the hardest. Jill made her stay in her room and wait for the evening plate and drink. Annie passed the time with the TV.

One night after Jill went upstairs, Annie was extra hungry so she tiptoed to the kitchen and when she opened the refrigerator door, she saw some chocolate chip cookies on a plate. She grabbed a handful and ran back to her room. She sat on her bed and ever so slowly ate the cookies and savored each bite. She couldn't remember ever having any thing taste as good as they did.

That night she dreamed of an afternoon long ago when she went to the ice cream parlor with Harriet. In her sleep, Annie smiled as she ate the whole cup and in the morning she was a little happier. It didn't last too long.

Annie was startled when Jill stormed into her room, ripped the cord to the TV out of the wall, and carried it out of the room. Annie was more scared than she'd ever been of her mother.

Within a few minutes Jill came back into her room and grabbed her by the arm. "You ate some cookies, didn't you? Did you really think that you could get away with it? I keep telling you that I can make you sorry for anything that you do? When will you learn? Are you deaf?"

Jill twisted Annie's arm so hard that the bone broke. Annie felt it and started to cry. Jill knew she had done something to her, so she let go. She stood looking down at Annie on the floor, and she finally said, "Maybe now you won't steal again."

Jill slammed the door and Annie lay on the floor and passed out from the shock and pain of having a broken bone. She lay on the floor for two or three hours. It was Sunday so they didn't have to go anywhere and Jill was glad that she wouldn't have to explain what Annie had made her do. Inside her own head, Jill really thought that she was blameless.

She did worry about how bad Annie was hurt, and that evening she went in to check on her. Annie was still lying in the floor and Jill walked over to her and made her stand up. Annie held her broken arm up with the other hand. Jill went to the bathroom closet and got a towel and wrapped around her arm. She knew she would have to take her out tomorrow when they went to the office, so she told Annie she was going to go to the pharmacy and get a sling.

When she got back, Jill put Annie's arm in the sling and helped her on the bed. She told her that she'd be right back. She came back to the room and sat Annie on the chair in the corner and pulled the nightstand over to it. She went out and came back with a plate with two sandwiches and a glass of milk.

A part of Jill was sorry for hurting her arm, but not enough to take her to see a doctor. She left Annie alone, and came back in a half hour later to get the dishes. She never apologized to her, she never touched her, she just took the plate and left. Annie was used to the pain by now. As long as she held her arm still, it didn't hurt too much.

At the office all the girls were concerned about Annie's arm. Jill told them that Annie was dopping around and had sprained her arm. She told them that the doctor told her it was sprained, but that in time it would heal. No one took the sling off, so they had no idea how bad the arm was hurt.

Within three weeks, all the girls at the day care facility had to go back to school. The company hired two full time attendants, and when Jill met them she told them that Annie had a bone disease from birth and her arm had always been deformed. No one questioned the real reason Annie didn't have full use of her right arm. Jill's lies came so natural that everyone saw her as the beautiful perfect mother.

Jill wasn't satisfied with physical abuse of her daughter. She would often make Annie scrub the bathroom floor with a toothbrush. The maid kept it clean, but Jill would see one of Annie's hairs on the floor and make her scrub it for at least an hour.

One time Jill didn't like the way Annie's bed was made so she wouldn't feed her for three days. The verbal abuse never stopped. She berated Annie everyday and often would call her an imbecile. From the first day Annie was alone with her mother, she never heard a good word from her.

The advertising company agreed to feature Jill's clothing line in their summer ads. This kept Jill busy for quite a while and Annie spent most of her days alone in her room.

Annie got used to being by herself and was withdrawn and quiet. She was no longer the happy smiling child she once was. Her eyes hardly ever made contact with anyone. Some people thought she was slightly retarded. Annie had no idea how to bond or relate to others because her own self esteem had been beaten down by her mother.

The one bright spot in her life was Sam. Annie loved him, and he visited their house often. Jill knew she had to behave when Sam was there and Annie soon figured out that she could have fun with him and her mother couldn't touch her. Jill would usually catch her after he left and poor Annie endured the cuts on her body and beatings. Jill tried to be careful where she hit Annie so she wouldn't have to explain the marks on her.

Sam hoped that Jill was falling for him like he was for her, but after a while he got the picture that she wasn't into him and he slacked off on his visiting. Annie would receive presents in the mail from him on a regular basis. He knew Annie loved dolls and he was constantly looking for new ones to send. Jill sometimes would take them from Annie and cut them into little pieces while she watched. Annie grew to hate her mother. Even at her age, she wished she could escape to another world.

At the end of the summer, Jill enrolled Annie into a nearby preschool. She dropped her off every morning and Annie looked forward to it. Their home life was getting worse, but Annie had learned how to play the game, and she would use the hours at school to forget what happened at home. Jill warned her almost every day that if she let it slip about her punishment, the punishment would get worse. Annie knew that she meant what she said, and she didn't say a word of how mean her mother was.

About three months after Annie started in the preschool, Jill met a man named John Hawkins. He was a distributor of the software for the advertising industry and was well known and well liked in his field. John made a presentation at one of the staff meetings, and Jill was enthralled by him. She noticed that he kept looking her way and when the meeting was over, he asked her to have coffee with him. She agreed immediately and they talked for an hour. John was fascinated by Jill's beauty and could have listened to her talk about herself for days.

John had never had a serious relationship for any period of time mostly because he traveled so often. But when he met Jill, it was as though he had been missing a part of himself. He changed his travel plans for the next few months so he could be near her.

And when he met Annie, he was in double trouble. She stole his heart at first sight and he was hooked. The fact that she was so shy scared him at first but he was determined to win both of these beautiful girls over to his side.

Jill and John dated for six months and then John asked Jill to marry him. Jill was thrilled and said yes. The whole time they were dating, Jill was on good behavior with Annie. She hadn't physically hit her for a few weeks. She still verbally abused her when they were alone, but Annie stayed clear of her as much as possible.

Annie would sit on the porch for hours with her doll and watch the birds. She loved the birds. She would listen to their songs and try to mimic them. Jill looked for ways to remind her that she was in control, and Annie would shut everything else out when the birds sang in her head.

Jill punished her with taking away the TV or telling her that she couldn't have anything to eat for twenty-four hours. She started a ritual of promising Annie ice cream on a certain day but when the day came; she told her that she didn't deserve it.

Annie would sit for hours and hum a tune she remembered from Sesame Street. She learned to shut out her mother and the pain that she inflicted on her body. It was a hard life for the small quiet child.

The difference between time spent at home and time spent with John was like two different worlds. Annie had a chance to experience a different environment since John had entered their life. John wanted to spend all his free time with Jill and Annie, and take his two ladies to all the finest restaurants.

Jill was in the habit of showing Annie the dresses that she designed and made for her, but warned her if she touched them there would be consequences. Now that John was in the picture Jill had to allow her to wear the dresses. She couldn't take her daughter out in public wearing her old clothes, what would people think.

Annie didn't really care about the dresses, and she made a point of spilling at least one thing on herself just to aggravate her mother. Jill would shoot Annie a look and Annie sometimes could hold her mother's stare, but Jill usually won and Annie's gaze wavered and her eyes would drop to the floor.

The relationship between Jill and John grew stronger and John didn't want to wait any longer and begged Jill to marry him, and Jill gave in and they were married in a small private ceremony. Jill designed her gown and the ad company featured a picture of the gown and the bride in "Bride's Book". Jill was a beautiful bride and John was proud to be her husband.

Jill hid her relationship with Annie by telling John that she was a difficult child who needed discipline almost every second of every day. John didn't think that Annie was that difficult, but he didn't try to get in between them.

After they were married, Jill and Annie moved to John's big home on the top of a hill surrounded by a canyon. The view was spectacular. Annie seemed to brighten up some during the few weeks while they moved. Jill was so busy that she didn't take the time to control or correct Annie as often.

John was extremely patient and kind with Annie and she slowly started to love him. He was gentle and caring, not like her mother. For the first time in a long time, Annie started bonding with someone. She looked forward to John coming home every day. Annie was opening up with him and he was content with his two beautiful ladies.

John's love for Annie was genuine and he would have given his own life for her. John began to wonder about the way his wife treated her only daughter, but he tried not to interfere when Jill punished Annie.

John came home one afternoon and Jill and Annie weren't home. He called Jill's cell phone and she told him that they were at the hospital. John asked, "Jill what happened? Are you or Annie hurt? Should I come and meet you?"

"No, we're okay. Jill fell off her bike and split her lip open and knocked out two teeth. They put stitches in her lip and a few in her

152

chin. She'll be fine, she just looks bad. I swear that child is a handful."

"I was worried about you when you weren't home. Are you sure Annie is okay?"

"Yes John, kids fall off their bikes everyday. We should be home soon."

John met them at the door when they got home and hugged on Annie for the next hour. She never said one word about what happened and agreed when John told her that she had to be more careful. Annie wished that she could've told him the truth.

Two weeks later Annie saw her mother out in her flowerbed at the side of the pool, and she snuck in her mother's room and was looking through her jewelry. She loved to touch the pearls her mother treasured. She would take them out and hold them sometimes, but today her mother caught her. Jill grabbed the back of Annie's head and slammed her face into the wall so hard that it broke her teeth and split her lip and her chin. The blood wouldn't stop flowing and Jill worried about John getting upset if she didn't take Annie to the hospital, so she loaded her in the car and took her.

John believed their story and the next day he surprised Annie with a new bike and helmet and promised he would spend the weekend watching her ride and giving her pointers on how she could keep herself from getting hurt again. Jill was furious and told him he shouldn't baby her but John came back at her and said, "Jill she's my daughter too and I always wanted a child to waste my money on."

Annie wanted to stick her tongue out at her mother behind John's back but he turned too quick and she didn't get the chance.

A few months later John got another call at work and Jill told him that she was at the hospital again. This time she told him that Annie was messing with the treadmill and had caught her hair in the belt and the machine had pulled a chunk of her hair out. She neglected to tell him the real truth which was that she had demanded that Annie put the two cookies she had taken from the cupboard back and Annie walked away from her. Jill got her by the hair and drug her to the floor. Annie fought to escape but Jill held on and pulled so hard that the chunk of hair came out by the roots.

Jill again was afraid of John's reaction and she took her to the hospital, and since they believed the story about the treadmill, she thought John would be satisfied and wouldn't question her or Annie about the incident.

John noticed several cuts and bruises on Annie in the next few months and questioned her about them. Annie always came up with an answer of how she fell or wasn't paying attention. John knew that Annie's movements were hampered by her right wrist being deformed and came to the conclusion that what his wife always told him about Annie being accident prone was true. It was not in him to think that his wife was a child abuser and he thought she loved Annie as much as he did.

But John came home early one afternoon and wanted to surprise his family and overheard Jill screaming at Annie in the back yard. He was shocked at the language that was coming from her, and he hurried to see what the problem could be. As he rounded the corner of the side yard, he saw Jill swinging Annie around as fast as she could by her hair. He yelled for her to stop, and Jill was stunned to see him.

Jill let go of Annie and started to explain the situation to him. "John, this child just broke my favorite candy dish. She knew it was the only thing left from my grand mother. I just lost my temper and when I reached for her, she almost got away but I caught her by the hair. I'm sorry. I've never lost my temper like that before. I need a vacation soon. Spending every day cooped up in this house is taking its toll. Annie, let mommy see if you are okay. Come here child."

Annie tried to escape the hands of her mother and almost got away but Jill grabbed her arm. "Annie, let me see. Oh, you are just fine. I didn't hurt you. Now, promise me that you won't steal candy again. I told you not to touch the dish, didn't I?"

"Yes, mommy I'm sorry. I won't do it again." Annie went along for her own protection and endured the bear hug that her mother gave her. As soon as she let her go, Annie ran into the house and hid in her room. She was really beginning to fear her mother and wanted to tell daddy John, but she knew that her mother would hurt her worse, so she just hid and cried. Her head hurt from having her hair pulled so hard.

"Jill, I hope you never do that again. If you need some time away why didn't you tell me. I'll take time off and stay with Annie and you can go wherever you want. You know that money isn't a problem, so please go somewhere and spend a week to just relax. I wish you'd have told me before that you were having a hard time with Annie. I'll hire someone to help you if you need me to."

"Oh John don't be silly. I can handle my own child. She's just so frustrating sometimes, and I just wish she'd listen when I tell her something. You've seen all the bruises and scars on her. She has to be the clumsiest child ever born. She can't even walk a straight line and bumps into everything. I just lost my temper a little. But you know, maybe I will plan some time to myself. It's been ages since I had a massage and pampering. I'll make some phone calls tomorrow and see what I can find to do. That's why I love you so much, you are just so sweet." Jill went towards him and hugged him and ran her fingers through his hair as she kissed him. John believed what Jill told him.

The next day Jill called their travel agent and arranged a spectacular week in the Bahamas. She insisted on having the best room and lined up the most expensive beauty regiment they offered. When she was done, she was in a mellow mood, and offered Annie a special treat for an afternoon snack.

Jill made her the biggest hot chocolate sundae that she'd ever seen. Annie didn't trust her mother, and wasn't surprised when after she took a few bites of it, Jill snatched it and taunted and laughed at her as she went to the kitchen sink and poured it into the disposal. Annie slowly climbed off the chair and went to her room. As she closed the door, she could still hear her mother's laughter and the words, "What a stupid child I have. She really thought she was going to eat the whole thing. Oh what a good mother I am."

While Jill was on vacation, Annie and John had a blast. The food and treats weren't pulled away while her mother was gone. Annie dreamed of a life with just her and her "Daddy John", as she often called him. Annie dreaded to see her mother come home and once she even had a thought about her mother being dead. She felt bad as soon as the thought popped into her mind. After all the abusive treatment from her mother, who could've blamed her?

Jill was only home a few days until she started to get agitated again. She begged John to let her work again but he wanted her to stay home.

"We don't need the money and I'd rather my wife stay home and raise our daughter. But you can do anything here that you want. Remodel the house, that'll give you something to do." So Jill took him up on it.

She remodeled and redesigned the whole house but as soon as it was done, she got bored. She went back to her old habit, when she was on edge, Annie suffered. John started noticing more bruises on Annie's arms and legs.

He came home one day and they were gone again. He called Jill's cell phone and she told him that Annie fell off the swing and fractured her collar bone, and that she would be home with her in a few hours. John didn't know whether to believe the story and was a little suspicious about what really went on when he wasn't there.

The next time he met Jill at the door as she was headed to the hospital, Jill told him that Annie had put her hand on the hot stove and that her hand had blisters. He drove them to the emergency room, and was in the room and picked up Annie's chart while they waited. He read about the past visits and questioned Jill about each of Annie's previous injuries.

Jill told him that Annie had always been an accident waiting to happen, and since John didn't have children of his own, he took her word for each one of them.

But Jill began to worry about what it may look like to the rest of the world, and after John left the room, she told the doctor that John had hurt Annie. She said that she wasn't in the room when the accident happened, and she was a little worried about their relationship. She told the doctor that John was a step-father, and not Annie's real dad.

The doctor said he would make note of it. He assured her that if she needed to, she could call the authorities for protection for either her or her daughter. Jill's old philosophy of looking out for herself before any one else still reared its head. Even to put her husband's reputation as a child molester on paper to cover up for her own guilt didn't stop her. She felt she had to do whatever it took to keep suspicion off herself. Besides she never expected any one in authority to question Annie's background. Even if they did, she knew men in high places in case she needed to call in some favors. She had attended a lot of charity functions and events as escorts to many of them and they would come to her side at her request. She left the hospital with Annie and John and felt good about the lies she had just told.

CHAPTER TWENTY-FOUR

John became a little concerned and kept a watchful eye on Annie after their latest trip to the emergency room. He began to notice how Annie reacted when her mother came into the room, and John worked extra hard to make Annie smile. The relationship between step-father and daughter was growing stronger and Annie learned to trust him. The two of them would play in the back yard for hours.

As a boy John collected matchbox cars, and at last count had over one thousand of them. He took Annie to the basement one Sunday afternoon, and she was fascinated with all the different models and colors. She wanted to touch them but he could see her hesitation. He assured her that she could hold them and said to her, "If they survived me, they certainly can survive a girl playing with them."

Annie looked up at him and was agitated at first but when she saw his smile she said, "Daddy John, don't call me a girl. Girls like to play with cars too."

"Oh they do? I thought all girls liked were their dolls. I bet I can build a better road then you in the sand."

"No you can't. I'll race you."

"You pick ten cars, and I'll pick ten. We'll start and whoever builds the best road can pick ten more."

They both counted out ten cars and ran to the sandbox. Within a few minutes they were both digging and laughing and John was glad to see the smile on Annie's face. He realized that it was a rare sight.

That night as they were dressing for bed he said to Jill, "Honey have you noticed that Annie seems withdrawn lately? I wonder if we should take her somewhere and have a doctor do a complete check up for her. I want her to be happy and I hope that she's happy with me. Do you think that she should talk to someone about accepting me as her father? I'm beginning to think of her as my own daughter and I want to be her father. Do you think that someday soon I might be able to adopt her officially as my own child? I would love that."

"John, you don't know how difficult she is. I swear that she's not the perfect child you see. There are days when I get so frustrated with her that I could scream. I know you don't discipline her, and I'm glad that you don't butt in when I do. We'll see what happens, and for now let's forget about her." Jill didn't want Annie to come between her and John, and she pulled her body next to his and within minutes made sure that he didn't give Annie another thought.

John and Annie began to look forward to the sandbox and the cars each week. Soon they each had roads, and farms, and buildings. At last count, they each owned three hundred cars and John made special trips to the hobby shop every Thursday after work to purchase all the accessories he could find for Annie. He loved seeing her face when he brought home his treasures. He watched as Annie relaxed and laughed openly as they played.

One Thursday night he was running late and by the time he got to the hobby shop it was closed. He felt so bad when he pulled into the driveway. He hoped that Annie wasn't too upset with him and he thought to himself as he got out of the car that he should have brought her something else. He hurried in the door and was going to her room to tell her that he wanted to take her shopping after supper so she could buy anything she wanted.

John walked into the foyer and had laid his briefcase on the stand when he heard Jill yelling. He followed the direction of the noise and saw Jill throwing all the cars into a bucket and stomping on all their buildings the two of them had spent hours on.

"Jill, what do you think you're doing? Those cars belong to me, and Annie and I have spent way too much time here for you to destroy it. What's the problem?"

"John I've told you before that this is between me and my daughter. It doesn't concern you, you aren't her father. Now, let me handle this."

"What in the world are you mad at? What did she do?"

"John please go back in the house. I'll talk to you later. I wanted to make a point and I do that by taking away the things that mean something to my child. I know what I'm doing."

"What did Annie do? What is so bad that you destroy all our work? Tell me."

"I was talking to her and she kept on walking. I demand that she stop when I tell her. She knows what she's doing. She deliberately ignores me and she knows what will happen. I wasn't finished telling her all the chores for today when she turned away from me. I warned her that I would throw all her cars away if she did one more thing, and she doesn't listen. So, I'm throwing all the cars in the trash. She will pay more attention from now on."

"Jill, these are my cars. I have spent the last few months with Annie building our properties and now you kick them over. Look I've tried to stay out of your way when it comes to daily care of Annie, but I'm beginning to wonder if you know how to treat a child. I want to love her, and I'm not sure you do."

John saw the anger boil in his wife's face. He took a step back as she headed for him. "John don't you ever tell me how to raise my child. I know what she needs, you don't and I'm her parent. The day you get in my way is the day that I will leave and take half of everything you have. She is mine, not yours, and I'll do as I please with her. I'm going in and I want you to put all of "your cars" into this bucket. I forbid Annie to play out here again. I don't want to hear another word from you, understand?"

Jill stood with her hands on her hips staring at him and he finally nodded his head and she stormed into the house. One by one John picked up the cars and put them in the bucket. With each one, his heart broke a little more. He knew that Annie wasn't his, and was almost certain that Jill would never allow him to adopt her. He wished that he could take her and run away, but that would only make Jill angrier at Annie and he didn't want that. After he was done he took the cars back to the basement. He was in no hurry to go back upstairs, but finally resigned himself to the fact that he had to see his wife sometime so he climbed the stairs.

He noticed that the table was set for two, not three when he entered the kitchen. Jill was seated at one setting, and he sat down across from her. "Are you ready to eat?" she asked him.

"Yes, where is Annie? Isn't she eating with us?"

"No, I took a plate to her and she isn't allowed out of her room for the night. And do yourself a favor and don't say a word. I'll deal with her more later."

"Fine Jill, but know that I don't agree. I realize that you need to have rules, but was it so bad that you had to do this?"

The look that he got from across the table silenced his next words. He was smart enough to know that she would make him sorry if he didn't keep his mouth shut. So he ate and silently went into the study. He wondered what Annie thought about her mother tearing down what the two of them had built. He thought about how on the way home he looked forward to taking her shopping, but now he couldn't even talk to her or Jill would punish her more.

John worked on some paperwork. He heard Jill go up the stairs around 9:00 and a little later he heard Annie crying.

Jill came down the stairs later and told him that Annie had soap in her eyes from the shampoo. "The way that girl acts you would think someone is trying to kill her."

After he watched the evening news, he turned the TV off and walked upstairs and down the hall. In order to get to their bedroom, he passed Annie's room. He wanted to open the door and she how she was doing, but he figured that Jill would see and it would start all over again, so he went straight to their own bedroom.

Jill was seated at the nightstand removing her makeup. She glanced his way as he went into the bathroom, and he found himself thinking that he had married a beautiful but cold lady. He had no idea how cruel Jill really was, and she wasn't quite ready to show him just yet.

The next morning John left early and had a hard time concentrating on his work. He wished he could call home and talk to Annie, but he knew Jill would answer and he didn't really want to talk to her today.

As he thought back about Annie, he began to remember a few times when he thought he heard Jill slap Annie and would go to check on them. Jill always smiled as he entered the room, and Annie never said a word, so he didn't push the issue. But now he was beginning to wonder just how mean Jill really was. He thought about the last time that he had seen Annie's hands burned from the stove. Surely Jill couldn't burn her own child, could she?

The more that John thought about everything, the more he drew the conclusion that maybe he should interfere and see if Jill was mistreating Annie. He thought all this time that Annie was a problem child, and from what Jill had told him, she had quite a few emotional problems and the doctors had been trying for the past two years to settle her down. He hadn't questioned Jill, and why would he?

He thought that when he got home today he would demand that he be allowed to take Annie shopping with just the two of them. He finished his work and hurried out to his car and couldn't wait to get home to tell Annie and see her smile.

So he parked the car, and dreaded seeing Jill, but wanted to see Annie. In the short distance from the car to the front door, he reconsidered confronting Jill and getting some answers. By the time he got to the door he decided he would just keep his mouth shut for Annie's sake. Maybe he would make some phone calls the next day and see what his options were as far as being a step-father and proving that Annie should be with him and not her mother. But was he willing to make those strong allegations towards Jill? Did he have the right?

When he went inside Jill met him at the door as though nothing was wrong, going on about her dinner and how much trouble she had gone to and he had played along to keep peace.

Then he found Annie on the living room floor. And now the evening had come full circle, ending with his wife accusing him of abusing her daughter, and now what? Did he have the guts to go against Jill and fight for custody? Did he have the evidence to accuse her and win? Would the authorities at the hospital believe the lies that Jill had already told them about him beating Annie. Would any court take his side, a mere step-father, against a child's real mother? Could any jury take a look at Jill, the most beautiful woman he had ever seen, and convict her of hurting a child? What chance did Annie have of surviving?

John pictured Annie lying in the bed and knowing that her body had been badly damaged by an abusive mother. His anger boiled over as he sat on the sofa in the study. He was glad of the things he had said to Jill. Tomorrow he would start the process of fighting for Annie, and gathering all the evidence he could against Jill. He finally laid back and tried to stop his speeding thoughts enough to get a little bit of rest. He wanted to get to the hospital early and would camp outside Annie's room until he could see her. He would protect her. He was ashamed of how he had allowed his infatuation for Jill and her beauty to cover up what she must have done to Annie.

John got up at 5:00 a.m. He had dozed off around 3:00 and had slept fitfully for two hours. His head felt like it would bust wide open. He grabbed some aspirin out of the medicine cabinet and thought to himself that the headache he had wouldn't come any where near the pain that Annie was feeling. Why was I such a coward until now, he thought? I'll do everything I can do to make Annie's life better.

John took his shower and went to the kitchen to make some coffee. He heard Jill's door open, and he braced himself for the confrontation and lies that she'd try to tell him. After the coffee was finished, he took his cup and went out to the deck. He sat and watched the sun climbing in the sky and wondered how Annie would feel this morning. He thought about the burns on her legs and a chill ran up his spine. How could he have been so gullible? I have to accept some blame for this, he thought. I should have seen what Jill was doing. I'll do everything in my power to make it up to Annie, and I'll make sure that the rest of her life is easier than the first six years have been. He felt his back stiffen when he heard the door sliding open and didn't turn when Jill sat in the chair beside him.

"John, I hope you're over being mad at me. I don't like sleeping by myself. Are you hungry, do you want breakfast? I thought we could go for a drive today, if you want to. I remember the last time we went away, I want to do it again, just the two of us."

"Jill, you have to be the most despicable person I've ever met.

You come out here this morning and ask me to go away with you. Do you realize that Annie is lying in a hospital room right now with injuries that were done by your hands? You put your own daughter in a tub of hot water and burned her legs. You kicked her in the back so hard that her ribs were broken and they punctured her lung. Jill, Annie would have died if I hadn't taken her to the hospital. Don't you even care about her at all? And Lord only knows what else you've done. And then you cover it up by telling the police that I did it. I want you out of my sight today and forever. I'm going to spend the day at the hospital even if they won't let me see her. I hope she'll know that I'm there, and that at least someone loves her. I beg you to consider letting me take Annie away. You can have your life back. I promise I'll never tell anyone what you've done. I just want rid of you and I want to raise Annie. Please think about it. I have to go. I think it is best if one of us stays at a motel until Annie comes home and we decide what to do. Do you want me to go, or would you rather take time away?"

John looked into Jill's face and saw anger. He saw no remorse for her actions, only selfishness. She was angry that someone had enough nerve to go against her.

"John, I warn you that you don't want to go against me on this. Believe me when I tell you that I have power over my own child. There will never be a day that I let you take her and throw me aside. I know people, John. I'll follow through with what I told the police. I can make them believe that it was you that hurt Annie. I think that you should consider what your future might hold if I press abuse charges against you. Don't get too high and mighty, John. I think if you have any feelings for Annie, you will keep your mouth shut and thank your lucky stars that I'm not a vindictive person. If you promise that we can go on like we have been, I'll drop the charges and bring Annie home. We can be happy, just like we were."

"Jill, I have to get out of here before I hurt you. I'll never give Annie back to you. You'll continue to abuse that poor little girl and ruin her life. I'd rather give my own life than let that happen. I'll come back later and grab some clothes and stay downtown for a while. I don't want you Jill. I have no idea why I ever thought that I loved you because you are a monster."

163

John tried to step around her but Jill raised her hand to hit him and before he knew it he grabbed both her arms and gripped them as tight as he could. "I could hurt you Jill. I would love to make you feel what you made Annie feel. I know that I could make you fear me, and I know exactly how to do it, but I'm not you. I don't want to harm another human being. And I would never abuse a sweet girl like Annie. What did she do to you Jill? Why do you hate her, do you have a reason?"

"I never wanted a child. I told Kurt that when we were married. But he was so stupid that he was murdered after making fun of an ugly girl. The girl's brother followed Kurt and hit him and killed him for calling his sister ugly. Can you believe such a thing? I thought about giving the thing that grew inside of me away, but I didn't want people to think badly of me, so I kept it. She's just a thing to me, not a daughter. I don't want her, but I won't let you slander me by telling everyone that I hate my child. I'll never let you have her John. So it is either both of us, or neither of us. You let me know."

Jill pulled away from him and stormed back into the house. It took John a few minutes to calm down. Jill had hardly mentioned her first husband. John hadn't heard the story surrounding Kurt's death before now. He was stunned and taken by surprise. He felt a twinge of sympathy for Jill, but it would never excuse her for what she had done to Annie.

He went into the study and got his keys and jacket. He just wanted away from here, and he needed to reassure Annie that he loved her and that he would protect her. He silently prayed for God to help him find a way to convince the authorities that it was his wife that was the abuser, and not him.

On the way to the hospital, John called his office and told his secretary that he wouldn't be coming into the office, and that he would call her later in the day. She asked him if he was sick and he told her that he had some personal business to take care of and that his daughter was in the hospital. He promised to call her back by noon.

John entered the hospital and approached the nurse's station outside Annie's room. He asked permission to visit her, and wasn't surprised to hear that Annie wasn't allowed to have any visitors without supervision. They informed John that they would call Children's Services and ask that someone come to the hospital as soon as possible to talk with him. John told them that he would be waiting in the waiting room.

"Would you please tell me how she's doing? I need to tell her that I'm here and I love her. Is she doing better this morning?"

The nurse glanced at Annie's chart and said, "I see here that she ate a good breakfast and slept well last night. I'll tell her that you are here, and I'm sorry for this delay, I'm only following orders."

"I understand. Please just tell her that daddy John is out in the waiting room."

"Yes, I will. And as soon as someone comes, I will let you know."

John went to the waiting room and found a seat in the corner. His headache was returning and his stomach felt queasy. He thought that he would find something to eat in a little while and hoped that his stomach would settle down.

He had no idea how his life had turned into a nightmare. If only he had seen Annie's injuries before and reacted to them, she wouldn't have been hurt this badly. He wanted to turn back time and give her back the innocence that her mother had taken from her. He vowed to love her more and make up for what she had endured.

Nurse Sharon went into Annie's room and smiled at her as she checked her IV. "Hi there sweetheart, how are you this morning? I wanted to tell you that someone is waiting for you. He told me to tell you that he is here."

"Is it Daddy John? Can he come in please? Why isn't he coming in to see me? Is he mad at me for telling mommy?"

"No honey, he isn't mad. We have to wait for the doctor to come in. In the meantime do you want anything? Can I turn the TV on for you? Do you want to read?"

"No thank you, I just want daddy John to come and sit with me. I won't say anything. I promise. I didn't mean to be bad."

"Annie, you're not bad. I'll do my best to find the doctor so you can see your daddy. Okay?"

"Okay. I will just sit here and wait then."

CHAPTER TWENTY-FIVE

Jill felt as though the top of her head was going to explode. The lack of sleep and the stress was driving her over the edge. She wasn't used to not having control and she had to find a way to remedy this situation, and do it quickly. The thought of letting one person think she was an unfit mother was definitely not on her list of things she was willing to put up with. How dare John think that he could talk to her the way he had done last night and then go to the hospital and make everyone believe that she was the one that hurt Annie. She tried to set it up so he would take the blame, and now she wished that she wouldn't have kicked Annie so hard. She just got so mad and she was tired of making excuses for having such a dim-witted child, and how could anyone blame her for losing her patience.

Jill got dressed and went to the kitchen. The coffee was still hot and she guessed that John hadn't left too long ago. She grabbed a cup and sat at the table to try to clear her mind. According to what the police and the children's services were saying at the hospital, charges might be forthcoming against one of them for the injuries to Annie.

How could she avoid being accused, and get rid of John while she did it. Jill was tired of him, and she certainly didn't need him trying to take Annie away from her. Boy that would do wonders for her perfect reputation, and how would she be able to deny it? She would have to think of a plan that would throw the suspicion to John and reinforce that as a mother, she was only looking out for the welfare of her child. Maybe she would have to request a few favors from some of the people that had the power to do just that.

Jill went upstairs to grab her purse and noticed that the lack of sleep had left black circles under her eyes. She ran to the vanity to hide the bags under her eyes, but she thought to herself maybe she needed to look a little less like a movie star. It might work in her favor if she met with the authorities and gave the impression that she was the one that was under John's rule, and not the other way around. Just maybe she would play the part of the abused wife, and thus throw more suspicion on him as the mean and abusive step-father.

So Jill wiped all the make up off her face and for the first time in her life, set out to make herself look like a poor haggard worried mother. She felt naked without her face made up, but she had a mission and it was the price she had to pay.

After she finished, Jill dialed John's cell phone. The phone rang and rang in her ear, and she almost threw the phone across the room. How dare he not answer her phone call, who did he think he was fooling with? She dialed the cell again but it just rang and rang. Jill thought to herself, "Mister, I'll show you how determined I can be."

She wondered if she should risk going to the hospital. She was afraid that if John saw her he may not allow her to play the poor hurting mother, and she wasn't sure that she could pull it off. Jill, she thought to herself, if ever there was a time for you to be in rare form, it was now. If she let the authorities accuse her of abuse to her child, it would put an end to everything she stood for and she was going to do her best to keep that from happening.

She sat down at her computer and scanned through the list of names and acquaintances that she had got to know quite well when she was at the ad agency. The formal parties that she attended with the company allowed her to befriend many powerful people. She often attended the gatherings on the arm of a well known judge or a high profile attorney. Jill knew that if she worked it right, that she could get Annie home, and she wanted to shift the blame for her injuries on John.

First, she needed to at least go to the hospital and do her best to assess the situation surrounding Children's Services and the police. If Annie's room was off limits to her and John, she'd have to start forming a plan to work her magic and get out of this with her good name.

She went out to her car and spent the time it took driving to the hospital trying to formulate the best scenario in her mind. She had to get out of this mess, and unfortunately she would take it out on John and Annie if she had to.

Jill hurried up to the floor and approached the nurse's station. "May I help you?" Nurse Sharon asked.

"Yes, my daughter Annie Lawson is here and I would like to see

167

her please."

"Annie Lawson and you are Mrs. Lawson?"

"No, I am Mrs. Hawkins. My daughter is from a previous marriage."

"Let me check. Yes, she is in Room 3211. Oh, I'm sorry; she isn't allowed to have visitors. We have strict orders not to let anyone in the room with her unless Children's Services is present."

Jill wanted to reach over the counter and get hold of the nurse but she forced a tear to form in her eyes. "I need to see my daughter. I haven't slept all night and I can't stand it until I know she is okay. My husband hurt her, and I have to see for myself how she is. Can you tell me if she's hurt bad? I won't stay but a minute, or can I at least peek in her room?"

"Ma'am your husband is in the waiting room. If you're afraid of him I can call security and we can take you to a secluded room to wait for someone to talk to you."

"My husband is here? I thought he went to work. I can't let him see me. Please, where can I go until he leaves?"

"Let me call security and have them meet you. I'll put you in an empty room until they get here."

Nurse Sharon made the call and asked Jill to follow her down the hall. She opened the door to an empty room and told her to wait and someone would be with her in a few minutes.

Jill nodded her head and slipped into the room. After the door closed she got a sly smile on her face. The ball is rolling into my corner, she thought.

A few minutes later she heard a knock on the door and she went to open it. She peered through the pane and saw a uniformed officer outside and hurriedly opened the door. "I'm glad you're here. Did my husband see me? Is he outside the door? I don't want to upset him any more than he is. He gets so mean and I just want to see my daughter, Annie. I need to know that she is alive. Please, can you take me to her room? The last time I saw her, John took her out to the car and told me that I'd never see her again. I'm so scared."

The officer reached out to steady Jill. He led her to a chair and asked her to take a seat.

"Ma,am, I need you to calm down. I'm Officer Charles Lane and

168

I'm sure that your husband didn't see you. Are you hurt in any way? Do you need a doctor?"

"No, I'm not hurt. I'm scared for my life and the life of my child. John is getting worse and this last time I thought he killed her. He hurt her awful badly this time and I want to be with her, please. I just need to see her. Why can't I see her?"

"Mrs. Lawson, I'm not sure what is going on, but I was told on the way in here that Children's Services has been notified and they are on the way. I can't take you to your daughter yet, I need to wait for them. I'll go out to the desk and see if I can find out what condition your daughter is in."

"My last name is Hawkins, but Annie's is Lawson. I married John Hawkins after my first husband, Annie's father died. John is not Annie's father and I never changed her name."

"And your husband John Hawkins is here in the hospital. Did you see him when you came in?"

"No, the nurse told me that he was in the waiting room and she brought me in here because I was scared."

"I want you to stay right here until I get back. I'll only be a minute."

Officer Lane went back to the nurse's station and asked them where Mr. Hawkins was sitting. They directed him to the first waiting room on the left and pointed to John sitting in the corner. John stood when Officer Lane came toward him.

"I am so glad you're here. Can you please go with me so I can see my daughter? I'm positive that she's waiting for me. I told her that I wouldn't leave her alone. May I see her now?"

"Are you Mr. John Hawkins? I'm Officer Lane. I just spoke with your wife and I need for you to come with me now. I'll take you downstairs and ask you to wait in our security shed until the Police department can get here. I understand that you brought your step-daughter in last night. Your wife is afraid of you and I'd like it if you come with me peacefully and I won't cuff you. If not, I'll use force to make sure that your wife and step-daughter are safe. Can I ask you to do that for me?"

"I'm not the threat to our daughter, she is. My wife is a liar and I need to tell Annie that I'm here. She's afraid of her mother, and I promised that I wouldn't treat her like her mother does. What can

169

I do to convince everyone that she is the one that hurt Annie? I want to take Annie with me and protect her, not hurt her. I need you to believe me."

"Sir, it's not up to me to believe or not believe. I want to make sure that no one is hurt today. I can't trust you to be with your wife right now, and if you co-operate we can avoid a situation. Will you come with me, sir?"

"I don't mind going with you, but can I at least tell Annie that I'm here? I promised, you have to understand, and that is the most important thing. I can't let her think that I doubt her anymore. I know what her mother is capable of. She has broken Annie's bones, and she put her hands on a hot stove, she pulled her own child's hair out. I have to see her."

"Mr. Hawkins, I can't allow that. I'm asking you again to come with me. We will take care of this somewhere else, not at this hospital. I'm going to walk towards you and if I can ask you to put your hands behind your back, it will go smooth."

John resigned himself that he must stay calm for Annie. He knew if he made a scene that all involved in this mess would think that he was capable of doing what Jill was accusing him of, so he turned and put his hands behind his back.

Officer Lane grabbed both his hands in his and pushed him gently toward the doorway. John allowed himself to be led down the hall and when they got on the elevator he said, "I understand you are doing your job Officer Lane. I'll do whatever I can to help my daughter. I won't be a problem I promise."

"I appreciate that Mr. Hawkins. I have to handle this as a domestic dispute and I'll request that you are escorted out of the hospital for now. I can't risk a confrontation in front of the patients. I met your wife and I'll leave you with my other officer and I'll go back upstairs and speak with your wife. If I see that she is a threat in anyway, I'll treat her just like I'm treating you, as a threat until proven otherwise. Unfortunately it may take some time before this is settled and your step-daughter's safety is a priority at this time. You do understand, don't you Mr. Hawkins?"

"Yes sir, I do understand. Will you at least take a note to Annie and read it to her? I'll do anything you ask me to. I need her to know that I'm with her in spirit. I'd never hurt her. I love her."

"I can take a note upstairs and leave it for Children's Services. They'll decide what to do with it. I'm sorry about this. I have kids of my own and if one was hurt it would kill me to think that I couldn't be with them. Now, we are going to go outside and walk to the security building to your right. I ask that you remain quiet until we get there, and that you don't try anything at all."

"I'll do whatever you say."

The two men walked outside and Officer Lane pointed to a door to the right and John did as he asked. Officer Lane directed him to sit in a chair and after talking to the other officer, John was taken to a back room and after he went in, he heard the door being locked from the outside. As the sound of the door clicked, John's heart broke and he sat and sobbed for several minutes. He cried for Annie and the despair he felt for his sweet little girl. How could he miss all the signs of what Jill was doing to her? A picture of Annie came to his mind and now he understood the frightened look that he had seen more than once when she was with Jill.

John was surprised when he heard someone unlocking the door and he stood as Officer Lane came and handed him a tablet and a pen. "I told you that I would take your note back upstairs. I'll give you a few minutes. When you are done, knock on the door and I'll come and get it."

"Thank you Officer Lane. You've no idea how much this means to me."

The officer nodded his head and softly closed the door. He thought to himself that Mr. Hawkins didn't seem like the type to hurt anyone.

John took the pen and started writing. "My dear Annie, you are my favorite girl in the whole world. I can't come to see you right now, but I'm thinking of you. I want you to be brave and listen to what the doctors tell you. I want you to tell them what your mother has done to you. Don't be afraid of her, she won't hurt you ever again, I promise. Remember what I told you, I won't let her hurt you. You get better and we will leave, just the two of us. Please don't be scared Annie. Be a brave girl and I will come and see you as soon as I can. I love you." He signed it Daddy John.

John rapped on the door several times and handed the note to Officer Lane. He went back to the chair and sat down and felt drained. How had it turned so ugly? He wanted to have a happy family with a wife and a daughter. He'd waited for the right woman, and thought he found it in Jill. And now he may be blamed for hurting Annie. Did Jill have the skill to shift the blame on him? And would Annie have the nerve to go against a mother that had tortured her for years? He had no idea how long he had to wait and he tried to send his love to Annie through his thoughts and hoped that everything would work out.

Lois Miller received a call from the Holy Spirit Hospital about a child abuse case around 8:00 a.m.

She talked to the nurse a few minutes and told her that she would contact Mrs. Branson and she would call her back as soon as she heard from her. Mrs. Branson was scheduled to come in this morning so she called her cell phone and asked her if she wanted to go straight to the hospital to see Annie Lawson. "Yes, I can go to the hospital. Will you call them back and let them know that I'll be there in fifteen minutes."

Lois called the nurses station and relayed the message. She had reviewed the case with Nancy Branson the night before and she agreed with her that proving who the abuser was in this case would take some investigation. The case workers were affected by the doubts and fears of trying not to falsely accusing either parent while protecting the child. They had worked in the field long enough to know that a usual suspect is a step-parent, but had to be careful not to make an assumption without proof.

Mrs. Branson went straight to the nurse's station and was told of the latest developments. She braced herself for the meeting with Mrs. Hawkins, and silently prayed that she would be able to decide what to do to insure that this young girl would be safe.

She had the nurse direct her to the right room and knocked on the door. Jill opened it and instantly went into action.

"Mrs. Branson I'm glad you're finally here. Can I see Annie now? I had a hard night and couldn't sleep a wink. I wanted Annie home with me, and I was scared being alone with John. He was here this morning and I begged the nurses to hide me, and they let me stay here. An officer went to take John away from us and told me not to worry. I'm scared, Mrs. Branson. I can't trust him to be around Annie. What am I supposed to do now? Can you help me?

I'm going to fall apart, I can't take it."

Nancy Branson sat down beside Jill and said, "Mrs. Hawkins, your husband has been removed from these premises so you don't have to worry about that. I'll go with you to see Annie, but you have to promise that you won't say anything that could be taken against you or your husband. We want your daughter to recover from her injury first. If I allow you to see her, you can't upset her. Do you understand that?"

"Yes, I would never to anything to upset her. She's the most important thing in the world to me. I thought that John loved her as much as I do, but I guess I was wrong. Have you talked to John yet this morning? He threatened me last night and I wondered if he had calmed down yet? He told me that I'd never see Annie again. I'm so afraid. I just want Annie to come home and I want it to be like it was before. I can't stand to see her hurt anymore."

"Mrs. Hawkins, can I get you anything before we go? Do you need something to drink?"

"No, I'm fine. I'm ready now."

The two women walked towards Annie's room. When Annie heard the door open she thought it would be John and she jumped down off the bed and rushed to the door. As the door opened and Mrs. Branson and Jill entered the room, she drew away and hid between the night stand and the bed.

Mrs. Branson saw Annie hunched down and bent down to her level. "Annie, don't be afraid. No one will hurt you again. I brought your mother to see you. Is that okay?"

"Where is Daddy John? He said he would come to see me before. He didn't come and I'm scared. I want Daddy. I need to see him, please."

Mrs. Branson noticed that Annie's eyes hurriedly went to her mother and then down to the floor. She wouldn't make direct eye contact with her mother. Why would a child that was abused by her step-father ask for him, but be frightened by a mother that claimed to protect her? This was going to be an extra ordinary difficult case.

"Annie, your step-father had to go somewhere and he'll come later. Do you want to spend a few minutes with your mother? I'll give the two of you a little privacy. Is that okay?"

173

Annie tried to look at Jill and felt her body tremble. She knew that she was supposed to act like the two of them were fine. Her mother often told her that she was to smile and make everyone think that they were so happy together.

"Yes, I will stay with my mother."

Mrs. Branson looked up at Jill and told her, "I'll stand in the doorway and give you a few minutes with her. Remember what I told you about saying anything."

Jill walked over and bent down in front of Annie. She looked her in the eyes and said to her, "Annie are you okay? Mommy was so worried about you. Do you hurt anywhere? I am here now and everything will be fine. Can I hug you, will it hurt you? Come here sweetheart."

"Yes, mother I'm okay. I'm sorry for causing trouble. Don't be mad mother, I'm sorry."

Mrs. Branson made a mental note that Annie was apologizing to her mother over and over. She knew that the classic signs of abuse were that the child would apologize to their abuser for being a bother, and the child had too much fear to tell on that parent. She was still leaning towards the fact that Mrs. Hawkins appeared guilty over Mr. Hawkins. She didn't get the feeling of compassion between mother and daughter that she got from John and Annie. Her gut feeling told her to tread lightly until she proved which one had hurt this child.

Nancy went to stand in the doorway and nodded to Jill that it was okay for her to help Annie back to the bed.

Jill sat down beside Annie on the bed and put her hand on her knee. Mrs. Branson saw the gesture and turned around and watched the people walking down the hall. She wanted Mrs. Hawkins to feel comfortable without seeming to stare.

Jill kept her hand on Annie's knee and asked, "Annie, how are you? I'm sorry that I couldn't stay with you last night. Did you sleep well? I didn't sleep a bit worrying about you here all alone. What did you have for breakfast? Hopefully they didn't make you eat oatmeal, since you hate it."

"I'm fine mother, I slept very well. Have you seen daddy yet? He said he was going to come and see me, but they told me that he had to go somewhere else. Is he coming later?"

Mrs. Branson was listening intently for Jill to reply, and she didn't see the hand squeeze Annie's knee so tight that her fingernails dug into Annie's flesh. Annie tried to pull her leg away but her mother hung on. She kept the pressure on and looked down at Annie and warned her with her eyes that she had better not say one word that hinted to what their relationship had been at home. And Annie also knew that she had made a mistake by asking for John.

"But I missed you mommy. I'm glad you're here and I love you."

The smile that came over her mother's face and the hand moving off of her leg told Annie that she had done what her mother wanted. Annie snuck a look at Mrs. Branson hoping that she would notice that her mother was hurting her, but Mrs. Branson had stepped a few steps into the hallway, and Annie thought to herself that she was alone and no one was going to stop what her mother had always done to her. Even Daddy John didn't care about her like he said he did. If he loved her he would come and take her away like he promised when he brought her to the hospital.

Jill saw a book lying on the table so she picked it up. "Sweetheart, look it's your favorite story. We read this one almost every night. Do you want me to read it to you?"

Annie looked up and nodded her head. Jill opened the book and started to read the story "Horton Hears a Who" by Dr. Suess.

When they were about half way through the book, one of the nurse's aide's came into the room. "Hi there Annie, how are you doing this morning? I need to take your temperature. Oh, you are reading the book I left. I remember you said that you'd never read it and I was going to come back later and start it with you. I see your mother is reading this one to you so I will bring "Green Eggs and Ham" later and we'll read that one? Are you feeling better?"

"Yes thank you I'm better now. I'm sorry I didn't wait for you."

"Annie, don't be silly there are many other books we can read. You and your mother just enjoy it."

Mrs. Branson overheard the conversation about the book and she wondered what benefit that Mrs. Hawkins got out of lying about the book. She had to wonder what else she had lied about and how she would get Annie to open up and talk about her mother.

After the nurse was finished, Mrs. Branson asked Jill if she needed a few minutes to say good-bye to Annie and that it was time to leave.

"I would rather stay with my daughter until I decide it's time to leave if you don't mind."

"Mrs. Branson, we discussed this before if you remember. I told you that there were rules you had to follow if I allowed you to see Annie. You said you understood them."

"I'll have you to know that I know certain people that will be eager to tell you what you can do with your rules. I plan on contacting a few the minute I leave here. I certainly don't need to ask your permission for anything when it comes to my child. I think it would serve your purpose well if you remember that."

"Mrs. Hawkins I'm not going to argue with you here. I asked you not to upset your daughter before we came up here. I must tell you if you don't leave on your own, I will have someone escort you out of the hospital. I'm more interested in protecting Annie right now than I am in listening to you. Whether you like that or not, that is the way it is."

"We will see how it is! I'll leave on my own accord. I just want to say good-bye to my daughter, if you don't mind."

"Fine, I'll wait in the hall then."

Jill went to Annie and hugged her and kissed the top of her head. "Sweetheart, I'll come back tomorrow. Don't say anything in front of these people; they just want to take you away from me. Okay?"

The look that Jill gave Annie was a warning of what would happen to her if she told anyone what her mother did to her. Annie nodded her head and smiled faintly in hopes of curbing her mother's anger towards her. Jill was secure in the fact that her daughter was more afraid of her than she was of any social worker.

Jill walked to the hall and said to Mrs. Branson, "Do you want to follow me down to the elevator, or am I allowed to go by myself? Remember what I said. I know people who will help me take your job away from you, and if I were you I would be concerned about that."

Mrs. Branson met Jill's stare without looking away and said, "Mrs. Hawkins you don't frighten me. I'm here to protect a child against abuse, and I don't really care who you know. If you have hurt this child, I'll do everything in my power to make sure it never happens again."

Jill turned and strutted to the elevator. She was certainly not going to let this woman make her look guilty. She had to hurry home and get the ball rolling to get Annie out of here and back home with her. There was no way that she would stand still and let a social worker say she was anything but a perfect mother. She determined to do whatever it took to assure that never happened.

Mrs. Branson went into the room and sat with Annie on the bed. She reached out and took her hand. "Annie, don't worry about this now. I want to see you get better and I made you a promise that no one would hurt you again, do you remember that?"

Annie nodded her head but couldn't look Mrs. Branson in the eye. She hung her head and wished that her Daddy John was here and then she wouldn't be so afraid.

Mrs. Branson reached over and lifted Annie's head and said, "Dear would you like to see your father for a few minutes? I can bring him if it won't upset you."

"I want to see him please. I love my daddy."

"Yes honey I know you do. I want to talk to you about your mommy and daddy soon. But right now you need some rest and I don't want you to worry about anything. I'll go downstairs and will be back shortly with your daddy, okay?"

"Thank you. I don't mean to be bad. I promise that I won't do it again."

"Annie, you aren't bad. Whoever hurts you is bad. Let's talk about that later. I will be back in a little while and I think the nurses will soon be bringing your lunch." Mrs. Branson squeezed Annie's hand and smiled at her as she stood to leave. Her heart was sorrowful for the pain and doubt that was evident on the face of this six-year old girl. She had already seen too much pain, and she hoped that after today that could be stopped. She hated this part of her job. Seeing children being hurt was something she would never understand, but if she could help one child it was worth the effort.

Mrs. Branson went to the security desk and asked where they had taken John Hawkins. They directed her to the room where he was and she knocked on the door and was surprised in the change she saw on his face. He looked like a man who was in torment. He stood up and waited for her to speak.

"Mr. Hawkins, I'm sorry for the harsh treatment the situation with your wife and daughter has put you through. You have to understand that until we can find the truth of who has harmed your daughter, we had to put her safety first. I'll allow you to see Annie on the condition that I'm to be with you in the room at all times. If I see that your presence upsets her, I will ask you to leave immediately. I'm determined that this child is to be protected from anymore physical or emotional trauma. Will you promise me that you will abide by my rules? I just came from her room and she is asking for you."

"I haven't harmed Annie in any way and I do promise that I will leave if I upset her."

"Will you follow me then and we will go back upstairs to her room. She is doing her best not to behave in a way that causes any one to be disappointed in her. I'm trying not to judge you until I can find the person that has hurt your step-daughter. I wish it was simple to get the truth but the children are so traumatized that they protect their abuser. For now though I'll supervise your visits until I see that they are causing a problem. Your wife was with Annie a little while ago, and in my opinion she did more harm than good. I don't want to forbid you to see her for that same reason, are we clear on that?"

"Yes, I agree with you. If I harm Annie, then I'll stay away. I promised her that I would stay with her and had every intention of doing that when I brought her in. I can't believe that my wife has hurt her this way. I loved them both and I told Jill last night that I'll do all I can to take Annie away from this treatment. I'm trying to cope with the truth too, and I wish I'd have reacted sooner. Now Annie is here, and I won't hide behind a rock again. I want to help her anyway that I can."

"We will go and see her then. I can't allow you to stay but a few minutes. Annie's well being is a priority and if that means we keep her secluded and away from the stress of the situation, then that is what I insist on."

Mrs. Branson led the way and when John walked into the room,

Annie's eyes lit up and her arms stretched out to him. John sat down on the bed and held Annie as tears ran down his cheeks.

After a while Annie spoke and said, "Daddy why didn't you come to see me before? I thought that you were mad at me too. I'm sorry Daddy. Mommy gets mad and I don't know why. I love you Daddy."

"Oh Annie, you aren't bad. It is your mommy's fault, not yours. I don't know if she knows how she hurts you, but I promise I will find out. But don't you worry about that now, you have to get better. How does your back feel, does it hurt? I know what happened to your legs. But Honey, it will never be the same again. I won't let her hurt you ever again, okay?"

John lifted Annie's chin and as they looked into each other's eyes Mrs. Branson thought to herself that this was a man that loved his step-child. She couldn't see him hurting Annie and that he truly loved her. She'd have bet her reputation on it.

She allowed John to stay with Annie for almost an hour. She walked to the nurse's station and called her office and told them that she would be in later in the afternoon, and that this case was crucial and she needed to push her other appointments to a later time.

Mrs. Branson walked back to Annie's room and told John that he'd have to leave soon. She assured him that he could visit the next day and she would meet him at the hospital anytime he wanted.

John held Annie and gently rocked her until she fell asleep. He tenderly laid her down on the bed and covered her with the blanket. As he stood over her bed he almost collapsed from the weight of guilt of not stopping the abusive treatment this little girl had suffered. Silently he vowed to do all he could to make sure that she was never hurt again.

At the door Mrs. Branson handed him her card and told him to call her the next morning. She wanted to tell him that she knew he was not the abusive parent, but held her judgment until she was absolutely sure.

When Jill arrived home she was furious. She tried to calm down but she needed to release some of her anger, and since she usually took it out on Annie, who wasn't home, she decided that she would

179

make some phone calls and call in a few favors. She got her address book and shuffled through it.

The first one she jotted down a number for was Judge Paul Calloway. She got to know him well a few years ago. His wife had passed away and she often attended the charity fund raisers as his guest. She remembered him as an easy person to talk to. She fixed a strong drink and dialed his number.

When his secretary answered she left her name and number and told her to tell Judge Calloway that is was urgent and she paced the floor until the return call came in about fifteen minutes later.

"Judge Calloway, how are you doing? I'm fine and yes I'll make a point of lunch real soon. The reason I'm calling is that I need a favor. I hope that you can help me, and you are the first one I called. No, I'm not in trouble with the law, at least not yet. Yes, I'm frantic right now, and I'd love to meet you and ask you a tremendous favor. I need your advice and your legal strong arm. Yes, I'll meet you at 3:00 this afternoon. Thank you and I'll see you soon."

Jill went upstairs to take a shower picked out one of her best outfits, and was ready to leave around 2:00. She didn't want to waste one more minute while the evidence with Annie piled up. She arrived at Judge Calloway's chambers in plenty of time. She took a seat after telling the secretary that she had an appointment.

Within a few minutes, Judge Calloway opened his office door and asked her to come in.

"Jill you're more beautiful than the last time I saw you. How are you and your new husband doing? I was so jealous when I saw the way he looked at you at your wedding. It made me wish that I had someone to look like that at me. I miss my wife, would you believe that is has been three years since she died. Enough of that, what can I do for you Jill?"

Jill paced around the room wringing her hands and talking as fast as she could. "I hate to tell you what has been happening to me, I'm so embarrassed. I thought John loved me and my daughter as much as I loved him, but evidently he wasn't what I thought he was. John has been abusing my daughter, and I just came from the hospital a few hours ago. She has broken ribs and a collapsed lung. John put her in a hot tub of water when he gave her a bath and now her legs are burned. I'm so upset and I don't know where to turn. John is saying that it was me that abused Annie, and I'm afraid that they might charge me and take my precious Annie away from me. John threatened to take her from me and I'm afraid that he'll hurt me if I argue with him. I should've said something a long time ago, but I was ashamed. Now it's dangerous and I have to do something. Will you help me?"

"Jill I had no idea. Why didn't you come to me sooner? I certainly will do all I can to help. Have they brought in a social worker? I need her name and I'll contact the agency before they close today. I'll get my secretary to call them immediately. Jill, sit down before you wear a hole in my carpet. Do you want something to drink? Let me get my secretary to bring some coffee. I could use some myself. Excuse me for one second."

"I know the person's name that they assigned to our case. She is Mrs. Branson. She had to stay in the room while I visited my own child. I was so humiliated. She doesn't like me; I can tell by the way she looks at me. I think she's taking John's side against me and I don't know how to convince them that is was him who hurt Annie, not me."

"Mrs. Nancy Branson? I'm surprised that she is treating you like that. I have dealt with her on other cases, and I always thought she was fair. Hang on one second and I'll try to get her office to call me before they leave for the day."

Jill's mind went a mile a minute while she waited for Judge Calloway to return. She had to get every thing taken care of before the authorities came to charge her. She would do every thing in her power to shift the blame to John. She regretted that it had to be this way, but she didn't feel guilty enough to stop. She thought to herself, John had no idea who he was dealing with. He honestly thought that he could threaten her. She could play hard ball when she had to.

Judge Calloway came back with coffee and they sat together for a few minutes talking about old times and mutual friends. Jill missed that part of her life and the anger intensified against Annie more than it had for a while. Jill thought that if she'd never had Annie, then her life would still be the same as it used to be. She would still be the center of attention and every one would be worshiping her like they used to. So in the end it came down to the fact that she had a right to punish Annie because it really was her fault that her life was so stinking miserable.

Judge Calloway's secretary buzzed the intercom and told him that the agency would call him back in fifteen minutes.

Jill rose to leave and told him that she'd wait to hear from him and that she hoped that he could help to straighten out the mess her life had become. She thanked him and hugged him and headed home. She was hoping that John would keep his promise and stay at a motel. She had to get started on her plan, and for that she needed privacy.

CHAPTER TWENTY-SIX

John left the hospital and drove to the Embassy Motel and booked a room. He carried his bag upstairs and unpacked. He spent the next hour making phone calls to his office and then calling several lawyers from his firm. He asked for advice on how he might beat Jill at this game before Annie was given back to her and she continued her behavior. He wasn't going to sit back and watch Annie being hurt any more. If it killed him he would protect her.

His lawyer told him that a situation involving a step child was difficult. The best advice they gave him was to gather evidence of the abuse before he and Jill were married. If Annie's injuries were documented before she met John, then the court would have to believe that Jill was indeed the abuser. John thanked him and decided that he needed to go for a walk and maybe he could think straighter. He couldn't get Annie's face out of his mind, and especially her petrified look when she talked about being bad and being punished again.

John walked several blocks and stopped in front of a hobby shop. The display reminded him of the good times he had with Annie as they played and built their roads and towns in the dirt. It seemed like a life time ago that he was rushing home to get her so they could go shopping for special items. His heart was heavy as he retraced his steps back to the Embassy Motel. He called room service to order dinner. He wanted to quit and crawl under a rock, but Annie needed his help and he decided that whatever he had to do with Jill, he would do his best to take Annie away and give her a life of happiness.

Jill arrived home and went straight to the phone. She got her directory and one by one she called all her old acquaintances in her life before John, and chatted with them. She was going to rekindle her relationship with as many as she could in the next few days and if she needed character references to stand for her, she would have a list.

After making quite a few calls her ear hurt and she took time to fix herself dinner. She kept one ear open for John's car to pull up in the driveway, but at 11:00 she took for granted that he had found a motel for the night. She had a couple minutes of regret and thought about calling him, but her old self preserving nature kept telling her that she had to stay strong and talking to him wouldn't be helpful. His face came into her mind and she stopped and remembered that at one time she truly loved John. He was a good man and had been a good husband to her. They fit well together, but when you put Annie in the equation it fell apart. She hated the bond between John and Annie, but so be it, she'd use Annie against him to save herself.

The next morning she put in a call to Judge Calloway's office. About a half hour later, he called her back. "Good morning Jill, I hope you got some rest. I wanted to call you and give you the good news. According to the law Children's Services can't hold your daughter. This is the first offense and I'll add my name to any document you need so you can end this rubbish. How could any court believe that you're a child abuser? I'll draft a petition to the agency that your daughter is allowed to come home with you as soon as she's physically better. They may put a stipulation against your husband if you want to charge him. And you may have to allow Children's Services into your home for the first month to do evaluations. But I know there is nothing to find and I feel comfortable with doing all I can do to make sure that you are protected against any further harassment."

"Thank you Paul, you don't know how much I appreciate this. I'm afraid of John right now. He said he was going to stay at a motel for a while, so he won't be around Annie, which is a blessing. I'm sure if he comes home, all I have to do is call you and you'll send help for us. I'd love to have lunch with you and repay you for your help. Will you call me this week whenever you have a free day?"

"I certainly will Jill. And you don't have to thank me. You call me if you need me any time of the day or night. Let me give you my cell number and please call me if you need to."

"I am so sorry to pull you into this mess. I don't really know why I married John. I thought he would love Annie as much as I do."

Jill wrote down Judge Calloway's number and when she hung up the phone she felt relieved. She wasn't sure she could recruit his help and she thought to herself, I told you John that you are going up against more than you bargained for. I will beat you yet.

She went upstairs and took a shower and phoned Mrs. Branson to ask if she was allowed to visit Annie this morning.

"Mrs. Lawson, I'll check my schedule and call you back and if I can clear up some other matters I'll meet you there later."

"Mrs. Branson I'm sorry for my attitude yesterday. As you can imagine I'm stressed to the point of madness about my daughter. I promise you that I would never harm my own child. You call me then and I'll do whatever you say. I want to cooperate fully with the agency's rules and I assure you that I only want what is best for Annie."

"I'll get back to you as soon as I can."

Jill again felt a sense of power. The old Jill was back and she would land on her feet like she'd done all of her life. She couldn't wait to see the expression on Mrs. Branson's face after she received the documents from Judge Calloway. Jill knew she would be tempted to say to her, "I told you not to mess with me."

Jill spent the time waiting for her phone call making notes in a small notebook she carried for important things to do. She wanted to make sure that when she acted on her plan that nothing was missed. If the plan went well it should prove to the whole world that Jill Lawson was innocent of any wrong doing. She studied what she had written and after she was satisfied that she covered all the bases, she put the notebook away and made herself a drink and walked out to the back deck to enjoy the beautiful day.

The phone rang around 12:30 and Mrs. Branson told her that she could meet her at the hospital at 2:00. She asked that Jill wait for her at the reception desk on the ground floor and not to try to go upstairs without her. Jill agreed and assured her that she would be waiting. Even though she couldn't stand the woman, Jill knew that it was in best interest to do as she told her. If things went as she was planning, Jill had to be seen as the scared wife and mother. She would have to spend time with Annie at the hospital and make others believe that she loved her daughter.

Jill entered the hospital, waited at the reception desk and concentrated on keeping her expression as calm as she could. When she spotted Mrs. Branson she ran to her and said, "Mrs. Branson thank you for taking the time to meet me. I just couldn't stay home another minute without being with Annie. I cried all night and I worried about her being here all alone. Do you think it's possible for me to sleep in her room? I can't sleep at home; all I did all night was worry about her. I promise I won't get in the way, do you think you could arrange it?"

"Mrs. Hawkins, I told you yesterday that I'm now the legal guardian of your daughter. I can't allow you or your husband to be alone with Annie until I find out for sure which one of you is responsible for her injuries. I can't make a snap decision if it will jeopardize your daughter's safety. Within a few days we might have the answer to that question. I want to wait for Annie to get a little better before I put her through the trauma of telling us what happened to her. I'm not sure she is physically well enough to put her through that. If the hospital decides to release her, I'd like to place her in a facility until we're sure who hurt her."

Before Jill could think about what she was saying she glared at Mrs. Branson and said, "Who gives you the right to decide anything about my child? I own her, not you or your agency."

Mrs. Branson stopped and turned around and glared back at Jill. "Mrs. Hawkins, this behavior is what I am afraid of. You aren't willing to let us do our job. If you insist on going against my requests, it might be a long time before you get her back. I don't listen to you, you listen to me. I'm not trained to worry about your wants and wishes; you lost that right when your daughter was brought here. Now I am putting Annie's safety above yours or your husband's demands. I told you this morning that I will allow you to see your daughter if you do as I say. Whether you like it or not, I'm responsible for your child. In the case of parental abuse the parents lose all rights. That is the way it is and if you don't believe me just try and go against me and we'll soon see who has the upper hand."

Jill clenched her fist and forced herself to calm down. "Mrs. Branson all I meant was that I can't be separated from my Annie. She is my whole life and I want to be with her. I am under tremendous pressure and I don't have any idea what I'm saying. Please forgive me. I promise I'll try to allow you to do whatever you see fit, I just need to see Annie and make sure she is okay."

Mrs. Branson stood still and looked at Jill for a few seconds. Her gut instinct told her to tell this woman to turn around and get out of her sight. But she knew that she had to be impartial until she could gather evidence against one or the other of these parents. In the meantime she owed it to the innocent party to not judge them too quickly.

"Very well, let's go see how Annie is doing. I hope she's stronger today, but if I see that you are upsetting her I will ask you to leave, understood?"

Jill nodded her head and tried to replace her angry look with one of a concerned mother. She hadn't had much practice with being a concerned mother but she tried to play the part.

Mrs. Branson started walking toward the elevator and held the door for Jill. They rode to the third floor in silence and as the door opened both women stepped out and headed in the direction of Annie's room. Mrs. Branson asked for Annie's chart and made a notation of their visit. She glanced at the report from the day before and according to the paperwork no one else had tried to visit after she and John left.

After looking at the chart Mrs. Branson turned around in time to see Jill walking into Annie's room. She muttered an exasperated comment under her breath. It was going to take a lot of patience dealing with her. She walked to the door of Annie's room and saw

Jill hugging Annie. She couldn't see Annie's face but felt the tension that Jill caused with Annie. Jill let go of her and sat on the bed beside her.

"How are you doing today? Are you ready to go home with me? I have all your favorite dishes waiting for you. I told our cook to make every dish that you like and I don't care if you eat all of it when you get home. I just want to see you better. Maybe we can plan a day at the zoo as soon as the doctor says it is okay. Would you like that?"

"Yes Mother I'd like that. Have you seen Daddy today? He was here last night and he said he was coming back. Can Daddy go with us to the zoo?"

"Sweetheart I'm not sure that Daddy is coming to see you today. We might have to live by ourselves for a while. But us girls can have more fun without him. He isn't happy with us right now. I don't want to worry you with all that now. What did you have for lunch? The cook made you a great big chocolate cake and you can eat as much as you want whenever you come home."

"Is today Wednesday then? I only get chocolate on Wednesdays remember?"

"Oh who told you that you little goof? You can have anything you want. I just want you to get well."

Mrs. Branson stood at the doorway and wondered if what Annie was saying was true. Did this mother restrict her daughter's food and then control what days she got special treats if she did as she was told. She'd only seen one case like this and it didn't end well for the child. The agency had to pull the little girl away from the home and now after a few months she was doing better. It took the counselors a long time to undo what some parents did to them, and in a few cases, the child never recovered.

"Mrs. Hawkins, I'm going to talk to the nurses for a few minutes. I'd like to have a chance to talk to Dr. Howard today if he's here. I won't be but a few minutes. Can I count on you to not upset Annie?"

"Good grief do you have to tell me how I should behave every second? I think I know what not to do. Ask Dr. Howard when Annie can go home. She looks fine to me so I hope I can make arrangement to take her home with me today. That would be great."

Mrs. Branson nodded to her and went to the desk to ask the nurses to page Dr. Howard. While she waited she asked the nurse how Annie was doing.

"She is such a sweet child. She never complains but she is always afraid of doing something wrong. We all reassure her that she shouldn't be afraid of us and we are all putting an extra effort to help her relax. Have you found out what happened to her yet? I watched her with her father last night and he seemed so gentle with her. Annie seemed to change with him. I can't imagine that he would harm her, I think he loves her."

"Well we are taking it slow with this case. Someone is guilty and I'm not sure if it is the father. I'll talk to Annie before she leaves the hospital but I'm not sure she can help without being afraid of punishment if she tells. These children learn fear because of the abuse and they think that no one can or will help it stop. So they won't talk about it because of the fear. It's a shame and I hope for Annie's sake that protection can be provided. Will you come and get me when Dr. Howard calls. I'll be in Annie's room."

"Yes, I'll let you know."

"Thank you and thank you also for caring for these children. I'm so glad the nurses here at the hospital take the time to give the children love and do it with an open heart. I've seen a lot of pain and it's good to know that you all care."

"I love this job but sometimes it is hard to see them go through the pain. We have several children on the floor this week that have cancer. They are troopers though. Most of them smile even with all they have to endure. But we have a special group of ladies and I enjoy working with them."

Meanwhile Jill sat down on the bed with Annie and told her, "You know if you tell anything about what we do you'll be sorry. I can hurt you and you know it. No one is going to help you Annie. I'm depending on you to keep your mouth shut. Do you understand? Remember how we talked about how we act in front of people? I want you to be polite and call me mother and remind them that we love each other. Can you do that? If you don't when we get home you will pay."

Annie looked up and nodded her head. "Yes, mother I'll be good

I promise. I won't tell."

Jill grabbed Annie's arm and squeezed as hard as she could. She wanted to make sure that Annie stayed more afraid of her so she'd never tell on her.

Mrs. Branson walked back to Annie's doorway in time to see Jill grab Annie's arm. She saw fear on Annie's face and she ran towards them. Jill looked up and caught sight of her and let go of Annie. "I thought she was going to fall off the bed and I was trying to hold on to her. I wasn't trying to hurt her."

Mrs. Branson held Annie's arm and saw red marks where her mother's hands had been. "Annie was your mother hurting you?"

Jill tried to squeeze into between the two of them and Mrs. Branson pushed her aside. She gave her a look that dared her to interfere. "Annie look at me. I'm here to help you. Tell me if your mother hurt your arm. You don't have to be afraid. I just want to hear from you what happened."

"Mommy wasn't hurting me. I fall all the time. She tells me to be careful but I still fall down and I hurt myself. I love my mother."

Jill gave Annie a little nod over top of Mrs. Branson's head. She was confident that Annie understood her and that she wasn't about to accuse her of anything.

"How can you think that I would deliberately hurt her? You have no right to accuse me. I'll make sure that her step father never hurts her again. I promise when we get home that John will never be alone with my daughter. All this time I've been too scared to fight him, but Annie's well being comes first."

Mrs. Branson continued to rub Annie's arm and noticed that her eyes never left her mother's face. It was going to be impossible to break the hold that Jill had on her daughter until they could separate the two of them.

The nurse came into the room and told Mrs. Branson that there was a phone call for her at the desk. She rose and said, "Mrs. Hawkins, I want you to keep your hands to yourself. I'm not sure what you were doing, but while Annie is here you will not touch her. I'm going to take this call and I want you to say good bye and make sure that you don't try to visit until I say you can. If you can't abide by that rule, then I will be forced to restrict your visits altogether. Now, remember I'm right down the hall. Annie I'm sorry but I have to take this call. It may be your doctor and I want to know how you are doing. Okay?" Annie nodded her head yes and gave a slight smile.

The nurse handed her the phone and she said, "Hello this is Mrs. Branson."

"Mrs. Branson, this is John Hawkins. I was wondering if it would be possible to meet you and visit Annie this afternoon. I bought her a gift and I can't wait to give it to her. I'll come in at your convenience and I'll only stay as long as you allow. I made some phone calls this morning and I'm working to file abuse charges against my wife. I need help to find record of any abuse to Annie before I met Jill. My lawyers advised me to do it as quickly as I can to counter attack her charges against me."

"Mr. Hawkins I'm at the hospital right now. Your wife is in Annie's room and I'd like to talk to you about her before you go to see Annie. Could you be here in a half hour? Please do me a favor and have the receptionist page me from the information center? I don't want you to argue with your wife in front of your daughter. She is fragile right now and she needs to have some peace."

"Yes I can do that, and thank you for your help. I can't imagine being in your position and not knowing who you can believe. I only want what's best for Annie. This isn't a power trip, but a concerned father. I don't want to see my wife at all and I have booked a room at a motel. I'll have you paged as soon as I get there, and Mrs. Branson thank you again."

"So I will see you shortly then."

Mrs. Branson went back to the room and found Jill standing in the corner of the room and she could tell by her demeanor that she wasn't pleased. "Mrs. Hawkins, would you tell your daughter good bye, I have something I have to take care of."

"Yes, I'll leave for now but I'll be back. Did you talk to the doctor to see if Annie can go home today?"

"No, I haven't got to talk to him yet. I did leave a message for him to call me. I'm not sure if that is possible, but we'll discuss that later. I'll call you at home as soon as I know what he says. I do owe you the courtesy of a phone call."

"Fine I'll call you later if I don't hear from you in a few hours. Good bye Annie, I'll be back soon. And Annie, remember what we talked about."

"I will Mommy, I promise."

Jill gathered her things and gave Mrs. Branson one last glare before she headed down the hall. Mrs. Branson went to the bed and sat beside Annie. "Sweetheart, how are you doing? I just talked to your daddy and he's coming to see you shortly. He told me that he has a gift for you."

"Mommy said he couldn't come to see me anymore. I can't wait till he gets here."

"Do you think you could lie back and rest for a while? You look tired today. How are your legs doing?"

"They hurt when the nurses put the medicine on them. I didn't cry when Mommy held me down though."

Annie didn't realize what she had said and Mrs. Branson asked, "Annie are you saying that your mommy held you down in the hot water?"

She saw the fearful look on the poor little girl's face as she said, "No, I did it myself. I made the water too hot and I couldn't get out so fast."

"Are you sure that your mommy didn't hurt you and make you stay in the water? It's okay to tell the truth, Annie. I won't let her hurt you again. I need to know the truth so I can help you. Will you answer questions about what happened to you? Did your mommy also kick you and hurt your back?"

"No mommy loves me. And I love my mother."

"Okay dear just lie down and we'll talk later. See if you can't go to sleep for a while and when you wake up your daddy will be here."

Mrs. Branson pulled the cover over her and smiled at her. "I'll be back soon. And Annie don't worry now. We'll keep you safe."

Annie looked up at her with a wishful look. It broke Mrs. Branson's heart to see the poor child so confused.

Mrs. Branson left the room and went back to the nurse's station. She asked if she had received a call from Dr. Howard. One of the nurses told her that Dr. Howard was in surgery and he wouldn't be available for at least an hour. Mrs. Branson thanked her and asked where the cafeteria was and that she was expecting a page from someone shortly.

They told her that the cafeteria was on the second floor and she should hear the page from anywhere in the hospital.

Mrs. Branson ordered a chicken sandwich to go and sat at the table. She was just finishing when she heard her name announced that she had a visitor waiting at he information center. Since she was close she decided to go and meet Mr. Hawkins and take the time walking to the third floor to talk to him. She saw John sitting in the lounge area and went over to him.

"Mr. Hawkins I hope I didn't make you wait too long."

"No it's only been a few minutes. How is Annie today? I brought her a new car. We used to play with the ones I had as a child, that is until Jill took them away. I promised Annie that we would build more roads when she gets better no matter what her mother says."

"I have to ask you some questions before we go upstairs. I saw your wife grab Annie's arm earlier and when I questioned them about it, Annie said she was falling off the bed. I swear to you that the marks on her arm looked like your wife was hurting her deliberately. Annie also let it slip that her mommy held her down in the hot water and burned her legs. Again she denied it when I questioned her. I don't blame her for being afraid. I know that whoever has hurt her also threatened her with not telling the truth or there would be more pain."

"I'm so ashamed of myself for not seeing the evidence before. Jill told me that Annie was accident prone and a difficult child. I've never had children of my own and I hate to admit that I didn't want to interfere with her discipline. I wish I'd have reacted sooner. Can you help me gather the information of any injuries before I met them? If we can prove that Annie was abused before, I can't be the guilty one if I wasn't there."

"I certainly will do my best to get the documents, if any exist, on prior reports on her. I can tell you that your wife has almost threatened to take my job if I pursue the charges against her and try to take Annie out of the home. I must tell you Mr. Hawkins that both you and your wife may lose her for a while until this is worked out."

"Where will she go? Am I allowed to have a say in this? I'll take her with me. I can handle Jill and I promise you that she won't get a chance to do anything else to Annie."

"I fully understand what you are saying, but I'm afraid that the courts will have to decide what is best for your daughter. I can't make that decision. I only report on what I see. Let's go visit your daughter, she's waiting for you."

When John entered Annie's room it was as if a bright light was shining on her face. Annie reached her arms out and John held her for a long time.

"Look what I brought you Annie. This car is just like the favorite one you used to have. I also brought you a book that tells about the cars and shows how to build the best city. I know your mother didn't want you to have any more but this can be our secret. We won't let her know about it and she won't take this one. I'm sorry that I let her do that to you sweetheart. I know I promised you a lot of things lately, but I am going to do my best to keep you safe. Okay?"

"Okay daddy I won't tell her, but she'll probably already know it. Mommy knows everything. I'm sorry that I told the lady that mommy held me in the tub. I hope mommy don't get mad at me. I don't want to be bad, but mommy says I am. I want you to stay with me daddy. I won't be bad with you."

"Annie I'm going to do everything I can to have you with me. I'm afraid that we might have to wait a little while, but I want you to tell me if mommy is mean to you. Can you do that?"

"I will daddy I promise. Will you look at the book with me now?"

"I sure will. Scoot over so I can sit with you. You're just too big for this bed, look I'm almost falling off the side."

Annie laughed and scooted way over to the side and John sat beside her and for the next half hour they read the book.

Annie was a different child when John was with her and Mrs. Branson was more determined to right the wrong that had been done to this little girl. She walked down to the lounge and found a book and let the two of them have their time together. She didn't worry half as much about this step-father as she did the mother.

Jill Hawkins was becoming guiltier in her eyes as she spent more time studying the child and parents together. She thought to herself that she would go into the office and prepare the legal papers to have Annie Lawson removed from the home as soon as possible.

Mrs. Branson allowed John to stay for over an hour and went back to the room to check on them. John was lying back on the pillow and Annie was snuggled down in his arms. She hated to wake them so she went to the desk and asked the nurse to note on the chart when John left for the evening and she left the hospital and headed back to her office. She knew that is was not proper protocol but she trusted John and felt that Annie deserved to spend the evening with him after all she had been through.

She wanted to get some paperwork finished and before she left for the day she would call the hospital and make sure that things there were fine.

Jill had left the hospital in a fowl mood. The more she was around the hospital the more perturbed she became. How dare that woman try to tell her what to do with her own child? She rushed home so she could call Judge Calloway and ask if his office had filed the petition against Child Services. The sooner she got Annie home, the quicker she could implement her plan.

The secretary told her that the judge was in his chambers and she would get a message to him as soon as she could. Jill almost pranced around the house in anticipation of seeing the look on that Mrs. Branson and John's face when the papers were served. Her thoughts of getting her daughter back home took a backseat to knowing that she had her power back.

Judge Calloway called her a half hour later. "Jill I have great news. I had the papers filed this morning and they will be expedited to the Children's Service's office in the next hour. They can't hold your daughter for one second and the petition gives you all your parental rights to do with your daughter as you see fit. I'm also filing a document against Mr. Hawkins that he isn't allowed to see your daughter without you being present. Since I feel that you aren't a danger to your child, I made sure that these documents are binding and it will take quite a while before they can file anything that will jeopardize this."

"Oh Paul, thank you for your help. I went to the hospital today and that woman acted like she owned Annie. I can't believe that she stood and stared at me the whole time I was with Annie. I just want her to come home so I can take care of her. I promise I'll repay the favor so let me know what I can do for you no matter what it is."

"You promised me a lunch date remember? I'm looking forward to it. And Jill don't hesitate to call me if you need anything else. I'll call you later in the week for that date when I'm free. Like I said, the papers should be filed before 5:00 today and you should have your daughter with you in no time."

"Thank you again Paul. You don't know how much you've helped me. I'd be a basket case if I lost my little girl. Call me next week and we'll do lunch."

"I'll talk with you soon Jill, and don't worry everything will be fine."

Jill looked at the clock and saw that it was 3:55. She decided to go out to the deck and relax for a while and took the phone with her so she would get it the second it rang. Oh how sweet is the victory, she thought. That child is mine, and after all I have had to do, no one will take her unless I say so.

When Mrs. Branson got to her desk she noticed a priority package on her desk. She got the letter opener and ripped the package open and when she pulled the petition out, she felt anger against the system. She knew what this meant, and it wasn't good for Annie. She would have to call the hospital and ask the nurses to tell John to leave and lift the restriction on the charts for Mrs. Hawkins. Judge Calloway was a kind decent man and she wondered what kind of relationship that he had with Mrs. Hawkins for these papers to have been drawn up so quickly.

She read over the details and knew in her heart that it would take weeks to fight Mrs. Hawkins for guardianship. A mother's legal right to her child was difficult to undo, and she wished the system was geared more towards the child. Ever so often she hated the laws that governed her office. A person would think that a child's protection would override in every case, but a lot of times it depended on who you knew and how fast you could use the system. Evidently Mrs. Hawkins wasn't lying when she had told her that she knew people in high places.

Mrs. Branson searched the file for John's number. She thought that it was best if she tried to explain to him about the document he'd be receiving shortly.

195

When he answered she identified herself and told him about the legal documents that had been delivered to her. "You can't see your step-daughter at any time unless your wife is present. And your wife has all rights to her care. I'm sorry Mr. Hawkins, I wish I could say that it isn't so, but I'm afraid that the system sometimes works for the guilty as well as the innocent."

"Are you telling me that I can't take Annie with me and that she has to go home with Jill? Annie is frightened and if she goes home with her mother I'm not sure what Jill will do for punishment. I know that if you cross Jill her fangs come out. Do I have any legal rights at all?"

"No, your wife is the natural parent and until we can prove that she has abused your step-daughter our hands are tied. I have to notify Judge Calloway's office that I received the papers and I'll start the appeal first thing tomorrow morning. Will you call me and let me know if you hear anything from your wife?"

"Yes, I hate this but I understand your position. I appreciate what you did for me today by letting me stay with Annie for a while. I pray that we're wrong and that Jill will be too scared to hurt her again with all of us watching her. For Annie's sake I won't make any static until I have the right to take her away from her mother. Do you think I have any legal means to fight her?"

"If we can prove that Annie was abused before then we can start a petition against your wife. If we can't, I'm not sure that we could win. Have you talked to your attorney yet?"

"Yes, I'll call them again and ask their advice. I'll do everything I can to stop this treatment of my step-daughter. I'll fight Jill to the end. I owe her nothing and I owe Annie a chance of a normal life. Thank you Mrs. Branson I can't imagine the frustration that your job brings when a child's welfare is at stake. I love Annie as though she were my own and I'll do all I can to help her."

"Call me tomorrow and I'll let you know in which direction I think we should go in order to keep her safe."

"Thank you again for your help and I'll call you as soon as I talk to my own attorney."

Mrs. Branson hung up the phone and it rang again. "Hello, this is Mrs. Branson."

"Mrs. Branson, this is Dr. Howard. I got your message about

Annie Lawson and I wanted to give you an update. She's doing well and I think she can be released tomorrow. Her legs will need to be treated. I want to see her in my office in a few days to make sure that the burns heal with no infection. Has your office decided to go ahead with the investigation of abuse? I don't want to falsely accuse someone of harming Annie, but it seems like there is a definite pattern when I read her chart. I don't think that this is the first incident."

"Dr. Howard I appreciate you returning my call. My office had filed petitions for guardianship, but Mrs. Hawkins, the mother, had her lawyers file legal papers to fight our petition. Right now, as it stands, Mrs. Hawkins can take Annie home and all we can do is file an appeal for the right to remove the child if we win. The whole process takes several weeks. I just hope if her mother is deliberately hurting Annie, that she won't try again until we get evidence to legally take her from the home. Mr. Hawkins has moved out and he's willing to take Annie, who is his step-daughter. I'm convinced that the guilty party is the mother after witnessing some of the signs between the two of them together. I wish that there was more I could do, but my hands are tied."

"So you are saying the courts can't legally take the child out of the home even though you suspect that there's a definite problem with the mother?"

"I can't say beyond a doubt that the mother is abusing Annie and that is another reason that the process will take a while. Until we obtain concrete evidence we don't file charges. I know that the laws are present to protect children and also protect parents against being falsely accused. Most of the time the balance of the two work quickly, but like this case, it may not work fast enough. I do think that Annie hasn't suffered any life threatening injuries yet. Her previous visits, except for her arm being broken, are classified as mild abuse. I know that doesn't sound fair, but legally things sometimes are handled differently."

"I haven't had an occasion to treat a young child for abuse before. I have to authorize Annie's release. The hospital won't hold her any longer than is necessary for medical treatment. I wish I could keep her for the time it takes for you to follow up on the investigation, but also my hands are tied with my superiors."

"I understand fully, and I appreciate that you care about your patients. All we can do is make sure that if we prove beyond a shadow of doubt that Annie Lawson is being abused by her mother that we can pull her out of the environment before something worse happens. I won't be back at the hospital again to see her. I'm forbidden by the petition to get near her. But will you tell her that I want her to know that I'll be thinking of her and that help is on the way."

"Yes I'll tell her. Am I supposed to call Mrs. Hawkins and tell her that Annie is being released tomorrow?"

"Yes, she is the one that you have to notify. A step-father can't have any legal hold on a child unless it is given by the law. In this case, Mrs. Hawkins has complete control over her daughter."

"I'll call right now and tell her that Annie can be picked up and taken home tomorrow morning. Thank you Mrs. Branson for doing what you can for all the children. I'm so thankful that there are agencies in place that do stop the abusive treatment of our children. And I hope that you do help Annie before she is hurt again."

"I do too. And I hope that if I see you again it is under better circumstances."

Dr. Howard got the file and looked up Mrs. Hawkins's home number and dialed the phone. He had no choice but to tell her that Annie was to be released.

"Hello, this is Jill Hawkins."

"Mrs. Hawkins this is Dr. Howard. I've treated your daughter Annie while she's been in the hospital. I'm calling to tell you that Annie can go home tomorrow morning. Her ribs will be sore and I want you to make sure that she isn't to do anything but rest until her ribs heal. If they are injured again, they may puncture her lung again. As far as the burns on her legs, I'll give you ointment that's to be applied three times a day. I want you to bring Annie to my office in a few days so I can make sure that they are healing properly. Do you have any questions that I can answer for you?"

"No, I think I can care for my daughter just fine. I'll make sure that she lies on the sofa until she's better. And I can apply ointment on her legs, how hard can it be?"

"Mrs. Hawkins let me assure you that 2nd degree burns are serious. Infection can set in within a matter of days, and then we have a problem. The infection can spread throughout her body and it could be a serious condition. I wasn't saying that you're not capable, I was saying that you have to make sure to follow my instructions or your daughter's health could be at risk."

"I understand Dr. Howard. I'll make sure that Annie is taken care of properly. And I'll bring her to your office next week. I just want her to come home and get well. I've been stir-crazy without her. I love my daughter more than anything and I'll do whatever it takes for her to come home."

"I'll leave the instructions on her chart and the nurses will give you the prescriptions your daughter will need. If I don't see you when you come in to get her, I'll see you in a few days in my office."

"Yes, thank you Dr. Howard."

After she got off the phone Jill was aggravated with the bother that her daughter was becoming. She wasn't pleased with having to worry about doctor appointments, and up until now she just let Annie heal on her own. There was absolutely no concern about her broken ribs or the burns on her legs. If she'd behave and do as I say she wouldn't get hurt, she thought. Oh well her plan was coming together and she had to remain calm and collected or she would mess it up. The last thing she needed was to feel sympathy for a child she didn't even want.

CHAPTER TWENTY-SEVEN

John was surprised when the nurse came into the room and asked if he could step outside. "Mr. Hawkins I'm afraid that I have to ask you to leave. We just got a call from Children's Services telling us that you are restricted from any visits with your step-daughter. The court has filed a petition taking away your visiting privileges and I'm sorry but we have to follow what we are told. I'll give you a few minutes to say good bye and I guess you'll have to call Mrs. Branson for the details."

John hung his head and thanked the nurse for giving him a chance to tell Annie good bye. He went back in the room and gently shook Annie awake. "Sweetheart I've to go soon. I enjoyed our visit today. I don't want to make you tired and I've been here a while. Maybe you can go home soon."

"Daddy, are you going to come to get me when I go home? I want you to come okay?"

"Annie, I might have to work and I'm not sure if I can take off. You'll be fine with your mother, won't you?"

"Yes, but mommy told me that you didn't want to be with me. I'm sorry if I'm bad. I'll try to be good if you'll stay with me."

"Honey you aren't bad. Mommy just loses her temper sometimes but it'll be fine. I promise that I'll do what I can to make you happy. I love you Annie. I think you are the cutest, and the most special, and the prettiest, and the smartest, and the best road builder that I know."

"Oh daddy you're silly. I'm just a stupid, dumb, and ugly girl. I love you too daddy. You're the best daddy that any girl ever had."

John sat beside Annie on the bed and hugged her to him. He was afraid for her and as he thought about Jill, it came to him that he'd never heard Jill tell Annie that she loved her. As a matter of fact, he'd never heard her say one nice thing to her daughter. What a shame to treat your own child so cruelly. He didn't want to leave, but he didn't want to stay if they would have to bring in the security and throw him out in front of Annie.

When John was ready to leave he turned in the doorway and blew Annie a kiss. He watched her smiling face and wanted to do whatever it took to keep that smile from fading. He made his way to the elevator and pushed the button for the first floor.

Meanwhile Jill decided to gather Annie's clothes so she could bring her home. She picked out the highest priced outfit she could find. She wanted everyone to see how well she took care of her daughter and how beautiful they both were. Let them envy me, she thought. When she packed everything in a small suitcase, she got ready to take them to the hospital. She wanted to make sure that the security in the hospital wouldn't question her right to bring Annie home. As she drove, Jill congratulated herself on beating her enemies once more.

She went to the main elevator and pushed the up button. When the door opened, she was shocked to see John. She waited for a few seconds and then stepped on the elevator. John turned and looked at her as the door closed. Wow, she thought, I didn't expect to see him. She brushed the thoughts of him aside and walked to the nurse's station. She asked them if Annie was awake and if she could go in to see her.

"Yes, Mrs. Hawkins, she's wide awake. She's such a beautiful young lady and a good patient too."

"Thank you, I'm glad to hear that she's being good. You know how most kids are when they get sick, they can drive you crazy. But Annie doesn't complain. I brought her clothes for tomorrow. What time should I come to pick her up?"

"The doctor makes his rounds early, so your daughter should be ready to leave by 10:00. We will leave a note for the doctor to call you if there's a problem. He noted on her chart that she's doing fine, and we'll have all the instructions for her care ready for you then."

"Okay, I'm going in to see her for a little while, and I thank you for your help."

When she entered the room Annie glanced up and saw her mother standing in the door. Her face changed instantly as though a light had gone out. Annie wished that daddy John could've stayed longer. When he was with her, she wasn't as afraid.

"I brought your clothes for you to go home in. I want you to make sure that you look pretty when you leave. Do you think you can handle that small task?"

"Yes, mother I'll try to be beautiful like you. I wanted daddy to come with you to take me home."

"Let me tell you one thing, and I don't want to repeat it. I don't want to hear John's name mentioned again. He's out of our lives and all you have is me."

Annie looked up at her mother and slowly nodded her head. She was all alone and not even her daddy could help her. It was though her life had been sunny for a little while, but now the darkness was back.

Jill hung the dress so carefully in the closet. She put Annie's shoes on the floor and laid the case on the small dresser. She showed Annie the brush and mirror she had brought her. For the next several minutes she explained how she wanted her to dress and how she wanted her hair to look. When she was finished she told Annie that she would be in at 10:00 to get her. Jill picked up her purse and stood in the doorway and she turned and pointed her finger and said, "Remember what I said. You know what I want and you will do as I say, okay?"

"Yes, mother, I will."

There was no wave, no kiss, no good bye, just a pointed finger and Jill turned and marched down the hall. Annie got out of the bed, walked to the dresser, and looked at the things in the suitcase. She carefully laid the brush and mirror on the vanity and tried to get the tangles out of her hair so it would look nice for her mother tomorrow. She was afraid if she waited until the last minute that she might not have time to get it as soft as her mother demanded. So for the next fifteen minutes Annie stood and looked in the mirror brushing her hair. As she stared she saw a pathetic ugly girl looking back at her.

John called home and didn't get an answer so he hoped that meant that Jill wasn't home. He needed to grab some clean clothes so he rushed to the house and when he went in the house was silent. He wondered to himself if he'd ever see the time again when he would come in the door and see his wife and his daughter again.

He went upstairs, found his suitcase, and hurriedly packed what he needed. He wanted to get out of the house before Jill came home. He sure didn't want to have to confront her after what had happened. He wasn't sure that he'd be able to control himself and right now he thought he could strangle the woman without feeling sorry.

John couldn't remember another time in his life when he felt such hatred towards another person, but he did feel hatred and anger for his wife and he hoped that he could make things happen and he could rescue Annie from her life with such a hateful mother.

He left Jill a note on the table telling her that he'd stopped by to get some things and hurried out the door. Staying at a motel wasn't like being home but for now it would have to suffice.

Jill left the hospital and stopped at the dress shop on the way home. She needed to treat herself to something expensive to make up for the day that she had. Shopping always made her feel better.

Jill looked around for a while and finally found a perfect dress.

It was so silky and flowing and it was done in a pale lavender, a color that she adored. She thought that after her plan was finished she would dress up and attend a formal gathering on the arm of a high powered sexy man. It had been too long since the world admired her beauty and to Jill nothing lifted her spirits like being the center of attention in a room filled with people. Why had she let John talk her into quitting her job and staying home to be a dreadful mother and wife? She had better talents and soon she would set her sites on reclaiming what she once had.

She got home and saw the note from John on the counter. Her first thought was that he was sorry for the things he said to her, and he wanted to come home. But as she read the note she got angry again. How dare he think that he could get away with calling her names and then walk away? No one did that to Jill Hawkins, no one!

The next morning after the nurse took her breakfast tray away, Annie dressed in her dress, put on her shiny shoes, brushed her hair the way her mother told her, and sat on the chair and waited.

The nurses were impressed with Annie's expensive dress. They thought she looked like an angel and everyone complimented her. Annie smiled at each comment, and politely thanked each one.

Annie knew that her mother would punish her if there was one wrinkle in the special dress or one spot on her shoes, so she sat as still as a mouse on the chair. She was so used to spending time waiting; her life mostly consisted of sitting in her room waiting for the next summons from her mother.

Annie looked like the perfect child, but if you looked closely you might notice the scars on her arms, or the disfigured wrist, or the burns on her legs. You might start to question what kind of life this beautiful angel had to endure. If you noticed, your heart would break for her.

Jill arrived at 9:45 and the last instructions were given, and the prescriptions were gone over, and the good byes were said to Annie. Jill reached for Annie's hand and was led by her mother down the hall. Nurse Sharon watched as the walked past the doorway where she was tending to another little girl. She felt a chill run up her arms, but for the life of her she couldn't understand why. Sharon was very perceptive of people, and she felt coldness exude from Mrs. Hawkins and she felt sorry for Annie. It was almost like she could sense what was going to happen.

When they got home Jill ordered Annie to take off the dress and hang it in the closet where she had gotten it from.

"Don't think for one minute that I'll baby you like the nurses did. I expect life to be normal again. The ointment is on the table and if you want it on your legs, you put it on. I've never touched your legs and I don't intend to start now. After you hang up your clothes, you can stay in your room until I send for you. I have a million things to do and I don't need you in my way."

Annie just turned and walked to her room. She took off the dress and carefully hung it on the hanger where it came from. This was the first time she'd ever worn it, and she didn't expect to wear it again. But it felt good to look pretty for a little while. She slowly made sure everything was back in place and grabbed a shirt and jeans from her drawer and after she was finished dressing, she climbed on her bed. She had no idea how long it would be before her mother let her out, probably hours. She reached for a book from her shelf and lay back on the pillows to look at the pictures. Within minutes she had dozed off, her body was tired from all the stress.

Jill opened the door to leave Annie's lunch, which consisted of a jelly sandwich and a glass of orange juice. She saw that Annie was sleeping and for once she didn't bother her. "I can get something done now that I don't have to hear you. But don't get used to it because the laundry is waiting and you have to clean your bathroom floor," she muttered as she slammed the door shut.

The sound of the slamming door scared Annie and when she finally realized that it was only the door she sat up on the bed and reached for the sandwich. She slowly ate it and got up to use the bathroom. Her legs were sore and she remembered that the doctor said to put ointment on them.

She opened the door and peeked out hoping that her mother wasn't in sight. She tiptoed to the foyer and grabbed the ointment and ran back to her room. Annie opened the tube and rubbed it on the blisters on her legs. She went into the bathroom and washed her hands and returned to her bed.

She leafed though another book and when she was sleepy again she got up and put on her pajamas, brushed her teeth, brushed her hair and went back to the bed. She climbed in and pulled the covers over herself and her last thoughts before she drifted to sleep were of her daddy and how she wished he was here so he could lie beside her and hold her like he had at the hospital. But in reality she was home and in her own prison made by her mother. There wasn't much hope and she accepted defeat as much as her young mind could handle.

The next morning Jill sat at the table and thought that she had to put her plan into action that night. She didn't want too much time to pass in case she would make a mistake and let Annie get under her skin and then she might do something she would have to answer for. She knew exactly how she wanted it to play out and even though it would be hard, it was something she had to do.

Around lunchtime she called John's cell phone. He didn't answer but she put a message on his phone.

"John, its Jill. I have to talk to you right away. I'm sorry for what I did and I need you to help me. I don't want to be like I am, but I have a problem. I love you and Annie and I want you to come over tonight so we can just talk. Will you help me John? I need you and I promise I'll be better. I have to take Annie to the doctor and I won't be home until 5:00, so can you come over around 8:00? Please John call me back and let me know."

Jill hoped that she had gotten to him with her message. She knew that John cared about Annie and she hoped that would make him come to the house. She had no intention of taking Annie anywhere but she needed to gather a few things before tonight and she wanted it to be dark before he got there.

She went into Annie's room and told her that she had to go out for a while and that she wasn't to answer the phone or let anyone in. She gave her two sandwiches and even a few cookies. Annie was surprised since she rarely got anything special. She'd learned not to expect anything and usually the treats were taken away before she could enjoy them, so she waited to hear the front door shut before she dared to eat them. After she was done she took the plate back to the kitchen.

She was still hungry so she went to the cupboard and poured herself a bowl of cereal and sat at the table and ate every bite of it.

Most of the time she went hungry and whenever she could steal food without her mother knowing it, she did. A lot of the times her mother discovered what she had done and the punishment wasn't easy. But today Annie didn't care. She went and sat in the living room on her mother's fancy sofa. She thought about going to the cupboard and getting some chocolate syrup and pouring it out on the sofa, but she was afraid that her mother really would hurt her, so she just sat for a while.

She got bored with just sitting and she went out to the backyard and got on the swing set. Her mother usually didn't allow her to use it, but since she wasn't here Annie swung as high as she could and loved the feel of the wind on her face. She thought she heard a noise in the front and she darted back inside the house and ran to her room. A few minutes later she heard the front door.

Jill unloaded her bags and put most of the stuff in the garage. She'd have to put things in their proper place later. She checked the refrigerator to see if she could spot anything that Annie had taken. Everything looked to be in its place so she didn't fret about it. Her mind had to be clear for more important things and she would deal with Annie later.

Around 4:30 she asked Annie to come out to the living room. She handed her the phone and said, "I want you to call your daddy and tell him that you want him to come here at 8:00 tonight. I miss him and I know you do too. I want you to do this for me and I promise that I'll be nice to you if you convince him that we want to see him. Can you do that?"

Annie took the phone after her mother dialed the number and when she heard the beep to leave a message she said, "Daddy I wanted to call you and tell you that I miss you. Will you come and see me and mommy please. I'll be waiting for you, okay?"

"That was good. Now you can have a cookie if you want to. I laid three of them on the table for you. If you want you can even have a glass of milk with them."

Annie was suspicious of what her mother was telling her but she went to the refrigerator and got the milk. After pouring some in her cup she went and put it back. The whole time she was doing this, she watched over her shoulder for Jill to come and take it away. Slowly she returned to the table and climbed on the chair.

One by one she ate the cookies and finished the milk. Her mother didn't come after her so she rinsed the cup and put in away.

Jill finally came into the kitchen and told her that she could go and play in the back yard for a while. "I want you to call your father back if we don't hear from him shortly. Now, do you want to go play or not?"

Annie walked to the door and slowly made her way to the swing. It wouldn't be as much fun now, but she did get on the swing and pushed herself with her feet. She had no idea what to expect, but she knew enough to stay out of her mother's way.

About an hour went by and finally she heard Jill call for her. "Come in here Annie. Your father wants to talk to you."

Annie jumped off the swing and ran to get the phone.

"Daddy are you coming to see us later? I want you to come."

"Hi sweetheart, how are you doing? It sounds like your mother is being nice to both of us. I'm glad that she is, but I want you to tell me if she does anything to you, okay?"

"Daddy mommy is being nice to me. She let me have some cookies and milk and I was outside on the swing. Please daddy, will you come home?"

"Yes I will be there in a few hours okay. Can I talk to your mother again?"

Annie handed her mother the phone and she heard her say, "John why do you think that I'm lying. I want you to come home and Annie does too. We both miss you. Okay, I'll see you around 8:00 then. No, I promise that I won't call the police."

She hung up the phone and told Annie that she'd done a good job. "You can go in the study and watch a movie if you want. I left them in the cabinet for you."

Annie still couldn't believe that she was getting special treatment today. "Thank you mommy and I promise I'll sit real still."

Jill watched her as Annie went into the study and almost lost her cool when Annie tripped on the rug and almost fell. She thought to herself how she wanted to go after her and ring her neck. How did I give birth to such a clumsy child?

After she heard the movie start, Jill went to the garage and brought the things she had bought that day out to the kitchen and hid them in the bottom cupboard. She wanted to make sure that when she needed them they'd be close at hand.

The next few hours passed quickly and when the movie was over, Annie hadn't heard anything from her mother so she put another one in the machine and climbed on the sofa to watch it. About half way through the second movie she heard the door open. She ran out to see if it was John and as soon as she saw him she ran to him. He picked her up off the floor and spun round and round while hugging her tight.

"Annie I missed you. Are you alright? Where's your mother?"

Jill came into the foyer and watched as John put Annie down. She waited a few seconds and then walked to him and kissed him.

"John thank you for coming. I wasn't sure you would. See there are no police here, only me and Annie."

"Jill I'm making no promises of staying. I came for Annie. I hope you will change and I'll try to help you, but you can't go on hurting Annie. We'll talk about this later, okay?"

"Yes John we'll talk later. Now, I want you both to come into the kitchen and eat. I fixed your favorite dishes and it's getting cold."

John reached for Annie's hand and the three of them went in the kitchen and sat down at the table. Jill had outdone herself and the table looked great and the food looked delicious.

Jill smiled at both of them and passed the dishes to them and the three of them filled their plates and started eating. John thought to himself that Jill might really be trying to change and he wished that their family was going to be whole again. Annie was confused but happier since John was here. She was too young to understand, but she also wanted things to stay this way. She smiled at John and picked up her fork and took a great big bite of her mashed potatoes.

CHAPTER TWENTY-EIGHT

The police were surprised when they got the call to go to 3876 Mainstream Drive. The Highmark Development was home to most of the wealthy families in the city. No one in the department could remember ever getting a call of this kind for this part of town.

After the call of distress went over the airwaves, six patrol cars raced to the address. A neighbor had reported that she heard gun shots coming from the home across the road. They discussed the possibility of a firearm in the home and used caution as they entered the residence. None of them were prepared for what they found.

When they reached the front door, they shouted that they were coming into the home and that they had their weapons drawn. Three of the officers stayed outside to inspect the perimeter and radioed that they saw nothing suspicious on the grounds.

The officers slowly walked through the door of the residence. They approached the first room and again shouted that they were armed and entering the room. When the first officer entered the room, he saw a victim lying on the floor. He approached and could see that it was a woman with multiple stab wounds. She had a pulse but not responsive and she had been badly beaten.

Another officer walked slowly to the second victim lying face down on the floor. He stooped down to take the pulse and shook his head to the others to let them know that the male victim wasn't breathing. They noted the time to be 11:10 p.m. The first officer radioed for medical help a.s.a.p.

When Officer Dean, the team leader, determined that the victims were taken care of, he sent two officers to search the rest of the house. They returned and reported that the house seemed to be empty and if someone had been in the residence, they didn't see any sign of a break-in.

Within minutes the emergency vehicles pulled into the driveway. They entered and went to work on the female. As they assessed her condition, they asked it anyone knew what had happened to her. Officer Dean informed them that they had only been on the scene for fifteen minutes and they had not determined if it was a robbery or a domestic situation.

They scanned the room for weapons and found a hand gun lying next to the female. They carefully put it in an evidence bag and continued with the search. They also found a baseball bat lying a short distance from the male victim's right hand. The room was quickly filling with detectives and other officials.

The paramedics arrived and examined the female and asked if they could take her to the hospital for immediate attention. Officer Dean gave permission and they put her on a stretcher and wheeled her to the ambulance. The screaming siren slowly faded away and the officers went to check for identification on the male.

The detectives put on their gloves and searched the man on the floor. They found a wallet in his jacket and opened it. The driver's license stated that the man's name was John Hawkins and the address was this residence so they assumed that he was the owner of the property.

Someone shouted from the other side of the room that another victim had been found. Everyone rushed to the where the officer was bent down and they saw a young girl curled up under the end table. Officer Dean asked her if she was okay and could she give them her name.

The young child didn't respond and they shouted for the paramedics to assist. The paramedics bent down to try to see if the young girl was injured and determined that as far as they could tell she had no injuries, but she didn't respond when they asked her more questions. One of them asked her to take his hand and crawl out from under the table, but she had a blank stare on her face and the paramedics knew she was in shock.

Steve Snyder, the first responder, had a daughter of his own and knew he had to be gentle with Annie. He stretched flat on the floor and while talking softly to her, he put his hands on her arms. When she didn't resist, he pulled her towards him and quickly looked to see if there was any blood on her. As he held her he saw a tear roll down her cheek and felt her body tremble. He didn't see an immediate danger and turned and asked if anyone had identified either of the adult victims and if the child lived here.

One of the detectives, Officer George Randall, walked over and showed the wallet from the male victim's body. "According to his license, his name is John Hawkins. I'm running the name right now and we should be able to get further information on him in a few minutes. Has the young girl given you her name yet?"

Steve replied, "No, she hasn't said one word yet. Her eyes aren't responding to light which means that we probably won't get any info from her for a while. I'm going to transport her to the hospital in a few minutes. When we get her in the E.R. they can run further tests. Do you know if John is her father, and if the female was the mother?"

"No, the female should be at the hospital by now. Hopefully she is able to fill in the details of what happened here. Do you think maybe the child witnessed the murder of her father and the attempted murder of her mother? Will she be able to tell us any details, and can we question her now?"

"No, the state she's in right now, I don't recommend that we push her deeper by harassing her for details. We'll certainly tell the hospital to call if she's any different after they work with her. But after whatever happened here she may be gone from us for quite a while. Children have a tendency to blot out tragedies and it may take months for her to be able to remember. I'll try to get her on the stretcher without upsetting her."

The men in the room agreed that this small child may have witnessed an awful sight in this room, and their hearts went out to her. They noted her disfigured arm, and the blisters on her legs and small scars on her body. They also noted that there was a hand print on her forearm that seemed as if someone may have grabbed her. The medical team did their evaluation as fast as they could in order to keep the child calm. Whenever someone touched her, her demeanor didn't change. It was as though they weren't even there.

Officer Dean and his team started the report on the crime scene. The male, John Hawkins had been shot in the chest two times. The initial report was that he died from these two wounds. He did have a cut in his right hand, which may have been from the knife found underneath his body. If he was the one that inflicted the wounds on the female, his cut on his hand would be consistent with a slip of the knife if he stabbed someone. The report continued with notes that the bat was covered with blood and had bloody fingerprints on it. They looked large enough to belong to the male.

As they walked through the rest of the residence they noted that in the kitchen the table had three table settings and food on each plate. Several of the bowls filled with food were found broken on the floor. It looked like someone had scattered them in anger. Two broken glasses were on the floor. One large bowl filled with mashed potatoes was found on the other side of the kitchen like someone had thrown the bowl. On the bar several items were knocked over. The report stated that an argument may have started here in the kitchen. As they continued, they found several small bloody footprints leading to a small table in the den where the bodies were found. The front drawer was open and a small gun case was inside. Their initial findings pointed to the conclusion that the female may have been injured and went to the gun case to get the gun for protection. If this proved to be true, they thought that this case may be domestic violence.

The coroner, Wayne Nyles, arrived and pronounced the male victim John Hawkins had died from the two gun shots. He took swabs from his hands and fingernails. There was a deep scratch on his right cheek. He asked if he could move that body and when they gave him permission he prepared the body to be taken to the morgue for further tests.

The detectives ordered that the phone records be pulled for that day. They worked for another hour making sure that all the evidence was properly photographed and documented. They found a woman's purse on the hall table and opened it and found a wallet. The picture on the driver's license matched the female victim and gave her name as Jill Hawkins, which they assumed was the wife of the male victim.

Officer Dean's phone rang and he asked the others to excuse him for a minute. "Hello, this is Officer Dean. Yes, I'm the lead detective on the investigation. Yes, I understand and I'll be right there?"

He turned and asked another officer, Dan West, to accompany him to the hospital and that the female victim was awake but hysterical. She wanted to talk to them and tell her side of the incident. He left instructions for the team to finish here and keep everyone out and left strict orders for the crime scene to be off limits to the public.

Officer Dean went to the front desk and asked if the receptionist could tell him exactly where he could find the female victim that had been brought in by ambulance. "Could you tell me if the patient gave her name?"

"Yes, she was signed in as Mrs. Jill Hawkins."

"I'm Detective Dean and I'd like to speak to her."

She checked the screen and directed him to the private rooms of the emergency department. He'd been in this part of the hospital before and knew that crime victims were kept away from the regular traffic because of contamination of any evidence.

Officer Dean and Officer West entered a room at the end of the hall and showed their identification. The nurse told them that Mrs. Hawkins had been given a mild sedative to try to calm her down.

Mrs. Hawkins was lying back on the pillow and there were several doctors present. One of them was in the process of taking her pulse. Dr. Shepperd said, "I think she is finally settling down. Mrs. Hawkins I need to examine your wounds if I may. You have two deep wounds in your shoulder and we may need to put stitches in them. Are you feeling less faint now?"

"I want to see my daughter. You don't understand. My husband tried to kill me because I wanted to protect her. I shot him and I think he's dead. You have to let me go and make sure she is alright. I don't care about me, I need to see her. Please, help me to find out if she is alive. I don't remember seeing her when they took me out of the house. My husband may have killed her."

Jill tried to get up off the bed and the doctors pushed her down and told her that they had to take care of her and that they promised that they would get someone to check on the daughter for her.

Officer Dean said, "Excuse me doctor, I just came from the scene and I can assure you Mrs. Hawkins that your daughter is safe. We have transported her here to the hospital. Are you able to tell me what happened?"

"Officer, I'm afraid that Mrs. Hawkins needs immediate attention. Her wounds must be dealt with as soon as possible. Can this wait?"

"I'd rather speak to her now if you don't mind. If her injuries are not life threatening, can they wait until we take her statement?

We need to get the details as soon as we can. I promise that we'll try not to upset her, but I need to speak with her now."

Dr. Shepperd replied, "Mrs. Hawkins needs to have her injuries taken care of as soon as possible but I understand that you need to take her statement. I'll give you a few minutes, but she is bleeding and we need to get that stopped."

"I promise I won't take any longer than I need to. Mrs. Hawkins, can you tell us exactly what happened at your residence tonight?"

Jill pushed the cover away on the bed and tried to stand. "I want you to take me to see my daughter. I'll deal with my own problems later. Is my husband dead?"

"Yes ma'am he was pronounced dead at the scene. Are you saying that you are the one that shot him?"

"Yes I shot him. I was afraid for my life and my daughter's life. It was either stop him or both of us would die. I tried to stop him, but he was hurting her and I couldn't stand by any longer and watch how he treated her. All this time I allowed him to punish her but I thought this time would be different. He promised that he would stop if I let him come back home."

"Has your husband hurt your daughter before?"

"Yes, I just brought her home from the hospital and I called him around 5:00 and he asked me if he could come over. I was going to say no, but he begged and I really thought he meant what he said. I fixed dinner and things were going good until Annie dropped her fork. Several months ago my husband broke Annie's arm and he wouldn't let me take her anywhere and now she has limited use of that arm. She drops things, and he just went crazy. I swear I was afraid of him. You do believe me, don't you?"

"Mrs. Hawkins, what's important right now is that we get the details of why your husband is dead."

"He got so mad and he knocked all the food off the table and broke the dishes. Then he threw a bowl of potatoes at the wall and everything just went chaotic. He grabbed Annie's arm and was going to take her into her room and hurt her again. I screamed for him to let her go and he ran to the garage and came back with a long knife and a baseball bat."

Jill stopped and put her head in her hands and her shoulders

214

shook from her sobs. She settled down and continued, "I've never seen someone look like John did at that moment. I couldn't believe that the man I loved meant my daughter and me harm. I tried to get to Annie and run but he cut me off. He held the knife in the air and told me that he was going to cut my throat and when he was finished with me he said he'd start on Annie. Are you sure that my daughter is okay? I can't live without her."

"Ma'am I can assure you that she is alive."

"Annie wanted him to love her. My first husband died and Annie has never had a father. She's been hurt so many times."

Jill stopped and sobbed some more and then said, "I was petrified of John, but for once I knew I had to take his rage to protect my daughter so I stepped in front of Annie and told her to hide. Before I could turn around John came at me with the knife. He lunged at me and stabbed me. I fell down and before I could move he started beating me with the bat. I tried to protect myself, but he kept hitting me. I didn't know what else to do. He hit me so hard I thought I was going to pass out."

"Ma'am where did you get the gun? Did it belong to your husband?"

"John finally quit hitting me and he turned to find my daughter and I crawled as fast as I could to the end table where I knew he kept the gun. I didn't have any idea if it was loaded, but I shouted for him to leave Annie alone. He got angrier and I yelled his name and when he turned and looked at me I just knew he wanted to kill both of us. I pointed the gun at him and I think I pulled the trigger twice, I just don't remember."

"Mrs. Hawkins can you prove any previous injuries to your daughter by your husband?"

"Yes I took her to the hospital several times over the past year. John would punish Annie in the worst ways. He slammed her into the wall and split her lip. He would get so angry he actually pulled her hair out by the roots. A few months ago Annie wouldn't listen to him and he put her hand on the hot stove and burned her. I just took her in the past week because he kicked her so hard that he fractured her ribs and they punctured her lung. I told him that she would die if he didn't take her for help. I think that he wanted to cover his guilt and he told the authorities that I was the one that kicked her. I told that social worker that my husband was the one hurting her but she tried to blame it on me. I was afraid for my life. If I lost my daughter, I would have never forgiven myself."

"We will check on these incidents."

"The last thing I remember is calling for Annie and then I passed out. Can I see her now?"

"I think you should let the doctor take care of you first. You say her name is Annie?"

"Yes, Annie Lawson, my daughter from my first marriage. She didn't tell you her name?"

"No ma'am, she was in a state of shock. She's not physically hurt, but the doctors here will check her out. I think we have enough for now. I'll be back to take a more detailed statement later. I'll let the hospital know that you would like to see your daughter."

Jill was thrilled. If Annie couldn't talk, her plan worked out even better than she had hoped for. She hoped that Annie never talked again and since she was the only one who knew that truth, it meant that her secret was safe.

"Before we leave may we photograph you for evidence of the bruises on your body? I need documentation of what your husband allegedly did to you."

"Yes of course. I want every one of them photographed to prove what a monster he was. He hit me with the bat over and over. I thought I was going to die."

Jill sat up in the bed and pulled her sleeves up so Mr. West could take pictures of the massive bruises on her arms. There were several on her legs and one big bruise on her left cheek, and her left eye was going to be black by tomorrow. Jill looked to find each one of the marks and stood perfectly still as the camera flashed. She thought, "I earned each one of them, and they served their purpose."

They thanked her and assured her that they would contact her soon.

After the officers left Jill said, "Okay now you can do whatever you need to do. But I warn you if I see any marks after I'm healed, I'll sue this hospital for a lot of money. I make a living showing off my body and I need it perfect, understand?"

The doctor was baffled by the change in Jill's attitude. He thought, "A few minutes ago she was ranting about her daughter's life and now she was more concerned about scars."

After the doctor examined her he decided that the two stab wounds in her shoulder weren't that deep and he told her he would numb the area and do the sutures with no problems.

"You don't think for one minute that I'm going to lay here and let you hurt me, do you? I demand that you put me to sleep so I won't feel it. Believe me you don't want me to start screaming again."

"But Mrs. Hawkins it won't hurt after the Novocaine takes effect. I promise you won't feel a thing."

"Listen the only way you can do it is to knock me out. I will raise the roof otherwise."

"But Mrs. Hawkins it will only take a half hour and I'll be done."

Jill let out a scream that would have wakened the dead. Dr. Shepperd turned to the nurse and asked her to schedule the O.R. for him.

Jill settled down and gave the doctor a satisfied smirk. Dr. Shepperd thought, "I wonder if she bullied her husband and that's one reason why he wanted to hurt her. Oh yes, she is beautiful but she knows how to get her way."

The O.R. was available within the hour and he told Jill that he would prepare for the surgery and he would see her again in the operating room. Jill won again. Did they really think that she was going to lie here and let some stupid doctor stitch her up? She sure didn't want to feel pain and really why should she when it was now the modern age and that was why medicine was invented. No one should feel any pain, and she didn't intend to put up with it. No one was going to hurt Jill Hawkins if she could help it.

The stitches were done in less than an hour. Dr. Shepperd did his best to make the tiniest stitches he could and hoped that Mrs. Hawkins wasn't serious about suing the hospital.

CHAPTER TWENTY-NINE

Dr. Wes Livingston was waiting for the young girl when she was wheeled off the elevator. He instructed the nurses to put her in room 490. He followed the gurney down the hall and asked the head nurse, Miss Smith to meet him there.

They lifted the young girl onto the bed and they quickly took her vital signs. Her heart rate was high and Dr. Livingston asked Miss Smith to get the blood pressure cuff on her. They did a full body assessment on her and didn't find immediate dangers since there were no signs of life threatening injuries. The report stated that this young child was found in a room where apparently her mother had killed her father. The report also stated that the child's name was Annie Lawson.

Dr. Livingston took his light and performed a test to see if she would follow it with her eyes. The young child showed no response to the light. He noted the injuries to her body which included the deformed arm, the burns on her legs, and many scars. He asked the nurse to get him the information of the previous hospital admittances. The fact that the child was not responsive worried him and he made a call to the psychologist on staff, Dr. Derek Van Horne.

Dr. Livingston asked the nurse to dress the burns on Annie's legs. Several of the blisters looked like they may have become infected and he left instructions for them to start an IV for antibiotics. He sat down beside the bed and softly asked if she could tell him her name and how old she was. Annie never even blinked. She gave no indication that she could hear him at all. He put his hand on her arm and again asked her name. Still there was no response.

Dr. Livingston walked to the nurse's station and asked to have Dr. Van Horne paged. The phone rang within a few minutes and he answered it. "Yes, Derek, I appreciate you calling me back. I have a young girl age six that is non-responsive to any of our tests. From what I understand she may have witnessed the murder of her father, and I'm assuming that she is now in shock. I need you to take a look at her if you would."

"Okay, I'm with a patient right now, but I can see her in about a half hour. Was the child hurt at all?"

"No, I don't see any injuries on her. But from what I do see, I'm afraid that the child may be a victim of abuse. She has old scars on her body and her right arm seems to have been broken and didn't heal properly. Also she has 2nd degree burns on her legs which seem to be only a few days old. I'm waiting on her records now."

"I'll be there as soon as I'm finished with my patient."

"Thank you, Derek. I'll wait for you on the floor."

Dr. Livingston went down the hall to another patient's room and asked the nurse to page him as soon as Dr. Van Horne was on the floor. When his pager went off, he headed back to Annie's room. Dr. Van Horne was sitting beside Annie's bed holding her hand. "Annie, can you hear me? My name is Dr. Derek and I want to help you. Are you hurt in any way? Can you squeeze my hand?"

Dr. Van Horne turned around when Dr. Livingston entered the room. "How are you Derek? I haven't had a chance to talk to you for a while." The two men shook hands.

"I'm busy, and I've been well. How are you?"

"I'm busy too. I guess in our profession there is no time off. What do you think about Annie? Do you think that she'll be okay?"

"I see what you mean about her not being able to respond. Did you say that she witnessed her father's murder? And can I ask who is responsible for his death?"

"According to what the police are saying, it was her mother. Evidently Annie's father had a history of abuse and the mother claims that he would have killed her and Annie so she shot him."

"Oh my, how awful. A child shouldn't have to see such things. I'll try to work with her in the next few days. In these cases the child sometimes blocks everything out in order to protect themselves. It may take a lot of work to bring her back."

"I also was told that the mother was injured and is in the hospital too. She has requested permission to see her daughter. Do you think that would be okay?"

"If it was the father that abused her I don't think it would do any harm. It may help to comfort her and right now I imagine that she needs someone that is close to her to cling to."

"I'll notify the authorities to allow her mother to see her as soon as she is able. I appreciate your help. Do you think that we should medicate her to help her stay calm? Would that help her to recover and be able to deal with all that has happened to her?"

"In most cases it does help to use medication to allow the mind to rest. From what I've seen it may take a while for the mind to be able to handle a tragedy like this. I'll leave instructions for the nurses to use a sedative if they see that the child is upset. By tomorrow we should see a change if she's going to respond quickly. When she can speak, I'll begin to counsel her and try to help pull her back to reality. And in her case, that isn't going to be an easy road. Reality is ugly in these cases."

"I'll keep in touch with you and again I thank you for seeing her so quickly. I wish her well. I can't put myself in her place and I sure can understand why the mind takes an easier road to deal with what she must have seen."

"I'll stop and check on her in the morning and make sure to stay in contact and hopefully we can help this poor child."

Dr. Van Horne stopped at the nurse's station to glance over Annie's chart and to prescribe medication if Annie became upset. He waved to Dr. Livingston as he headed to the elevator.

The nurses kept an eye on Annie all night and made sure that she was as comfortable as possible. The young girl never moved even when they changed the bandages on her legs and applied medication. By the next morning, all the nurses had fallen in love with the sweet beautiful little girl in room 490.

Dr. Derek came to check on her around 10:00 and saw no change in Annie. The light in her eyes sparked absolutely no reaction. Wherever the mind had gone, it wasn't going to right itself without a lot of help.

Jill spent the morning examining her stitches and wasn't sure if the doctor had done what she told him to do. The wounds in her chest were swollen and it was an ugly sight to look at. She thought to herself as she stood at the mirror, "I hope I didn't take this plan too far. Maybe I shouldn't have been worried about my story being believable. I hope that these ugly marks were worth it."

She had just crawled back in the bed when Officer Dean knocked on her door. "Mrs. Hawkins, how are you doing this morning? I wanted to ask you a few more questions if you don't mind."

"I'll answer any questions you have. I have nothing to hide, and I want this behind me as soon as possible. I still want to see my daughter. I asked the nurses how she was, but they wouldn't tell me a thing. I will call some people if I'm not allowed to see her soon. I just want to make sure she's okay. Have you seen her?"

"No ma'am I was going to go see her after we are finished. I wanted to ask you if you have remembered anything else about last night. We do believe that you acted in self-defense and I hate to make you go back over it, but it's necessary that we gather all the information we can before we decide what actions to take."

"Are you telling me that I may be guilty of anything except defending myself and my daughter?"

"No, I didn't say that. But I need you to help us make sure that we get all the facts. I do wish that your daughter could help by telling us what happened at your home. It helps to have a witness as to what went on."

"Have you asked her what she saw?"

"From what I understand from the doctor that is treating your daughter, your daughter hasn't spoken one word and isn't responding at all."

"Is she that bad? Oh how can I ever make it up to her? She's been hurt so many times by my husband and I hope we both can recover."

"Sometimes children cope by blocking it all from their mind. I hope that after a few days of treatment that she can tell us what took place and that your side of the story is true."

"Officer Dean, are you saying that I'm lying? Believe me when I tell you that it was a matter of life and death for both of us. I assure you that Annie will say the same thing that I've said. John grabbed her arm hard enough that I'm sure that she has the bruises to prove it. Besides, you have it on record that John was abusive before. I can't begin to tell you what fear I had for our safety. It was either him or us."

"Mrs. Hawkins I'm not saying that I don't believe you. I am obligated by law to ask you these questions. I'm going to ask your doctor about your injuries and if they are consistent with what you have told us. Did your husband stab you with the knife that we found under his body?"

"I guess it was the same knife. All I know is when he came back from the garage he lunged at me and I felt so much pain I couldn't stand. He stabbed me the second time and I fell to the floor. I tried to crawl away but he came at me with a baseball bat and hit me several times. I told you all this before. When he went after Annie I got the gun and because I thought he would kill her too, I shot the gun. I screamed for Annie before I passed out and that's all I remember. I'm not sure how much Annie can tell you. If she was hiding, maybe she didn't see John stab me. If she didn't see that, then her story won't tell you much will it? Besides how much can a six year old know?"

"Mrs. Hawkins, your daughter must have seen some of it and that's why she is now in shock. Hopefully this doesn't ruin her life. Some children can't handle a tragedy like this and they carry it for the rest of their life. I'm sorry to put you through this now, and by the way, the doctor has given permission for you to visit your daughter as soon as you're able. I hope that it will help her and that you and your daughter can overcome this together. I have to talk to the doctor, and the social worker handling the case, and I'll be in touch soon. I thank you for your cooperation and I wish you and your daughter well."

"Thank you Officer Dean, and may I ask when my home will be ready for us to go back. Will they clean all the blood away so we don't have to see it? I'm certainly not going back until everything is taken care of. Do I have to hire an outside service for that?"

"I will check and see how far the investigating team has gotten with all the evidence and I'll let you know what the department has in mind. I know the teams take fingerprints from everywhere and it does leave quite a mess. But you probably will have to hire someone to come and take care of it. I don't think our department offers that service."

"I'm not going to stay here one minute longer than I have to. I may decide to get rid of the house after all that has happened. I'm not even sure if I want to spend one night in my own home again. My daughter and I can stay somewhere else, which isn't a problem. Whatever it takes to help her through this, then that is what I'll do."

"I must ask you not to leave the area until all this is settled."

"I'm not guilty of anything Officer Dean. I defended myself and my daughter from a monster. And I would appreciate if you do your best to prove that fact by the evidence that I've given you."

"I'll follow that evidence Mrs. Hawkins. And if what you have said is true, then you have nothing to worry about. I've got to go and I'll be in touch soon."

After the officer left, Jill got agitated. After all the trouble I went to, you won't find anything that proves me guilty, she thought to herself. The nurse came in to take her vital signs and she asked her to find out what room Annie was in and get her a wheel chair so she could go upstairs to visit her.

"I'll contact your doctor and as soon as we get permission I'll help you."

"Thank you and do you have some towels so I can get in the shower? I need to have someone tape my bandages so they won't get wet."

"Yes Mrs. Hawkins I'll get them and help you wrap your bandages, just give me one second."

Jill hated the hospital. She couldn't wait to go back home to her own room. She needed to vent and she sure couldn't do that here.

After Jill was finished with her shower the nurse told her that the doctors approved her trip upstairs to Annie's room. "They're hoping that your visit will help your daughter. I feel so sorry for her; it must have been terrible what you both went through."

"Yes, I loved my husband but he was a monster. I didn't realize until it was too late and now we're all alone. I just want to take my daughter home and love her."

"I'll be right back with the wheel chair and we'll go and see that daughter of yours and you can hug her and make her better."

Jill's thoughts of Annie were ones of pure anger. She hated the fact that she had to pretend and would be happy when they could be alone again and quit this stupid game she had to play.

The nurse helped her in the wheel chair and they went upstairs to find the room. Jill was a little surprised by the look on Annie's face when she wheeled next to her bed. She had a few seconds of remorse for what she'd done to her but it didn't last long. "I really hope you stay like this forever and you'll be easier for me to put up with you if you just lie in a bed and don't bother me. I guess you could say that I killed both of you at the same time and now I'm free," she thought.

Jill took Annie's hand and said. "Annie, it's Mommy. Can you hear me? I'm here now and you don't have to worry anymore. Daddy can't hurt you now. Annie, will you look at me?"

Annie didn't move at all. Her eyes stared straight ahead. Jill sat with her for a while and every time she heard a nurse come into the room she grabbed her hand again and talked softly to her. After a while, Jill leaned down to Annie's ear and said, "Annie I know you can hear me. I want to tell you that when they ask you questions about what happened, you tell them that your father hurt you and that we were both afraid of him. Do you understand? If I find out that you said anything bad about me, you'll be sorry. And we both know how mean I can be. So you just make sure that you keep your mouth shut."

A nurse came in the door so Jill went back to playing the role of a concerned mother. After a short time Jill called the nurse and asked her to take her back to her room. "I can't stand to see Annie like this and I'm tired now."

The nurse wheeled her back to her room and helped her in the bed. Jill lay back on the pillow and was asleep in a matter of minutes.

CHAPTER THIRTY

Dr. Van Horne allowed extra time to run a few tests on Annie Lawson. He hoped that she'd be more responsive this morning. He was pleased to find that her heart rate and blood pressure were almost back to normal. When he performed a prick test on her feet, Annie didn't move at all.

Dr. Van Horne asked the nurse to help him to raise her head higher in the bed. He sat on the stool and asked her several questions. He turned her head towards him thinking that maybe she would respond to a direct sound, but still nothing. He spent several more minutes trying to get a response to sounds. But Annie was deep in a trance and he was afraid that it would take time for her to heal and have a desire to return to the world she had escaped from.

Dr. Van Horne made a phone call to Dr. Livingston and discussed the results of his visit. "I did work with Annie Lawson this morning and in my opinion she'll need time and gentle care before she's responsive. I'm going to set up therapy while she's here in the hospital. I'll leave it up to you the length of her stay. Does she have medical problems that I should know about?"

"No I don't think that she sustained any further injuries. I read her records this morning of her previous visits to the hospital and I have to confer with Dr. Howard's recommendations that Annie Lawson has been abused by someone. The burns on her legs may be a result of someone putting her in a tub of hot water. The records also indicate that the mother was accusing the step father of that abuse. And are you aware of the police report states that the step father was trying to harm Annie and that the mother shot and killed him?"

"Yes you told me that yesterday. It does explain why this child has retreated within herself. I'd like to have the full report to study if you can forward one to me. I think that Annie's condition can't be pinpointed to one thing, but is a result of continued events in her life. It may take some time before we can help her to deal with all of them. Do you have any idea how long she will be in the hospital?"

"No right now I don't, but I want to examine her arm and bring in plastic surgeons to explore that possibility of maybe giving her back some use of her arm. The records show that her arm was broken and left untreated because the step father wouldn't allow the mother to seek treatment. I'm hoping that the arm can be reset and heal properly. The range of what they can do nowadays is better than it used to be. I'll get these records to you and let you know any further developments."

"I'll schedule the therapy sessions to be done twice a day and I'll be in touch."

Dr. Livingston called Dr. Norris, the best plastic surgeon on staff. He asked him to consult on Annie's case and left his number where he could be reached. After all this poor child must have been through, it was the least that they could do for her.

An hour later Dr. Norris went to Annie's room and examined her arm. He called Dr. Livingston and told him that he was positive that he could make an improvement in Annie's arm.

"I would like to schedule surgery as soon as possible unless there are other conditions preventing surgery so quickly. I noticed that she doesn't respond to my voice."

"She went though a traumatic experience and has retreated. I have Dr. Van Horne working with her. Do you think that a surgery would make her worse as far as her emotional state?"

"No, I don't see why it would. Maybe it'll be easier to do it now while she's still and give the arm time to heal."

"Yes, I think that's a good idea. Can you work her in soon?"

"Actually I can schedule her as soon as tomorrow. I had a cancellation. I'd like to have my team look at her and I'll let you know if we can do it tomorrow."

"Thank you Dr. Norris. I'm going to check on her later today and if a problem arises I'll call you."

Dr. Norris's team met in Annie's room later that evening. They all agreed that their team could repair the arm and it would be close to normal. The broken bone needed reshaped and all the scar tissue cleaned up. Within a few weeks the arm would heal and look almost like it had before. Hopefully none of the nerves were damaged. If Annie would have been responsive they would've asked her to move her fingers to see if the use was limited. Since she wasn't, the surgeons would have to check them and repair all the damage they could.

Each one of the team fell in love with the tiny little girl lying on the bed. How could anyone want to hurt a beautiful child like this one in the first place?

The next day the nurses prepared Annie for the operating room. The whole time they worked, Annie didn't stir. The surgery went well and Dr. Norris called Dr. Livingston and told him that Annie should regain ninety percent use of her arm and there would only be two tiny scars running along each side. He was pleased with the results and was glad to be able to help.

Dr. Shepperd went to Jill's room the next morning and told her that she would be able to go home that evening if she wanted to. All the stitches looked good and the bruises on her body would eventually heal. Jill was thrilled. She needed to go home and soak in as many bubbles that the hot tub would hold. She asked the nurse to find Officer Dean's phone number for her and left a message for him to call as soon as he could. She asked him if they were finished at her house and could she go home.

"Mrs. Hawkins, I did ask my team to clean up as much of the mess as they could. The department brought someone in to clean up the blood and I apologize for the condition of your home. Are you sure that you want to go back so soon? I thought that you said you could stay somewhere else."

"I may stay at a motel for a while, but I have to go home sometime and face what happened and right now I'm just too tired to worry about it. So I'm allowed to go home and you're finished with your investigation?"

"I'm not saying we are finished yet, but I don't think that we need anything else from your home. I would appreciate if you would call me and let me know where you're staying if you decide not to stay at your house. I need you to be accessible to us if we need further information."

"Why Officer Dean that almost sounds like I'm a criminal. Surely you can't think that this was planned, do you?"

"I'm not saying that, but I insist that you stay in touch with me, understand?"

"Fine, I'll let you know if I'm staying any where besides my own house."

As she hung up the phone she wanted to scream. "I went through all this and you think that you can tell me what to do," she thought.

She didn't waste too much time worrying about what Officer Dean thought. She'd have to call a taxi to take her home and she was in a hurry to do just that.

Jill reached for her buzzer and asked, "Nurse, can you come to my room please. I'm going to go home in a few hours and I need you to take me to see my daughter."

"Yes, Mrs. Hawkins I'll be right there."

Jill didn't give a darn about Annie, but she had to stick with the caring mother act so she would put up with the aggravation. She even managed to cry when she saw the bandages on her arm. She asked the nurse what happened and she explained to Jill that the surgeons repaired the damage to her arm and that she would be almost as good as new. "Isn't that wonderful?" she asked.

"Yes, it's a small blessing for her after all that she's been through. Thank you so much for that. I wanted to have it fixed but my husband forbid me to. Now I can have my daughter back and even better than she was."

Jill spent a half hour sitting by Annie's bed then asked the nurse to take her back to her own room. "I have to go home and make sure her room is ready for her to come home. Do you know how long she has to stay? I hope it's not too long, I can't wait to start our new life without fear of someone hurting either of us ever again."

"According to the chart, Dr. Livingston hasn't made any notations of when she can go home. I'm sure that he will call you as soon as he knows. But you can come back and stay with her; we can even put a cot in the room if you want."

"No I want to rest and heal myself so I can take care of her when she does come home. But I'll be back tomorrow."

Jill went back to her own room and packed her things and called a cab to meet her outside. She couldn't wait to get out of here. She dreaded seeing what the idiot police had done to her house, but oh well, it came with the territory.

When they pulled into her driveway Jill forgot that she didn't have her purse to pay the driver. "Give me one second to go and get my money. I was taken to the hospital in the ambulance so I didn't have time to get my purse."

"That isn't a problem, ma'am. I'll wait for you."

Jill ran in the house and grabbed her purse, then hurried out to pay the driver. She went back in and was shocked when she entered the foyer. The blood was gone but things were still lying where they had been thrown. The bat and the gun were gone. She was glad for that fact.

Jill glanced down at the spot where she'd seen John fall and it finally occurred to her that she'd never see him again. She stumbled to the chair and fell into it. What had she done? She loved him and she'd miss him, but she had to keep her own reputation spotless and she believed that was more important than anything else. She sat still for a while until she was steady and finally stood and headed upstairs to her bedroom.

She went into the bathroom and turned on the faucet and ran herself a hot bath. Slowly she got undressed and climbed in the warm water. She lay back and closed her eyes and said, "Get hold of yourself Jill. You just did what you had to do. Now you have to get on with your life. And I will, just like I always have."

She walked to the mirror before getting dressed and couldn't believe the bruises on her body. She was black and blue everywhere. She might have went a little overboard with the bat but no one would have believed her without some marks on her body, so she'd done what she had to do.

The stitches on her shoulder still looked red and swollen. Hopefully all of the marks would soon disappear and she would look as good as ever.

When she was finished she went back downstairs and spent the rest of the evening going over John's papers and tried to make a list of the things she would have to do. Planning her husband's funeral was easier this time. She went up to bed around 11:00 and slept straight through the night.

In the morning she was up early and thought about her schedule. She would have to call Officer Dean and asked what arrangements had to be done for John. Then she had to go to the hospital and put in an appearance. It wouldn't be smart of her to abandon the daughter she professed to care about. She'd like to forget she even had a child, but for now the game must be finished.

The next morning she called the station and left a message for Officer Dean to call her back. She didn't want to see John's body again, and she wasn't sure if she could actually cremate his remains. But when she thought about it, maybe it would be accepted, given the circumstances of his death. She would call a funeral home and ask about a cremation service.

Jill sure didn't want to go to the hospital and sit and look at a dim wit child. She resolved herself to just go and get it done and she drove to the hospital. When she arrived in Annie's room she walked to the side of the bed.

Annie didn't look any different than yesterday but to see if she would react to her, she reached down and pinched her arm as hard as she could. There was absolutely no response. She pinched her again and still nothing. She hadn't realized that she had left a mark and when the red splotch appeared on her arm she tried to rub it away. That didn't help either so she decided to go and find a nurse.

"Excuse me, could you tell me if the doctor has been in to see my daughter and what he said?"

"Oh, Mrs. Hawkins, let me check and see. No, Dr. Livingston has not been in yet. But I see that Dr. Van Horne saw your daughter about an hour ago. I think Dr. Livingston makes his rounds soon. If I see him I'll tell him that you'd like to speak to him."

"Has there been any change in my daughter's condition? Has she spoken yet?"

"As far as I know she hasn't responded to any of us. I think she's so precious. I suppose this is so hard on you to see her like that."

"Yes it breaks my heart. I want her to come back to me. I miss her so much. Would you tell the doctor that I'll be in her room?"

Jill went back to the room and sat down in the chair beside the bed. As she looked at Annie she was so grateful for her condition. "Small blessings often come when you least expect them," she thought.

A few minutes later Dr. Livingston came in the room. "Mrs. Hawkins, how are you doing? I was going to call you later this morning. I spoke to Dr. Van Horne, the specialist that is working with Annie and we wanted to ask your permission to send her to a facility that will dedicate a full time staff to her and hopefully bring her back to us. I know this is a crucial time for you after what has happened and you're hurting too."

"I'm not sure I can stand it without her with me. I'm barely hanging on after what my husband did and I'm scared to death what will happen to Annie."

"I wouldn't recommend this if I saw any other way to help her. We don't have the staff on hand to give her the best care. I think highly of Dr. Van Horne and I know if anyone can bring your daughter back, it would be him. She may not have to stay long, it depends on Annie. I think we've done all we can do for her here."

"I understand Dr. Livingston. I want what's best for Annie. If you think this will help her I'm for it. How long do you think that it will take? Do children stay this way forever? I wish I could go back and undo it for Annie's sake, but I was afraid for our life. Dr. Livingston I want you to do whatever it takes for Annie."

"I have a meeting with Dr. Van Horne this afternoon and I'll call you and let you know what we decide. I'm sorry Mrs. Hawkins. I hope it doesn't take long to reach her. I want to check her vital signs before I go."

"Of course, I have things I must do this afternoon, and since Annie doesn't even know that I'm here I'll leave and wait to hear from you."

"No, I think Annie does know you're here, she just can't say it. I'm sure it's a comfort to her when you're here. But I'll call you later."

"Thank you Dr. Livingston. I'm grateful for the help you have given my daughter."

Jill was almost giddy with relief. If Annie stayed this way she could institutionalize her and no one would think anything about it. "Talk about good luck," she thought.

When she got home she saw that there was one message on her phone. "Mrs. Hawkins this is Officer Dean. I'll be in my office for the next few hours and if you don't mind coming down to the station, I'll discuss all the details with you then."

Jill changed and drove to the station. She asked to see Officer Dean and was directed to his office.

"Mrs. Hawkins, I appreciate you coming in. I got your message about your husband's body. I've discussed your case with my team and the conclusion this office has decided is that you indeed acted in self defense. There'll be no charges filed and you may make the arrangements for your husband's body to be picked up any time. I'm sorry to hear that your daughter is still in a state of shock. Do you have any further questions?"

"Officer Dean I'm grateful that I can put this tragedy behind me. When I got home yesterday I was overtaken by grief about my husband. I should have acted on his behavior a long time ago, but it won't benefit me or my daughter to dwell on what's happened. I'm going to do my best to go on with my life. When I visited my daughter yesterday, there was no change in her. Her doctor has recommended that I place her in a treatment facility so they can work with her full time. I'm going to go with their recommendation even though I won't have her home with me. I just hope that she remembers what happened and I'll hire the best doctor there is to make sure that she recovers and if it takes the next several years, I won't stop until she is normal again."

"I hope so. Your daughter has suffered a traumatic blow if she saw you shoot your husband after he beat you. On top of that, she was abused by him several times and I hope that the fact that you were protecting her can be explained and she'll somehow cope with what she's seen. I'm not an expert in this field, but when she understands that you only acted in self defense, it'll help her to heal. I'd appreciate you keeping in touch with the department as to your whereabouts if you decide to relocate. I don't see any problems, but if we would have any further questions I'd like to know how to reach you."

"Yes, of course, I'll let you know if I do relocate. Right now I'm not sure what I'll do. I guess it depends on where I have to take my daughter for treatment. I may sell my house, which would get rid of a lot of bad memories. I appreciate you taking time for me today and I'll stay in touch with you."

On the drive home Jill couldn't believe her luck. She had every intention of locking Annie away for a very long time if she could arrange it and not throw any suspicion on herself. Life did have a way of working out if you have the guts to make it happen.

CHAPTER THIRTY-ONE

Dr. Van Horne walked down the hall towards Annie's room. As he walked, he read the latest notations on her chart. According to the nurses, Annie hadn't made a sound. He was concerned that she was slipping deeper and he wanted to move her as soon as possible to the Children's Safe Haven, a facility that in his opinion, was the best in the state.

He entered Annie's room and went to the bed and softly asked her how she was doing. There was no recognition or response to his voice. He reached for her hand and held it and spoke to her again. He watched her eyes to see if they tried to follow his voice, but she stared straight ahead.

In cases with children like Annie, when they can't handle something that has been done to them or have witnessed a horrible act, they withdraw from reality. He'd worked with several children and he liked to use sounds or words that before had brought them comfort. He hoped to find Annie's comfort zone. If she felt comfortable she may respond and then they worked with her to help her deal with whatever had caused the pain in the first place. He wanted to have a meeting with Dr. Livingston that afternoon and would recommend transferring Annie by tomorrow if her physical condition would allow it. When dealing with situations like this it was easier on the children if they could reach them before they sank too deep into the depression.

Dr. Livingston told him that he was free at 2:00 and Dr. Van Horne said that was fine and he'd see him then.

The two doctors shook hands and after they both were seated, Dr. Livingston got Annie's chart and asked, "So you think that sending Annie to The Children's Safe Haven is the best treatment?"

"Yes, I do. I've had no response from her so far. I would like to move her tomorrow and have my staff start working with her immediately. We don't want to waste precious time. If the children go too far into a depression after witnessing something that they can't handle we have a harder time reaching them. As I understand, Annie was abused several years by her step-father. Considering that abuse on top of what she may have witnessed when her mother shot him, we have a lot of work to do. I hope that we can reach her and help her to deal with all of this. Annie may never be the same, but we can use our skills to help her to cope. She may never remember any of it, and I think that may be a blessing. If she can go on from here, she may recover quickly."

"I don't see any problem with moving her tomorrow. I did speak to Mrs. Hawkins and told her that we were leaning towards that possibility. She seemed fine with it, and she said she wanted her daughter to recover and come home to her."

"If I may ask you a question, do you suspect that her mother had any part of Annie's abuse? If that is true, we need to keep them separated because her presence may send Annie backwards. The information I gathered stated that it was indeed the step-father. If I see that the mother is a hindrance to Annie's recovery, I'd restrict the mother's visits."

"You know I never thought about it that way. I assumed that the two of them were close before the step-father came into the picture. I have observed her mother with her and I thought Annie related well to her. But I'm not trained to make that assumption, so I'll also leave that discretion up to you."

"I'll deal with that when I have to. I insist that the children come first with no exceptions. If that means keeping the family away, then they must respect my wishes. I'll make the arrangements for the transfer and if there are no objections, I'll move her to the center tomorrow."

Dr. Van Horne went back to his office and called the treatment center to set up a room for Annie. He contacted his head nurse, Mrs. Heather Spencer, to prepare for her arrival. After all the paperwork was complete, he went to Annie's room one more time to check on her. He saw no improvement in her condition and as he left he really hoped that she was not in a place they couldn't reach.

Dr. Livingston placed a call to Jill to let her know that Annie was to be moved the next day.

"Is this center reliable? I have money and I want the best treatment for my daughter. I don't care what it cost, and if I don't see improvement in her quickly, I'll pull her out."

"Mrs. Hawkins, I understand your impatience but believe me when I tell you that Dr. Van Horne is the best doctor to treat her. I've seen amazing results in children he's counseled. Your daughter has retreated from the pain of what she's been put through. I don't want to sound harsh but a child is not supposed to endure this kind of thing. They want to be loved and feel safe and when they don't they retreat. I do hope that you allow Dr. Van Horne freedom to treat Annie as he sees fit. I'm not trained in the field, but he is. If

234

you have no objection, Annie will be moved tomorrow. Her arm is healing quickly and the burns on her legs are also healing. The lung that was punctured is doing fine. Now the only thing we need to do is step out of Dr. Van Horne's way and let him help her emotionally."

"I'm fine with it, but if I see a problem arise, I won't hesitate to find my own doctor."

"Very well then, I'll call you tomorrow with the information on the center and give you the address and directions. I do hope that Annie gets better and can be a happy carefree child."

"I do too, Dr. Livingston. I know that my husband did a lot of damage and I want the rest of her life to be better."

After Dr. Livingston hung up he thought again about what Dr. Van Horne had asked about Mrs. Hawkins. He certainly did hope that she only wanted what was best for her child, and that she wasn't part of the problem.

The hospital staff worried about the beautiful girl named Annie Lawson. The story of what happened to her spread quickly. Dr. Howard heard the stories and was saddened by the outcome. Children's Services came in contact with many hospital workers and the story made its way back to Mrs. Branson, who was Annie's former caseworker.

Mrs. Branson was completely shocked by the whole thing. She was overwhelmed when she heard that Mr. Hawkins had been shot and killed by his wife Jill.

"How could I have been so wrong?" she thought. If she would've had to stake her career on a gut feeling, she thought that Mrs. Hawkins was the abuser. She wanted to pay a visit to Annie later that evening and hug her and apologize for being so wrong. She felt guilt for not stopping either parent from being around her. If she would've been more forceful, maybe none of this would've happened to a sweet young girl.

Mrs. Branson had another appointment at the hospital at 3:15, and when she was finished she went to Annie's room. When she walked to the bed, her heart broke for Annie. She couldn't look at her without shedding tears. It wasn't fair for two grown adults to mistreat a child like Annie's parents had done to her. It made her angry, and even though she wasn't sure if Annie heard her, she told her she was sorry and hugged her before she left. In this job she met children who hadn't got a fair shake in life, and it tore her heart to pieces. She often thought about quitting, but she knew that there were more children to help before she walked away from it all.

That evening as the hospital quieted down the nurses made several trips to Annie's room. Each one of them straightened the blanket on her bed. Each one of them spoke quietly to her and checked the bandages on her arm and examined the blisters on her legs. The burns were healing and hopefully would leave no scars. They left the light on over her bed hoping to give her comfort in case she was afraid of the dark. But Annie didn't seem to notice any of them. She slept without moving a muscle. The world was revolving around her, but she stayed oblivious to it and never made a sound.

The next morning they prepared Annie for the transfer. Jill made an appearance and kissed the top of her head as they wheeled her out of the room. She asked the attendants to be careful with her daughter and watched as they went down the hall. She even looked as though she lost her composure as the tears ran down her cheeks as she turned to leave. She was getting good at playing the grieving mother.

Jill returned to her home and called several funeral homes and finally found one that would cremate her husband's body. She made another call to Officer Dean's office to ask that he would make the arrangement for John's body to be picked up that afternoon. The chapter in her life as John Hawkins's wife was closing and she planned to start a new chapter that would give her back the freedom she used to enjoy and she'd do her best to get back into the fashion world and her real true love in life, which was promoting Jill Hawkins. She couldn't wait to start designing again and maybe do some modeling again. As soon as her body was healed, she would contact her old friends and make a comeback.

Annie was taken to a private room at the facility and all the staff came to welcome her. The beautiful girl didn't utter one word, or acknowledge any of them. The staff knew that this was going to be a delicate case. The story of what happened to Annie Lawson was certainly a heart breaker, but she was in good hands and with their help her life would be better now than it had been before, and they could give the poor child a new beginning to her future.

Where that future would take her was still a mystery. After witnessing her father's death and being abused mentally and physically for the last few years, Annie may be gone from the reality of the harsh world she'd endured for awhile.

Her mother, on the other hand, was thankful for the way things had worked out. She got her old life back, and now she wouldn't have to pretend to love her daughter. Her hope was that Annie would never come back and no one could accuse her of being a terrible mother if her daughter was locked away in a comatose state. She would bury her husband in a few days, and in a way she buried Annie too. Her old motto reared its ugly head once again, look out world Jill Hawkins was back and since she had no obstacles in her way, she could be whatever she wanted to be. And in her sick way of thinking, she didn't have to be a wife or a mother. The future was bright once again.

....................To be continued....................

OTHER BOOKS BY
DONNA LEE COMER

"A DAY FOR A DAY"

PUBLISHED MARCH 6, 2010

http://www.donnaleecomer.com

Made in the USA
Charleston, SC
10 August 2011